ARCTIC OCEAN

Barents Sea

Kara Sea

Laptev Sea

Norwegian Sea

S i b e r i a

A S I A

Sea of Okhotsk

Oslo   Stockholm

St. Petersburg

Glasgow

North Sea

Moscow

Copenhagen

Lake Baikal

Dublin

Hamburg

Minsk

London   Amsterdam   Warsaw

Shenyang

Sapporo

Paris   Brussels   Prague   EUROPE   Kiev

Beijing

Sea of Japan

Lyons   Vienna   Budapest   Odessa

Lanzhou

Seoul   Tokyo

Bordeaux   Belgrade   Bucharest

Caspian Sea

Aral Sea

Xi'an   Shanghai   Osaka   Kitakyushu

Barcelona   Rome   Sofia

Black Sea

Chengdu   Chongqing

East China Sea

Lisbon   Madrid   Naples   Istanbul   Ankara

Izmir   Tehran

Kabul

Kunming

Guangzhou   PACIFIC OCEAN

ablanca   Rabat   Tunis   Algiers   Athens

Mediterranean Sea   Beirut   Damascus   Baghdad

Lahore   Delhi

Hanoi   Hong Kong

Tripoli   Alexandria   Amman   Persian Gulf

New Delhi   Dhaka

Rangoon

Cairo   Riyadh

Karachi

Calcutta

Bangkok   Manila

Dakar   AFRICA   Arabia   Arabian Sea   Bombay

Bay of Bengal

South China Sea

Ho Chi Minh City

Abuja   Addis Ababa   Bangalore   Madras

Ibadan   Lagos   Colombo

Medan   Singapore   I n d o n e s i a

Abidjan   Nairobi   Mogadishu

Kinshasa   Dar es Salaam

Jakarta   Surabaya   Bandung

Luanda

INDIAN OCEAN

Madagascar

AUSTRALIA

SOUTH ATLANTIC OCEAN

Johannesburg   Maputo

Brisbane

Perth   Adelaide   Sydney   Canberra

Cape Town   Melbourne

ANTARCTICA

EXPLORERS & DISCOVERERS

**PALM BEACH COUNTY
LIBRARY SYSTEM**

3650 Summit Boulevard

West Palm Beach, FL 33406-4198

EXPLORERS & DISCOVERERS

From Alexander the Great to Sally Ride

Volume 6

Nancy Pear
•
Daniel B. Baker

Edited by Jane Hoehner

AN IMPRINT OF GALE

DETROIT · LONDON

Explorers and Discoverers

From Alexander the Great to Sally Ride

Volume 6

Nancy Pear and Daniel B. Baker

Staff

Jane Hoehner, *U•X•L Senior Editor*
Carol DeKane Nagel, *U•X•L Managing Editor*
Thomas L. Romig, *U•X•L Publisher*

Shanna Heilveil, *Production Associate*
Evi Seoud, *Production Manager*
Mary Beth Trimper, *Production Director*

Pamela A. E. Galbreath, *Senior Art Director*
Cynthia Baldwin, *Product Design Manager*
Barbara J. Yarrow, *Graphic Services Supervisor*

Jessica L. Ulrich, *Permissions Associate*
Margaret Chamberlain, *Permissions Specialist (Pictures)*

Marco Di Vita, Graphix Group, *Typesetter*

The following CIP citation is for Volume 6:

Library of Congress Cataloging-in-Publication Data
Explorers & Discoverers : from Alexander the Great to Sally Ride
   by Nancy Pear and Daniel B. Baker.
      p cm.
    Includes biographical references and index.
    ISBN 0-7876-2946-4
1. Explorers—Biography—Encyclopedias, Juvenile. 2. Discoverers in Geography—Encyclopedias, Juvenile. 3. Travelers—Biography—Encyclopedias, Juvenile. I. Pear, Nancy. II. Baker, Daniel B.
    G200.S22 1995
    920.02—dc20   95-166826
                                       CIP

Printed in the United States of America

10 9 8 7 6 5 4 3 2 1

Contents
of Volume 6

Biographical Listings

Reader's Guide

Explorers & Discoverers: From Alexander the Great to Sally Ride, Volume 6, features thirty biographies of nineteen men, nine women, one facility, and one machine that have expanded the horizons of our world and universe. Beginning with an ancient Egyptian queen and extending to a present-day marine biologist, *Explorers & Discoverers, Volume 6* presents the lives and times of well-known explorers as well as many lesser-known women and non-Europeans who have also made significant discoveries. Who these travelers were, when and how they lived and traveled, why their journeys were significant, and what the consequences of their discoveries are are all answered within these biographies.

The thirty biographical entries in *Explorers & Discoverers, Volume 6* are arranged in alphabetical order. More than eighty photographs, illustrations, and maps bring the subjects to life as well as provide geographic details of specific journeys. Additionally, sixteen maps of major regions of the world lead off the volume, and a cumulative chronology of exploration by region, list of explorers by country of birth, and index conclude the volume.

Comments and Suggestions

We welcome your comments on this work as well as your suggestions for individuals to be featured in future volumes of *Explorers & Discoverers*. Please write: Editors, *Explorers & Discoverers,* U•X•L, 835 Penobscot Bldg., Detroit, Michigan 48226-4094; call toll-free: 1-800-877-4253; or fax: (313) 961-6348.

Introduction

Explorers & Discoverers, Volume 6 takes the reader on an adventure with men and women who have made significant contributions to human knowledge about the earth, the plant and animal life with which we share it, and ourselves. Journeying through the centuries, we will conquer frontiers and sail uncharted waters. We will trek across treacherous mountains, scorching deserts, steamy jungles, and icy glaciers. We will plumb the depths of the ocean, live locked inside a giant greenhouse that simulates the earth and its life cycles, and share in intriguing rituals and customs of unfamiliar peoples. We will excavate the oldest human settlement on earth and dwell among the "gentle giants" that are the mountain gorillas, both experiences giving us tantalizing glimpses into our own far distant past. Encountering isolation, disease, and even death, we will come to know the grave sacrifices that discovery sometimes exacts. But we will also experience the joys of achievement!

Before joining the explorers and discoverers, however, it is worthwhile to consider why they venture into the unknown.

Certainly a primary motivation is curiosity: they want to find out what is on the other side of a mountain, or they are intrigued by rumors about a strange new land, or they simply enjoy wandering the world. Yet adventurers often—indeed, usually—embark on a journey of discovery under less spontaneous circumstances.

Many explorers were commissioned by the rulers or governments of their countries to lead expeditions with a specific purpose. **José Celestino Mutis,** for instance, was chosen by King Charles III of Spain to travel to the New World colony of New Granada (now Colombia) to gather plant specimens for the royal botanical collection. The explorer brought back many unknown species, some with great medicinal value; these included the *chinchona* tree, whose bark produced quinine, which would become the best treatment for malaria. Put in charge of extending telegraph lines through parts of Brazil and surrounding areas by his government, army engineer **Cândido Rondón** opened up new territories, collected important biological specimens, and made the first peaceful contacts with many little-known Native American tribes that dwelled in the Brazilian jungles. Rondón would later serve, in fact, as the first director of a national agency to protect Brazil's native population. In 1500 King Manuel I of Portugal sponsored an official voyage of exploration to investigate the recently discovered North American mainland, which—at that time—was believed to be northeast Asia. He asked **Gaspar Corte-Real** to command the expedition; on his second trip to what he thought was Asia, the explorer became lost sailing down the North American coast in search of China. The king authorized **Miguel Corte-Real,** Gaspar's brother, to lead an expedition to look for the lost voyager; Miguel, too, was never heard from again. Far more successful in his royal mission, navigator-turned-priest **Andrés de Urdaneta** left his quiet life in a New Spain (Mexico) monastery to fulfill the request of Spanish king Philip II, who was looking to found a colony in the Philippines and—especially—to find a safe way to the make the return trip back to the New World. Urdaneta made the first successful west-to-east crossing of the Pacific Ocean by sailing farther north than previous navigators; known as Urdaneta's Passage, the route would change the nature of Pacific travel and give Spain a practical link to the Orient by way of Mexico.

Explorers also received backing from private sponsors or were motivated by economic self-interest. The Association for Promoting the Discovery of the Interior Parts of Africa—also known as the African Association—was a private organization composed of twelve London gentlemen who commissioned explorers to investigate the little-known interior of the continent in the late eighteenth and early nineteenth centuries. Retired military officer **Daniel Houghton** was one of the early explorers the Association sponsored; his mission was to investigate the Niger River region, which was rumored to be an area of great wealth and the site of a rich trade center called Timbuktu. Traveling inland from the west coast of Africa, Houghton died before he could reach his destination. Swiss scholar **Jean-Louis Burckhardt,** too, was commissioned by the Association to travel to Timbuktu. His mission, however, was to approach the region from the north, by way of Cairo and the Sahara Desert. While years of delays prevented Burckhardt from fulfilling his mission as well, his travels in the Middle East—especially to the forbidden Islamic holy cities of Mecca and Medina—provided Europeans with valuable information about Muslim life. In an effort to expand the fur-trading operations of the British North West Company, of which he was part-owner, **Simon Fraser** traveled from British North America to the Pacific Northwest, into what is now British Columbia. There he established fur-trading posts and encampments, including Fort McLeod, the first European settlement west of the Rocky Mountains. His efforts opened up the territory for future British occupation at a time when the United States, too, was eager to establish claims in the Pacific Northwest.

Religious dedication has long been a strong motivating force behind exploration and travel into unknown lands. **I-Ching,** for example, was one of many Chinese Buddhist monks who made the trip to India—the birthplace of Buddhism—to visit holy sites and study original religious texts. But unlike most of these pilgrims, he was unable to take the usual land route to India across central Asia and the Himalayas because of political turmoil in the region. He was forced to take a more southerly route, most of it by sea, beginning in 671. The accounts he wrote about his years of religious travel provide a rare record of the early history, culture, and religion of the peoples of Indonesia. French missionary priest **Jordanus of Séverac** also left valuable written accounts that resulted from his years of religious travel. Arriving in India in 1321 to serve that country's small Christian population and make further converts, Jordanus traveled throughout the subcontinent, becoming a bishop of southern India in 1330. His *Mirabilia* (*Book of Marvels*) is considered the best description of medieval India by a Westerner. And under circumstances oddly similar to those of I-Ching's (but occurring a millennium later), Jesuit missionary priest **Johann Grüber,** working in China during the mid-seventeenth century, also had to find an alternative route to complete his religious mission. Because maritime warfare between the Dutch and the Portuguese along China's coast cut off the usual sailing routes, Grüber—a trained mathematician and geographer—was asked to find an overland passage from the Jesuit mission in Peking to Catholic headquarters in Rome. The difficult trip took him through the Himalayas and the little-known mountain kingdom of Tibet; he was the first Westerner to describe such wonders as the Potala, the royal palace and monastery that was the centerpiece of Tibetan Buddhism.

Explorers have been inspired, too, by the quest for scientific knowledge. British archaeologist **Kathleen M. Kenyon** spent five trying but exciting years in the Jordan desert, excavating the site of the ancient city of Jericho. At first determined to learn what she could about its most famous "era" (described in the Bible, when Joshua and the Israelites blew horns and shouted in order to collapse the walls that surrounded the city), Kenyon shocked herself and the world when she discovered that the town had been rebuilt dozens of times, and that it dated back to the Neolithic or New Stone Age, around 7800 B.C. Her findings also revealed that Jericho's Neolithic dwellers were surprisingly advanced. Years of studying the mountain gorillas that lived in the Virunga Mountain range of east central Africa led to surprising discoveries for American zoologist **Dian Fossey** as well. She found that far from the violent, chest-thumping beasts that they were thought to be, the mountain gorillas were really "gentle giants," who had strong family ties and cared for one another almost tenderly. With their population threatened by hunters and farmers, Fossey used aggressive methods to protect these endangered animals and brought their plight to the attention of the world; she was murdered in her wilderness camp in retaliation for her antipoaching activities. With similar passion, marine biologist **Sylvia Earle** has devoted her life to developing new ways and tools to make the deep sea and its little-known inhabitants easier to study. In 1979 she made a record-breaking dive in a specially designed suit that allowed her to explore deeper waters than anyone had done before; since 1982 she has been developing small, easy-to-use submersibles for deep-sea exploration. Earle believes that the more we know about the oceans and their wondrous inhabitants, the more concerned we will be about protecting them.

But perhaps the foremost motivation to explore is the desire to be the first to accomplish a particular feat. Scottish explorer **James Bruce** was determined to become the first Westerner to discover the source of Africa's great Nile River, a mystery for centuries. During a five-year journey in which he endured illness, imprisonment, and a near-death experience in the desert, Bruce managed to find the source of the Blue Nile River in the highlands of Ethiopia. Jubilant over the fame and honors he would receive upon his return to Europe, Bruce was bitterly disappointed when his fantastic tales of African adventure and discovery were thought to be made up. Experiencing similar grave disappointment was Arctic sea captain **Bob Bartlett,** who piloted the ship and participated in the campaigns of explorer Robert Edwin Peary as he attempted to become the first man to reach the North Pole. Bartlett joined Peary on the condition that he be allowed to accompany the explorer to the Pole. However, at the last advance camp—just 150 miles from their destination—Peary told Bartlett to turn back while he proceeded. Peary's controversial last-minute decision has since been the subject of much speculation. Also controversial are the claims of **Louis Hennepin,** the Franciscan missionary priest who accompanied French explorer René-Robert Cavelier de La Salle on a voyage through the Great Lakes into the upper Mississippi River valley. Sent with three others as advance scouts to try to locate the great river, Hennepin maintained that he and the scouts not only found the Mississippi, but in less than two months' time had canoed south to its mouth (beating La Salle to the destination by two years) and returned, an impossible journey of more than 3,000 miles. When Hennepin experienced ill fortune later in his life, he blamed it on a plot by La Salle to discredit him and his claim. Attempting her "first" before the eyes of the world, popular American newspaper reporter **Nellie Bly** took her challenge from a fictional character—Phileas Fogg from Jules Verne's novel *Around the World in Eighty Days.* During 1889–90 she rushed to circle the globe by boat and train faster than Fogg (or any real person, for that matter), and accomplished her goal, traveling 21,740 miles in 72 days, 6 hours, and 11 minutes. Conceived as a way of increasing readership of the newspaper she wrote for, Bly's trip succeeded wildly as people around the world followed her progress and cheered her achievement.

By concentrating on biographies of individual explorers and discoverers in this book we seem to suggest that many of these adventurers were loners who set out on their own to singlehandedly confront the unknown. But as a rule, explorers rarely traveled alone—they had help in achieving their goals. Therefore, use of an individual name is often only shorthand for the achievements of an expedition as a whole. Explorers were often accompanied by large groups of servants and porters and—most importantly—native guides. Sometimes the contributions of these guides were so vital to the success of an expedition that they received individual recognition; such was the case of **Sacagawea,** the Native American woman who accompanied Meriwether Lewis and William Clark on their journey of discovery across the American West. Many times during the trip the expedition leaders were grateful for her unique skills: she gathered nutritious food from the wild when provisions were low, guided the travelers through unknown territories, and acted as an interpreter when they needed to trade with other Indian tribes for horses for overland travel. While it took nearly a century, Sacagawea's invaluable contribution to the opening of the American West is at last publicly recognized.

Explorers & Discoverers, Volume 6 tells the stories of these men and women as well as those of others motivated by a daring spirit and an intense curiosity.

A final note of clarification: When we say that an explorer "discovered" a place, we do not mean that she or he was the first human ever to have been there. Although the discoverer may have been the first from her or his own country to set foot in a new land, most areas of the world during the great periods of exploration were already occupied or their existence had been verified by other people.

Picture Credits

The photographs and illustrations appearing in *Explorers & Discoverers, Volume 6* were received from the following sources:

On the cover: John Smith; **The Granger Collection, New York:** Beryl Markham and Matthew A. Henson.

Culver Pictures, Inc. Reproduced by permission: p. 1; **AP/Wide World Photos. Reproduced by permission:** pp. 2, 32, 38, 48, 50, 54, 57, 60, 72, 83, 88, 125, 128, 145, 148; **Corbis-Bettmann. Reproduced by permission:** pp. 7, 9, 18, 44, 81, 90, 95, 97, 139, 147, 150, 159, 162; **Archive Photos. Reproduced by permission:** pp. 11, 14, 67, 79, 92, 114, 181; **Mary Evans Picture Library. Reproduced by permission:** pp. 26, 35, 169; **The Granger Collection, New York. Reproduced by permission:** pp. 30, 64, 104, 107; **The Library of Congress:** pp. 58, 142, 156, 163; **National Aeronautics and Space Administration:** p. 132; **State Historical Society of North Dakota. Reproduced by permission:** p. 161.

Maps

The World

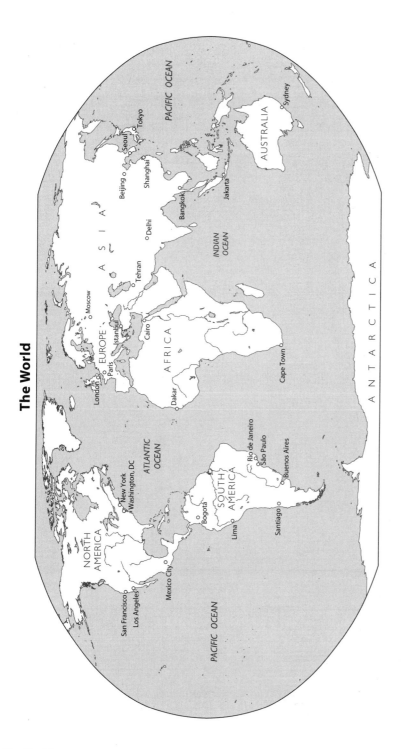

The World

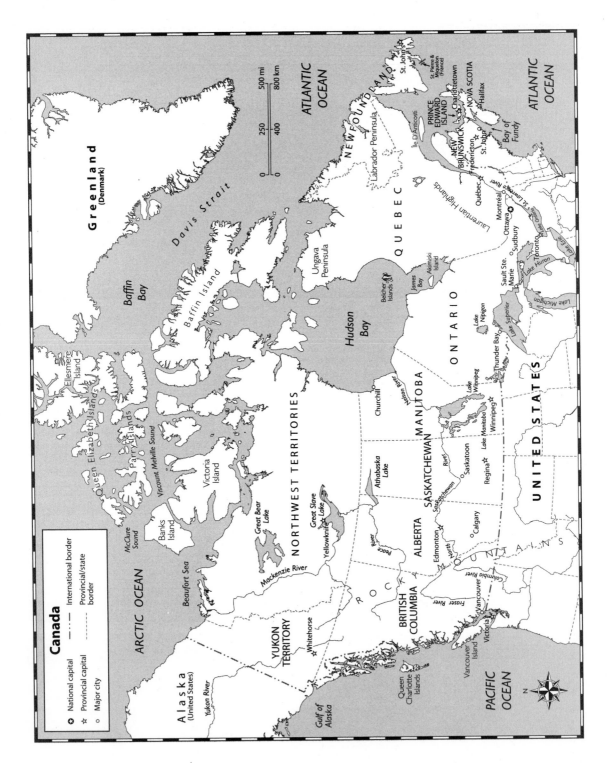

Canada

Legend:
- —·—· International border
- ----- Provincial/state border
- ✪ National capital
- ★ Provincial capital
- ○ Major city

ARCTIC OCEAN

ATLANTIC OCEAN

ATLANTIC OCEAN

PACIFIC OCEAN

Greenland (Denmark)

Baffin Bay

Davis Strait

Baffin Island

Ellesmere Island

Queen Elizabeth Islands

Parry Islands

Viscount Melville Sound

McClure Sound

Banks Island

Victoria Island

Beaufort Sea

Alaska (United States)

Yukon River

Gulf of Alaska

Queen Charlotte Islands

Vancouver Island

Victoria

Vancouver

Fraser River

Columbia River

ROCKY MOUNTAINS

BRITISH COLUMBIA

YUKON TERRITORY

Whitehorse

NORTHWEST TERRITORIES

Yellowknife

Mackenzie River

Great Bear Lake

Great Slave Lake

Peace River

Athabaska Lake

ALBERTA

Edmonton

Calgary

North Saskatchewan River

SASKATCHEWAN

Saskatoon

Regina

Churchill

Nelson River

Lake Winnipeg

Lake Manitoba

MANITOBA

Winnipeg

Hudson Bay

Belcher Islands

James Bay

Akimiski Island

Ungava Peninsula

QUEBEC

Labrador Peninsula

NEWFOUNDLAND

Laurentian Highlands

Île D'Anticosti

Québec

Montreal

Ottawa

Sudbury

ONTARIO

Lake Nipigon

Lake Superior

Thunder Bay

Sault Ste. Marie

Lake Huron

Lake Michigan

Lake Erie

Lake Ontario

Toronto

St. Lawrence River

UNITED STATES

St. John's

St. Pierre & Miquelon (France)

PRINCE EDWARD ISLAND

Charlottetown

NOVA SCOTIA

Halifax

NEW BRUNSWICK

Fredericton

St. John

Bay of Fundy

500 mi
800 km
250
400

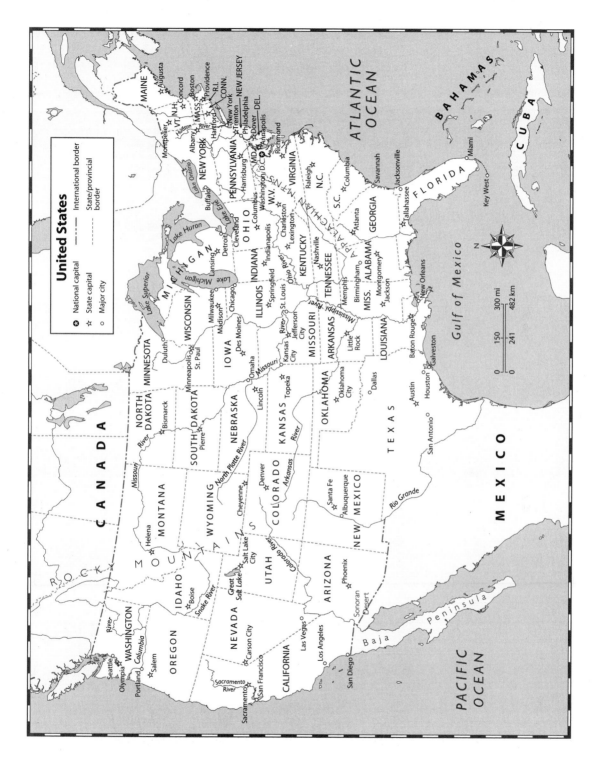

Americas–United States of America.

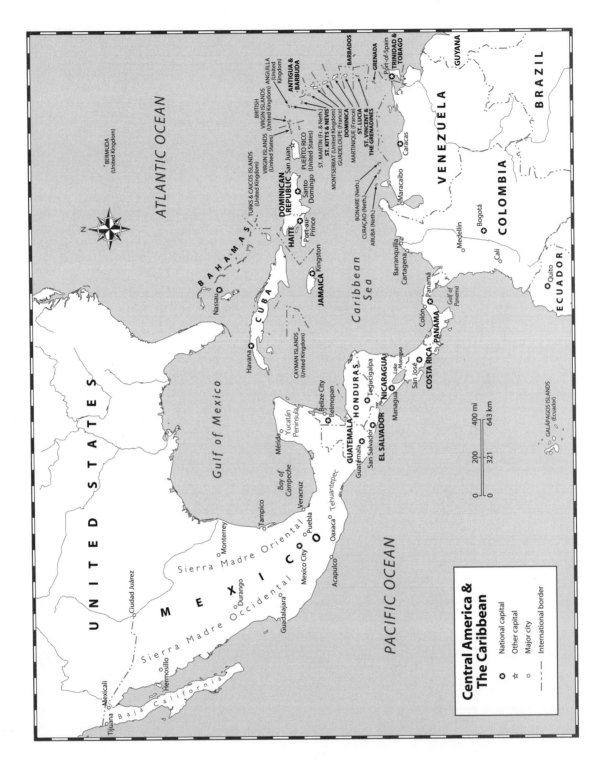

Central America &
The Caribbean

National capital
Other capital
Major city
International border

Americas—Mexico and Central America.

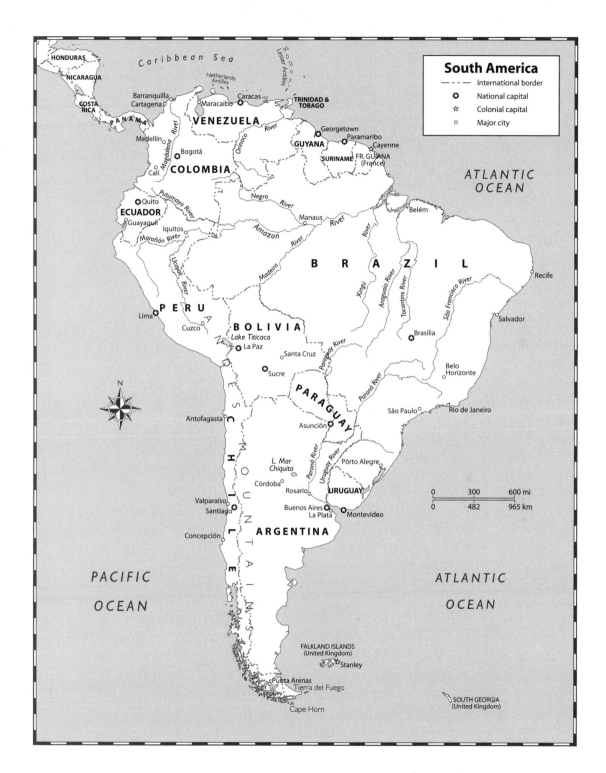

South America

- – – International border
- ⊕ National capital
- ☆ Colonial capital
- ○ Major city

HONDURAS

NICARAGUA

COSTA RICA

PANAMA

Caribbean Sea

Barranquilla
Cartagena

Maracaibo

Caracas

Netherlands Antilles

Lesser Antilles

TRINIDAD & TOBAGO

VENEZUELA

Medellín

Magdalena River

Orinoco River

Bogotá

Cali

COLOMBIA

Georgetown

Paramaribo

GUYANA

SURINAME

Cayenne

FR. GUIANA (France)

ATLANTIC OCEAN

Quito

ECUADOR

Putumayo River

Guayaquil

Iquitos

Marañón River

Ucayali River

Negro River

Manaus

Amazon River

PERU

Lima

Cuzco

BOLIVIA

Lake Titicaca

La Paz

Santa Cruz

Sucre

Madeira

B R A Z I L

Xingú

Araguaia River

Tocantins River

São Francisco River

Belém

Recife

Salvador

Brasília

Belo Horizonte

Paraguay River

PARAGUAY

Asunción

Paraná River

São Paulo

Rio de Janeiro

Antofagasta

L. Mar Chiquita

Paraná River

Uruguay River

Pôrto Alegre

Córdoba

Rosario

URUGUAY

Valparaíso

Santiago

Buenos Aires

La Plata

Montevideo

C H I L E

A N D E S M O U N T A I N S

Concepción

ARGENTINA

PACIFIC OCEAN

ATLANTIC OCEAN

FALKLAND ISLANDS (United Kingdom)

Stanley

Punta Arenas

Tierra del Fuego

Cape Horn

SOUTH GEORGIA (United Kingdom)

N

| 0 | 300 | 600 mi |
| 0 | 482 | 965 km |

Americas—South America.

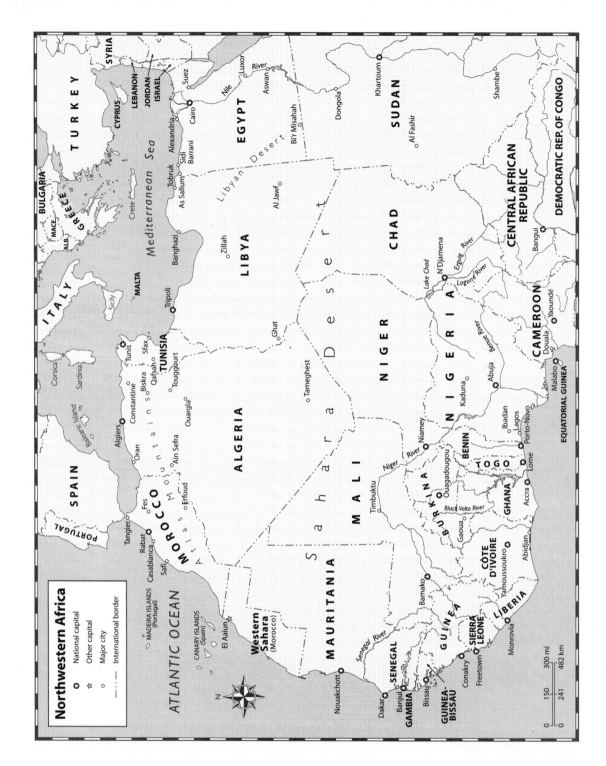

Africa and the Middle East—Northwest Africa.

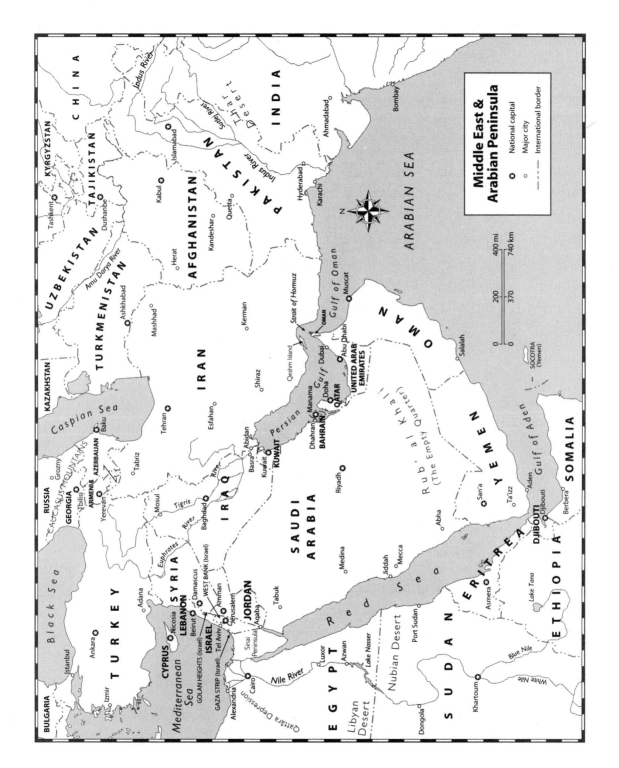

Africa and the Middle East—The Middle East and Arabia.

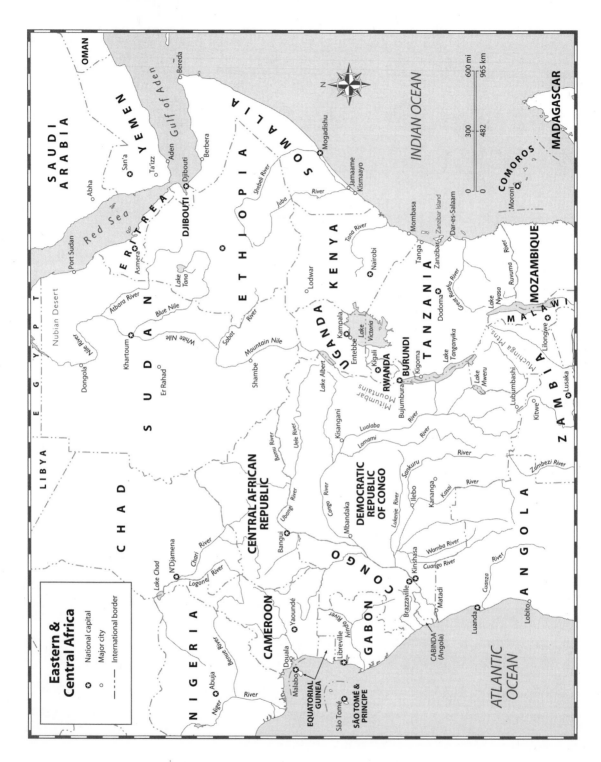

Africa and the Middle East–Eastern Africa.

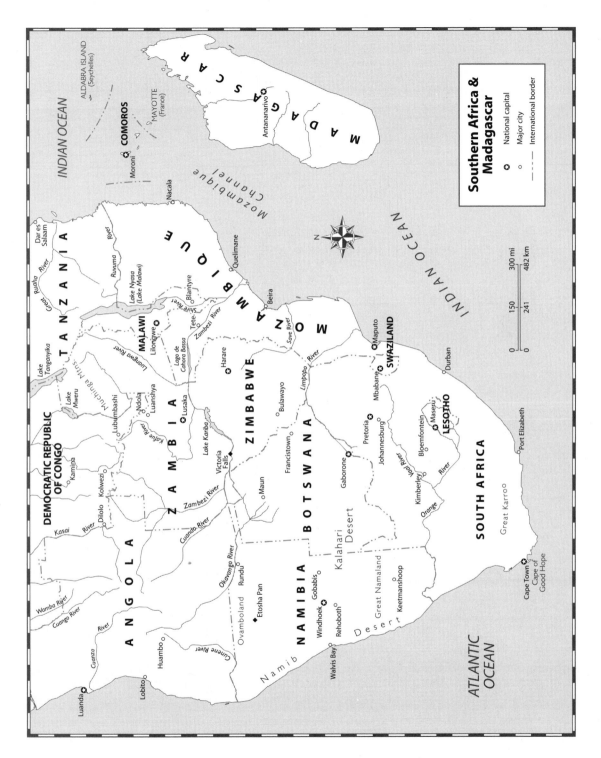

Africa and the Middle East—Southern Africa.

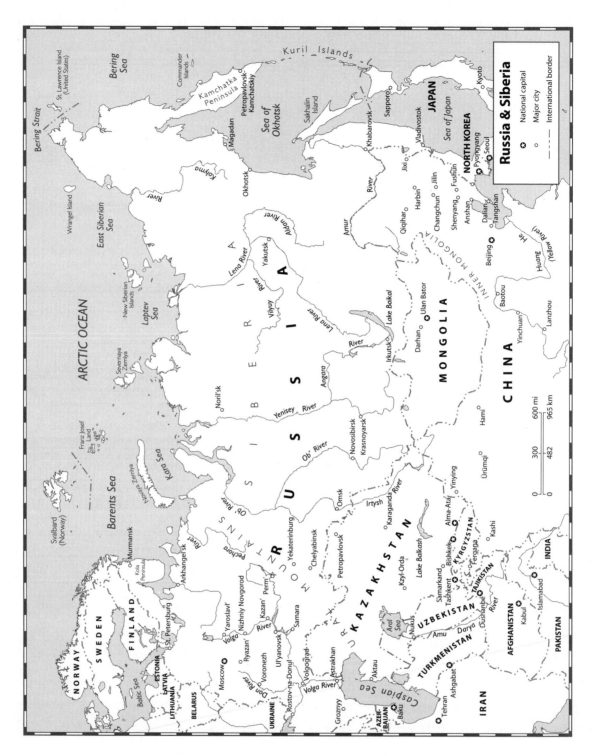

Asia–Siberia.

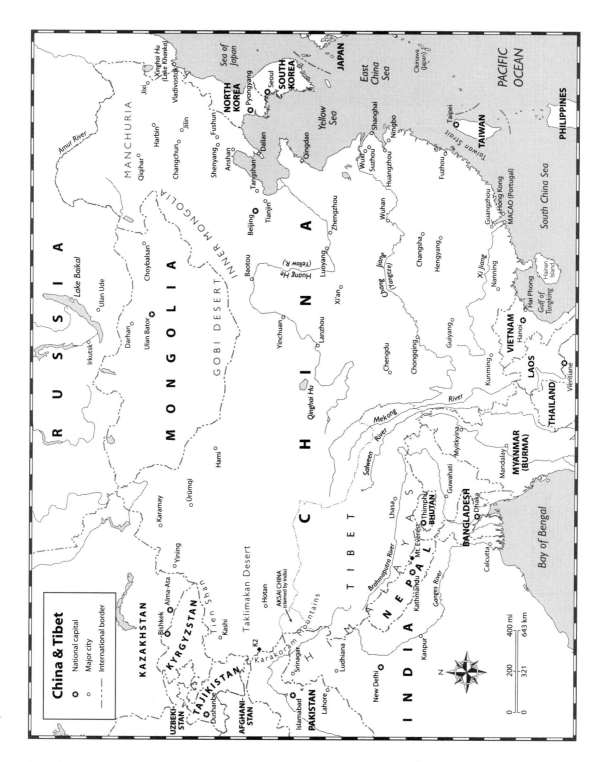

Asia—China and Tibet.

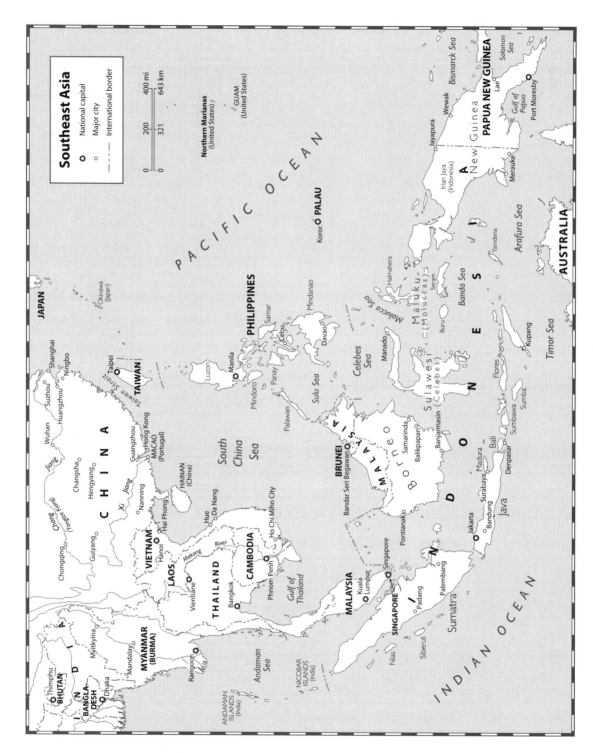

Asia–Southeast Asia.

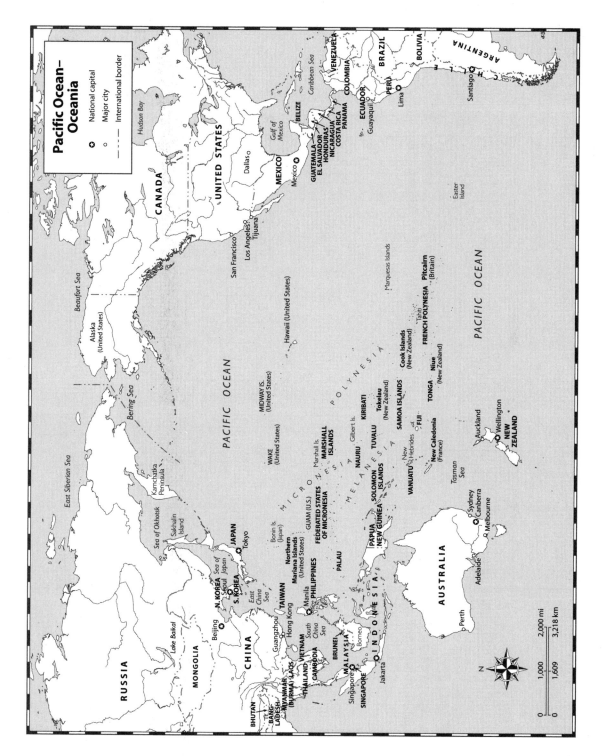

Pacific Ocean–Oceania

- ✪ National capital
- ○ Major city
- – – – International border

Pacific Ocean–Oceanea.

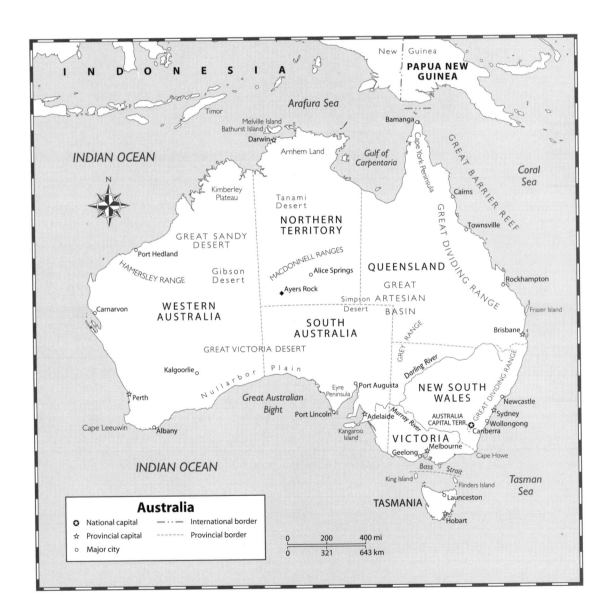

Australia

- National capital
- ✩ Provincial capital
- ○ Major city
- —·—·— International border
- ‑‑‑‑‑ Provincial border

| 0 | 200 | 400 mi |
| 0 | 321 | 643 km |

INDONESIA

Arafura Sea

PAPUA NEW GUINEA

New Guinea

Timor

Melville Island
Bathurst Island
Darwin ✩

Arnhem Land

Gulf of Carpentaria

Bamanga

Cape York Peninsula

Coral Sea

INDIAN OCEAN

N

Kimberley Plateau

Tanami Desert

NORTHERN TERRITORY

GREAT BARRIER REEF

Cairns

GREAT SANDY DESERT

MACDONNELL RANGES

Alice Springs

Townsville

GREAT DIVIDING RANGE

Port Hedland

HAMERSLEY RANGE

Gibson Desert

♦ Ayers Rock

QUEENSLAND

GREAT ARTESIAN BASIN

Rockhampton

Carnarvon

WESTERN AUSTRALIA

Simpson Desert

SOUTH AUSTRALIA

Fraser Island

GREAT VICTORIA DESERT

GREY RANGE

Brisbane ✩

Kalgoorlie

Nullarbor Plain

Darling River

NEW SOUTH WALES

GREAT DIVIDING RANGE

Newcastle

Perth ✩

Great Australian Bight

Eyre Peninsula

Port Augusta

AUSTRALIA CAPITAL TERR.

Sydney ✩
Wollongong

Cape Leeuwin

Albany

Port Lincoln

Adelaide ✩

Murray River

Canberra

Cape Howe

INDIAN OCEAN

Kangaroo Island

VICTORIA

Geelong

Melbourne ✩

Bass Strait

King Island

Flinders Island

Tasman Sea

TASMANIA

Launceston

Hobart ✩

Pacific Ocean–Australia.

Maps | xxxiv

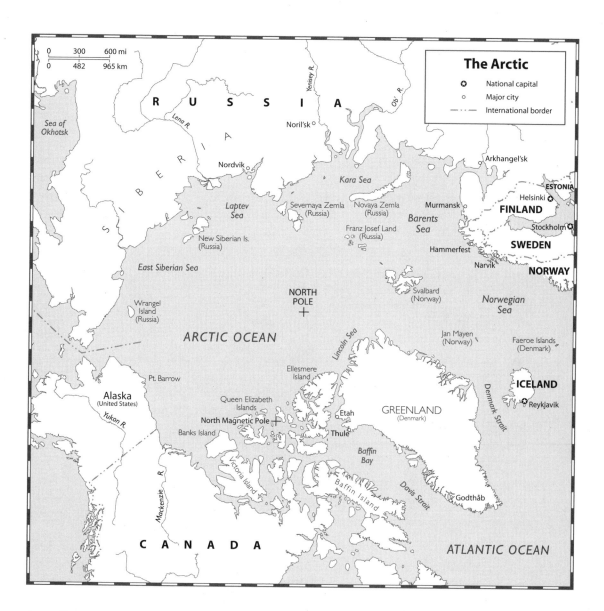

Arctic Region.

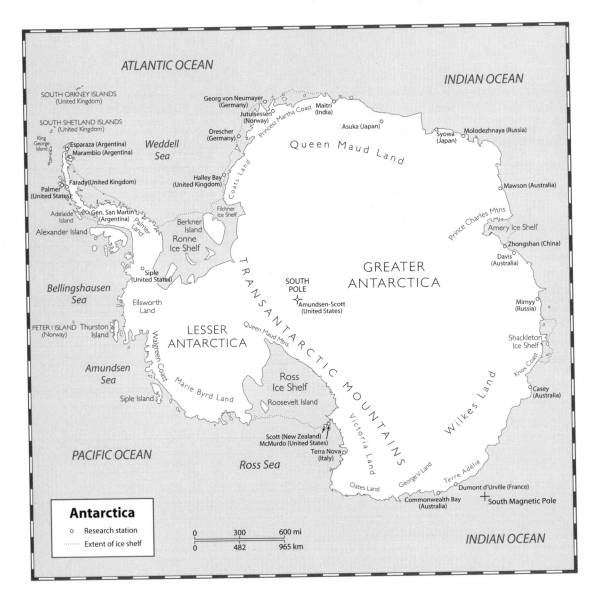

ATLANTIC OCEAN

INDIAN OCEAN

SOUTH ORKNEY ISLANDS
(United Kingdom)

SOUTH SHETLAND ISLANDS
(United Kingdom)

King
George
Island

Esparaza (Argentina)
Marambio (Argentina)

Farady(United Kingdom)

Palmer
(United States)

Adelaide
Island

Gen. San Martin
(Argentina)

Alexander Island

Palmer
Land

Berkner
Island

Ronne
Ice Shelf

Siple
(United States)

Bellingshausen
Sea

Ellsworth
Land

PETER I ISLAND
(Norway)

Thurston
Island

Amundsen
Sea

Siple Island

Walgreen Coast

Marie Byrd Land

LESSER
ANTARCTICA

PACIFIC OCEAN

Ross Sea

Georg von Neumayer
(Germany)

Jutulsessen
(Norway)

Drescher
(Germany)

Princess Martha Coast

Maitri
(India)

Asuka (Japan)

Syowa
(Japan)

Molodezhnaya (Russia)

Coats Land

Weddell
Sea

Halley Bay
(United Kingdom)

Filchner
Ice Shelf

Queen Maud Land

Mawson (Australia)

Prince Charles Mtns

Amery Ice Shelf

Zhongshan (China)

Davis
(Australia)

GREATER
ANTARCTICA

SOUTH
POLE

Amundsen-Scott
(United States)

Mirnyy
(Russia)

Shackleton
Ice Shelf

Queen Maud Mtns.

Ross
Ice Shelf

Roosevelt Island

Scott (New Zealand)
McMurdo (United States)

Terra Nova
(Italy)

TRANSANTARCTIC MOUNTAINS

Victoria Land

Wilkes Land

Knox Coast

Casey
(Australia)

George V Land

Terre Adélie

Oates Land

Commonwealth Bay
(Australia)

Dumont d'Urville (France)

South Magnetic Pole

INDIAN OCEAN

Antarctica

○ Research station

...... Extent of ice shelf

0	300	600 mi
0	482	965 km

Antarctic Region.

EXPLORERS & DISCOVERERS

Bob Bartlett

Born August 15, 1875, Brigus, Newfoundland

Died April 28, 1946, New York, New York

The oldest of ten children, Bob Bartlett was born in the small Newfoundland fishing village of Brigus on August 15, 1875. When he was fifteen he left to attend boarding school in St. John's, the capital city of Newfoundland. But he was unhappy there and, after two years, convinced his parents to let him go to sea aboard a sealing ship. He quickly earned a reputation as a skillful seal hunter, which was one of the chief ways to earn a living in Newfoundland at that time.

In 1898 Bartlett's uncle hired him to serve as first mate on the *Windward*, the ship used by American explorer Robert Edwin Peary (1856–1920) in his first attempt to reach the North Pole. After a winter in the far north, Bartlett and the *Windward* returned south. Peary stayed behind in the Arctic, learning Inuit (Eskimo) methods of travel and survival and improving his expedition equipment and tactics. He developed what was later called the "Peary system" of polar travel: sending advance parties ahead to open the trail and set up supply stations, which allowed the main party to spend its energy covering distance.

A native of Newfoundland, Bob Bartlett became known as the best Arctic sea captain of his time. He accompanied Robert Peary on his attempts to reach the North Pole and was captain of the first Canadian Arctic Expedition.

The Theodore Roosevelt.

Agrees to join Peary as ship captain

In 1904 Peary commissioned the building of the *Theodore Roosevelt,* a steamship specially designed to sail in polar waters. Ready to make his next attempt at the North Pole, he asked Bartlett to be his captain. Bartlett agreed, with the condition that he be allowed to accompany Peary to the Pole. They set out from New York on July 16, 1905, and first headed to Greenland to pick up a party of Inuit men and women and a team of sled dogs. (The Inuit were crucial to the success of the expedition, for the men constructed igloos to live in and the women made garments out of animal hides and furs.) From Greenland the *Roosevelt* fought its way through the ice of Smith Sound, arriving at Cape Sheridan on the northwest coast of Ellesmere Island on September 5. Beginning in February 1906, Bartlett led parties of Inuit north to cut trails and set up supply depots. On April 21 he reached as far north as latitude 85° 12', before a large expanse of open sea stopped him. Peary, too, tried to push farther, but bad weather and open water made it clear that the expedition was at its end. On July 4 Bartlett turned the *Roosevelt* south.

The return trip was a difficult one. Sea ice almost crushed the ship, destroying its rudder and making a large hole in its bottom. It took seventy-five days just to travel to the settlement of Etah in northern Greenland. There the crew made temporary repairs to the ship before continuing the trip. Off the coast of Greenland they were hit by several storms but managed to make it to Cape Breton Island in Nova Scotia. Peary disembarked there and took a train back to New York. Bartlett continued to sail the disabled ship down the coast until it reached New York Harbor on December 24, 1906— ninety-nine days after leaving Etah.

Sets sail on second polar expedition

During the next few years Peary worked to raise money to fully repair the *Roosevelt* and finance another expedition to the North Pole. Bartlett returned to Newfoundland and captained sealing ships. In June 1908 he received a telegram from

Peary telling him that the *Roosevelt* was ready to sail again. They set off on July 7, 1908, from Oyster Bay, New York. The ship's namesake, President Theodore Roosevelt, was there to wish them luck.

Angry Bartlett denied access to North Pole

The expedition reached Cape Sheridan on September 5. A base camp was set up several miles away, at Cape Columbia. Throughout the winter, small parties established supply drops to the north. On February 28, 1909, Bartlett left base camp and headed north to open up the main trail. As other support parties turned back, Bartlett pressed on, advancing to within 150 miles of the North Pole. Peary and his party set out along this route on March 14, and by the 31st had caught up with Bartlett at the farthest advance camp. That night Peary told Bartlett that he was taking his own party of four Inuit and his servant/companion Matthew Henson the rest of the way to the Pole, and that Bartlett would have to return to Cape Columbia.

Bartlett was furious at the news, believing that Peary had made him a firm promise that he would accompany him to the Pole. Bartlett left the advance camp on April 1, 1909, beginning his long journey back to Cape Columbia before Peary and Henson were awake. Peary and his group would go on to reach the North Pole, arriving on April 6.

Peary's decision to leave Bartlett behind was a controversial one that has led to much speculation. Did Peary not want to share credit for reaching the Pole with another white man (Henson was African American)? Did he realize that he could not reach the Pole, and was fearful that Bartlett—a skilled navigator—would know it? (Henson and the four Inuit in Peary's party were unable to take latitude and longitude readings and verify the Pole's position.)

Bartlett had a difficult journey back to base camp, the trip taking eighteen days. At one point he fell through the ice and had to be rescued by his Inuit companions. When Peary returned to Cape Columbia after his historic journey, Bartlett

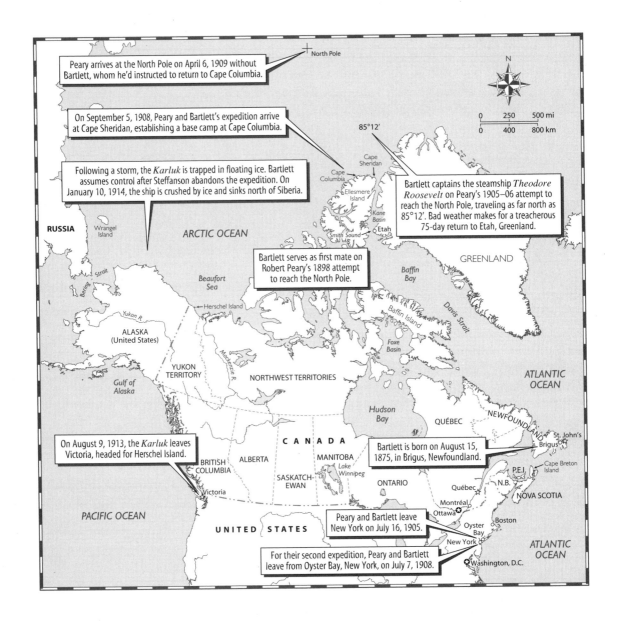

Peary arrives at the North Pole on April 6, 1909 without Bartlett, whom he'd instructed to return to Cape Columbia.

On September 5, 1908, Peary and Bartlett's expedition arrive at Cape Sheridan, establishing a base camp at Cape Columbia.

Following a storm, the *Karluk* is trapped in floating ice. Bartlett assumes control after Steffanson abandons the expedition. On January 10, 1914, the ship is crushed by ice and sinks north of Siberia.

Bartlett captains the steamship *Theodore Roosevelt* on Peary's 1905–06 attempt to reach the North Pole, traveling as far north as 85°12'. Bad weather makes for a treacherous 75-day return to Etah, Greenland.

Bartlett serves as first mate on Robert Peary's 1898 attempt to reach the North Pole.

On August 9, 1913, the *Karluk* leaves Victoria, headed for Herschel Island.

Bartlett is born on August 15, 1875, in Brigus, Newfoundland.

Peary and Bartlett leave New York on July 16, 1905.

For their second expedition, Peary and Bartlett leave from Oyster Bay, New York, on July 7, 1908.

congratulated him on his success. The *Roosevelt* headed to the coast of Labrador, where news of the achievement was telegraphed to the world. In 1910 Bartlett went to Europe on a lecture tour to talk about the expedition. He was then hired by a pair of American millionaires who wanted to hunt polar bears in Greenland and on northern Baffin Island. On this expedition they captured the first adult male polar bear ever taken alive and donated it to New York City's Bronx Zoo.

Pilots first Canadian Arctic expedition

In 1913 polar explorer Vilhjalmur Stefansson (1879–1962) convinced the Canadian government to sponsor an expedition to the western islands of the Canadian Arctic, in part to strengthen the country's claims in the area. The government bought an old wooden sailing ship, the *Karluk,* and hired Bartlett to be its captain; Stefansson was appointed scientific head of the first Canadian Arctic expedition. The *Karluk* set sail from British Columbia's port city of Victoria in July, heading for Herschel Island. But a frigid storm stopped the ship off the north coast of Alaska on August 9, and three days later it was frozen into its icy surroundings. Stefansson left the ship on September 19 with a small party of men on dogsled, saying that he was going to hunt caribou and would be back within ten days. But, in fact, he did not want to be detained in his mission, and set out for Herschel Island. Never intending to return to the ship, Stefansson remained in the Arctic for the next five years, traveling more than five hundred miles and discovering unknown territories. The care of the rather unseaworthy *Karluk* and its twenty-five passengers was left in the hands of Bartlett—and an Arctic winter was approaching.

Trapped ship drifts in Arctic waters

Shortly after Stefansson left, the *Karluk*—caught in a shifting sheet of ice—began to drift west, pushed by heavy winds and ocean currents. It was nearly crushed by floes as it passed north of the Bering Strait, which separates North America from northeast Asia. By October 10 the ship was north of Siberia near the place where the *Jeannette*—commanded by American explorer George Washington De Long (1844–1881)—was crushed by ice in 1881. In order to avoid the same fate, Bartlett had his crew and passengers move everything they could off the *Karluk* and onto an ice floe, building igloos for shelter. It was a wise decision, for on January 10, 1914, the ship was crushed by ice and sank.

Uses "Peary system" to reach land

On January 20 Bartlett sent a party of four men south across the frozen sea to a rock named Herald Island to see whether he could set up a base camp there. The men were never heard from again. Soon after, a group of the expedition's scientists set out on their own to try to reach the Russian mainland; they also disappeared. In the meantime, Bartlett was regularly sending out small parties to open a trail and set up food depots, using the system of travel Peary had used in his polar expeditions. Finally, on February 19, the survivors left "Shipwreck Camp," and reached land—Wrangel Island—on March 12.

Once camp had been set up on the island, Bartlett and an Inuit hunter headed for the mainland. Upon reaching it they were taken in by Chukchi hunters—the native people of northeast Siberia. The castaways then headed for the Bering Strait, where they met a Russian trader who was able to get word of the *Karluk* disaster to the outside world. Bartlett found a ship to take him to Alaska, which he reached on May 28. He then spent the next two months trying to find a boat that would take him back to Wrangel Island to rescue the rest of the expedition.

Bartlett found an American sailing ship that tried to make the voyage, coming within twenty miles of the island before being forced back, on August 24. On September 7, 1914, a Russian schooner was able to make its way to Wrangel Island and at last rescue the survivors—three more of whom had died during the wait.

Unfair investigation leaves Bartlett bitter

Afterward, an investigation into the *Karluk* disaster unjustly found Bartlett's actions partly to blame for the incident. After his heroic attempts to save the ship's crew and passengers, Bartlett felt—understandably—bitter. He moved to the United States during World War I (1914–1918) and became an American citizen. During the war he carried out routine assignments for the U.S. Navy.

In the following years Bartlett promoted several schemes for Arctic exploration but could find no financial backers. Discouraged, he began to drink heavily, which led to a serious accident that landed him in the hospital in 1924. Bartlett remained sober after that, and his life continued to improve when a millionaire friend bought him a sailing schooner, the *Effie M. Morrissey.* Bartlett used the ship to make twenty voyages to the Canadian Arctic, collecting large amounts of scientific data.

Left to right: Dr. Heinbecker, G. P. Putnam, Carl Dunrud, Bob Bartlett, and Ed Manley study a map for an upcoming scientific expedition to the Arctic aboard the Effie M. Morrissey.

Important expedition work

Bartlett's expedition work—in places including Baffin Island, Greenland, and Ellesmere Island—was sponsored by numerous scientific organizations. His collection of oceanic and atmospheric data in Greenland, for instance, was backed by the U.S. Navy. Bartlett wrote articles about his expeditions for various publications, including the *National Geographic,* and published two books about his experiences. During World War II (1939–1945) he made several trips to northern Canada and Greenland, setting up and supplying military bases for the Allied war effort. Following the war he caught pneumonia and died in a New York City hospital on April 28, 1946. The *Effie M. Morrissey* was later put on display at Mystic Seaport in Connecticut.

Sources

Baker, Daniel B., ed. *Explorers and Discoverers of the World.* Detroit: Gale Research, 1993.

Pear, Nancy and Daniel B. Baker. "Vilhjalmur Stefansson." *Explorers and Discoverers.* Detroit: U•X•L, 1997.

Saari, Peggy and Daniel B. Baker. "Robert Edwin Peary." *Explorers and Discoverers.* Detroit: U•X•L, 1995.

Biosphere 2

Construction began in 1987

In 1984, a scientific research company called Space Biospheres Ventures (SBV) bought land in Oracle, Arizona, in the foothills of the Santa Catalina Mountains, north of the city of Tucson. Over the next several years a number of ecological research facilities would be built on the site, including the most challenging and daring structure of them all, Biosphere 2. An enormous steel and glass greenhouse that reaches ninety-one feet at its highest point and covers an area the size of three football fields, Biosphere 2 was built to be a miniature replica of Earth. The purpose of studying Biosphere 2—complete with its own desert, rainforest, savannah, marsh, ocean, and plant and animal inhabitants—was to gain a better understanding of how the planet Earth and its life systems work. SBV hoped to use its findings to develop new recycling technologies that would help solve environmental problems. The company also hoped to use what it learned to improve enclosed life-support systems for eventual use in uninhabitable places like Antarctica, on the ocean floor, or even in outer space.

Part of a scientific research complex in the Arizona desert, Biosphere 2 is an enormous greenhouse-like structure that houses a mini-Earth with its own atmosphere and more than three thousand species of plants and animals.

A biosphere is a system of living things that work together in a shared environment. The largest natural biosphere is the planet Earth—which scientists often call Biosphere 1. Thus, when an international team of experts in science, agriculture, architecture, and engineering gathered together to plan their miniature copy of the world, they called it Biosphere 2.

Building begins

In 1987, after months of planning and performing tests in a small biosphere test module, construction of the $200 million Biosphere 2 began. Because life inside would be dependent on the sun, the structure would require thousands of glass windows. And since each glass pane (6,400 would be used) weighed about 250 pounds, a strong steel frame would be needed for support. The roof would also have to vary in height, so that the air inside could rise and fall and circulate just as it does in nature. A steel bottom would separate the structure from the ground below. It was vital that Biosphere 2 be airtight, so that no outside forces could ruin the experiment by affecting the miniature world inside.

But because Biosphere 2 was airtight, it presented air pressure problems. Heated air expands, and designers of the structure feared that during a hot day in the Arizona desert the air inside the biosphere might expand so much that it would blow out panes of glass. To solve this problem, they attached a pair of giant balloon-like "lungs" to the main structure. These would expand and contract as the air inside Biosphere 2 heated and cooled.

Choosing Biosphere 2's inhabitants

Scientists wanted to include as many of Earth's different plants and animals as possible in Biosphere 2, in order to give the enclosed environment the greatest chance for success. So they designed a number of ecosystems, called biomes, to sup-

Opposite page: The one-half acre agricultural biome, where the crew grew their food.

port these varieties of life. The structure contained a rainforest, a savannah (tropical grassland), a marsh, an ocean, and a desert. And because a team of scientists—Biospherians—would also live there, a place was included for them called the Human Habitat, where they could eat and sleep and conduct their scientific research. There was also a working farm in the structure, complete with farm animals, that would provide the humans with much of the food they would need during the two years they were expected to remain inside, sealed off from the outside world.

Because Biosphere 2 was such a small world, selection of the plants and animals that would fill it was a very difficult task. No poisonous plants or dangerous animals were considered. Plants had to be modest in size and, ideally, provide food for animals and humans as well. All animals also had to contribute something to the food chain, be easy to care for, and not weigh or eat too much. Even the farm animals had to be small; African pygmy goats would provide the Biospherians with milk and other dairy products, and a species of pygmy pigs would provide them with occasional meat.

Where did the nearly four thousand species of plants and animals that were finally selected to inhabit Biosphere 2 come from? Many of them were found in "tame" places like research centers, botanical gardens, and plant nurseries. But a great many more had to be hunted down in the wild. Scientists traveled to the Venezuelan jungle to look for candidates for the biosphere's half-acre rainforest—which would be densely packed with plants and animals. They brought back things like mosses, orchids, and rubber trees, as well as lots of frogs, snakes, and insects. (Before introduction into Biosphere 2, all "wild" specimens were quarantined for a while to make sure they were healthy.) For the savannah biome, the scientists collected grasses from Africa, South America, and Australia. Several types of coral, as well as hundreds of species of marine animals, were brought back from the Caribbean Sea and the Gulf of Mexico for the biosphere's 900,000-gallon saltwater ocean, which reached depths of twenty-five feet. Over 100,000 of those gallons were hauled in from the Pacific near San Diego, California, to supply the ocean with the microscopic organisms required for a healthy system. A special wave machine was added to keep the water moving—just like in nature—so that valuable nutrients would keep circulating instead of piling up on the ocean floor.

Imitating nature

Because Biosphere 2 was so much smaller than Earth, it needed the help of other manmade systems to maintain its cycle of life. Air was kept clean by being pumped through soil (soil-bed reactors), which contained microbes that filtered out and transformed unwanted elements. A separate energy system was used to heat and cool the air, and to help it circulate in the biosphere in the patterns that are found in nature. Rain was created by a computer-operated system of pumps and sprinklers. Fresh water in the biosphere was constantly recycled: pumped to the top of an artificial mountain in the rainforest, it plunged down a waterfall into a pool that flowed into the savannah, and then traveled through the marsh and into the ocean; desalination equipment housed in the biosphere's basement then removed salt from the water, and it was pumped back to the top of the mountain to begin the route all over again. Other recycling systems in Biosphere 2 included one that used bacteria and marsh plants to break down solid waste, which was then used for fertilizer on the farm. While scientists had originally hoped that solar power would provide the electricity needed to run all these mechanical and computer systems, they found that such equipment was too expensive, and used electrical generators instead.

Sealed away from the outside world

After all plant and animal inhabitants and life systems were in place, a team of eight volunteer Biospherians were ready to participate in the grand experiment. On September 26, 1991, before a worldwide audience of millions of television viewers, they were sealed into Biosphere 2's miniature world. They would be allowed out only if they became very sick, or if the atmosphere inside the structure failed. The team members—who had also helped in the development of the

The eight crewmembers on the eve of their two-year living experiment.

biosphere—had undergone months of training and acquired a variety of skills, for they would need to be completely self-sufficient for two years. Although a Mission Control building and staff would be located just outside, the crew could expect no supplies or physical assistance from them. The Biospherians needed to learn about electricity and plumbing, farming and first aid, and how to repair their own clothes. In addition, they were intensively trained in the biology, ecology, chemistry, atmospherics, and geology of our planet.

Teamwork was essential for the success of the experiment. All Biospherians worked on the farm, shared cooking and cleaning chores in the living quarters, and performed other maintenance activities. But each crew member also had special areas of study and responsibility. Abigail K. Alling, for instance, oversaw the marsh and marine biomes, and Linda Leigh managed the terrestrial biomes—the rainforest, savannah, and desert. Taber Kyle MacCallum was responsible for the computer-based environmental monitoring system, whose two thousand scattered sensors reported on the condition of the air, water, and soil in the biosphere many times each hour. English crew member Jane Elizabeth Poytner was in charge of the 150 crops that were grown on the farm's tiny half-acre plot—including food processing, canning, and freezing—as well as the care of the domestic animals. Another Englishwoman, Biosphere 2 co-captain Sally Silverstone, oversaw the quality and nutrition of the crew's diet, which was mostly vegetarian (although the team bred jungle chickens for meat and eggs, and raised tilapia fish in a small rice paddy). Belgian Mark Van Thillo, the biosphere's other captain, was responsible for maintaining the vast, complicated mechanical systems that kept the structure running, including its 200 electric motors and 120 pumps. Roy L. Walford, a physician, was the team's medical officer. SBV co-founder Mark Nelson was in charge of communications, serving as the link between Biosphere 2 and scientists around the world. (Throughout their stay, the Biospherians kept in touch with family and friends through telephone and video hookups.)

On September 26, 1993, the eight crewmembers of Biosphere 2 stepped out into the Earth's atmosphere, completing their mission. They had set a new record for living in a closed system, breaking the previous record of six months held by Soviet researchers during their Bios-3 experiments in Siberia.

Lessons learned

Just like planet Earth, Biosphere 2 had its share of problems and successes. The Biospherians had managed to recycle 100 percent of the water and waste in their environment, which was an extraordinary accomplishment. Despite two winters of record cloudy weather, they were still able to produce about 80 percent of their food (the remaining 20 percent coming from crops stored in the structure prior to closing). The food had been grown without toxic pesticides or chemical

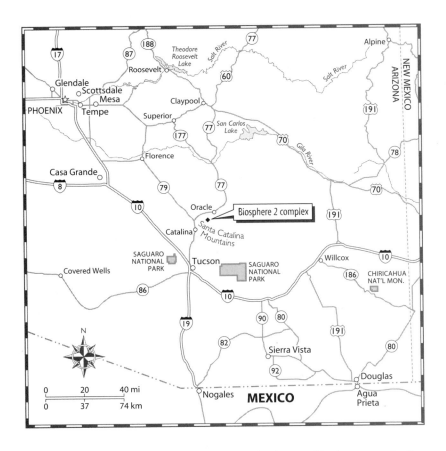

fertilizers. The health of the crew had actually improved after their two years on the low-calorie, low-fat, nutrient-rich diet that Biosphere 2 had provided.

The most serious and unexpected problem with Biosphere 2 was a consistent decline in oxygen levels in its atmosphere. Part of the reason was the unusually cloudy weather, which reduced photosynthesis in the plants, raising carbon dioxide levels. The Biospherians learned how to remove the excess carbon dioxide, but—twice during their two-year stay—oxygen had to be added to their air. The problem led to a greater understanding of the complexity of oxygen cycles.

Biosphere 2 today

In 1994 a team of seven more Biospherians were sealed in the structure for further experiments, staying six-and-a-half

Visiting Biosphere 2

The Biosphere 2 complex—renamed Biosphere 2 Center—is now open to the public. It offers research and educational programs, as well as daily tours of the center and of the Biosphere 2 structure. Tours include exhibits, multimedia presentations, interactive science activities, and a look into Biosphere 2's ocean by way of an underwater viewing gallery. There is a restaurant and cafe at the center, as well as three gift shops. There is also a hotel on the site. Group student educational tours and workshop programs are available. Biosphere 2 Center is open every day of the year, except Christmas Day, from 8:30 A.M. to 5:00 P.M.

months. Then on January 1, 1996, New York City's Columbia University formed a partnership with Biosphere 2, and the ecological facility began to be used for short-term scientific experiments. There were no further plans for human habitation in the biosphere, and the number of species living there was reduced to about three thousand—mostly insects and plants. Scientists working there now pass in and out everyday, through airlocks. The main focus of their research is to learn how different levels of carbon dioxide effect plant growth. Since concentrations of the gas are the highest they have ever been in Earth's atmosphere—due in large part to our burning of fossil fuels like coal and oil for energy—the findings made possible by Biosphere 2 will be of great importance to the future of our planet.

Sources

Biosphere 2 Center. [Online] Available http://www.bio2.edu/, March 7, 1998.

Gentry, Linnea and Karen Liptak. *The Glass Ark: The Story of Biosphere 2*. New York: Viking Press, 1991.

Press Releases Issued by Space Biospheres Ventures in September 1993. [Online] Available http://www.biospherics.org/, February 17, 1998.

Nellie Bly

Born May 5, 1864, Cochran's Mills, Pennsylvania
Died January 27, 1922

Nellie Bly was one of America's first female newspaper reporters. In 1889–1890 she traveled around the globe, setting a new speed record.

Nellie Bly had an adventurous spirit and a strong concern for others. These two qualities combined to make her one of the most widely read newspaper reporters of her time. In order to get a true sense of the subjects she wanted to write about—factory conditions, care for the mentally ill, prison life—she disguised herself and went undercover, one of the first journalists to do so. Her shocking revelations led to needed reforms, and her daring encouraged women to try new things at a time when their choices were limited. When Bly decided to beat the travel record of Phileas Fogg, a fictional character in Jules Verne's novel *Around the World in Eighty Days,* people around the globe followed her progress and cheered her success.

Bly was born Elizabeth Cochran on May 5, 1864, in Cochran's Mills, Pennsylvania. The town was named for her father, who was a wealthy businessman, lawyer, and judge. Elizabeth had six brothers and a sister. High-spirited, Elizabeth enjoyed the rough play of the boys—the tree climbing, horseback riding, and sports. She also liked to read books and write stories.

Elizabeth's father died when she was six. The family managed to live comfortably for many years with the money he had left them. But by the time she was twenty and her brothers had married and moved away, the Cochran home had to be sold. Elizabeth moved with her mother and younger sister to Pittsburgh, Pennsylvania, where they lived in a boarding house. She would have to find work there to help support the family.

Elizabeth looked hard for an interesting job that paid a decent wage. At that time most occupations, including writing, were closed to women. A few lucky women could be teachers or nurses, but most had to resort to factory or domestic work, which paid very little. The best job Elizabeth could find was in a laundry, washing and ironing clothes.

Lands first newspaper job

Around that time, Elizabeth read an article in the Pittsburgh *Dispatch* that made her furious. Called "What Girls Are Good For," it made fun of women like her, who wanted meaningful work and wages similar to those earned by men. She dashed off a letter to the newspaper's editor, talking about the unfair conditions working women faced and demanding that they be given a chance to prove themselves. He was so impressed by her writing that he asked to meet her. When she arrived at the newspaper office he offered her a job as a reporter. Elizabeth's dream of making her living as a writer had suddenly and unexpectedly come true!

Changes name to Nellie Bly

Elizabeth's first article for the *Dispatch* was an outspoken piece on marriage and divorce. Her editors at the newspaper liked the article but were sure that it would stir strong feelings among its readers and wanted Elizabeth to use a "pen name" to disguise her identity. She decided on the name "Nellie Bly," the title of a popular song by composer Stephen Foster (1826–1864). Elizabeth would go by that name for the rest of her life.

Becomes undercover reporter

Bly next wrote a series of articles about working women. In order to get a true picture of what their lives were like, she got a job in a large, bottle-making factory. Conditions were terrible. The women worked fourteen-hour shifts standing on cement floors, their feet wrapped in rags to keep their toes from freezing. The factory was dirty and full of rats and broken glass. Worse still, the women were paid half the amount that men made. When the article was published, people were shocked.

Stories bring reforms

Bly continued her undercover work, taking more jobs and reporting her findings about the horrible treatment that working women—and even children—received. Soon the residents of Pittsburgh were calling for stronger child labor laws and better working conditions for women. Thanks to Bly's investigative reports, reforms were made. But while more and more people bought the *Dispatch* to read Bly's stories, owners of factories and other businesses were not happy with her reports. They threatened to withdraw their advertisements from the newspaper if she did not stop writing them. So Bly's investigations were ended by the newspaper management.

Assigned to report on other topics such as fashion and society parties, Bly grew restless. Therefore, when a group of visiting Mexican officials asked her to come see their country, she jumped at the chance. Bly convinced her editors at the *Dispatch* that readers would be eager to learn more about Mexican life; they agreed, but were worried about letting the twenty-one-year-old woman travel there alone. But Bly finally convinced them to send her. In 1886, with her mother accompanying her, she boarded a train to Mexico.

Mexican adventures

Traveling around the country, Bly wrote about Mexico's beauty and rich history. She visited its grand churches, attended a bullfight, and enjoyed the country's spicy foods, even sending recipes back to the *Dispatch* for publication. But a reformer at heart, Bly couldn't help but comment on the things that disturbed her as well. She didn't like how Mexican women were treated by their husbands, and she wrote an outspoken article about freedom of speech in Mexico—how reporters there could be jailed if they wrote things the government didn't like. Mexican officials were angered by Bly's article and asked her to leave the country at once. She gave a sigh of relief when she, her mother, and her newspaper stories—which were hidden in a suitcase—safely crossed the border into the United States.

Bly's articles about Mexico were a success and her readership grew. Still, she knew that she would not be able to do the kind of investigative reporting she wanted to if she remained at the *Dispatch*. So in 1887 she headed for New York City, center of the nation's publishing industry. She was hoping to get a job with *The World,* one of country's most important newspapers, run by Joseph Pulitzer (1847–1911).

Becomes investigative reporter for *The World*

Bly spent several months in New York City, trying to get work with *The World*—or any other newspaper. No one would hire a woman reporter, not even one with experience. Finally, Bly stationed herself in *The World* offices and refused to leave until Pulitzer agreed to see her. Impressed by the young reporter's determination, the newspaper editor agreed to hire her if she could carry out a trial assignment. Bly wanted to go undercover at Blackwell's Island (in New York's East River), a hospital for poor, mentally ill women. Her plan was to get herself committed and pose as a patient for a week. Since few women left the grim place, she was frightened to go, but counted on Pulitzer to manage her release.

As Bly suspected, conditions at the mental hospital were horrible. The patients were poorly fed and did not have enough clothes or blankets to stay warm. For baths, caretakers poured buckets of cold water over the patients' heads. It appeared that some of the women had been beaten, and the doc-

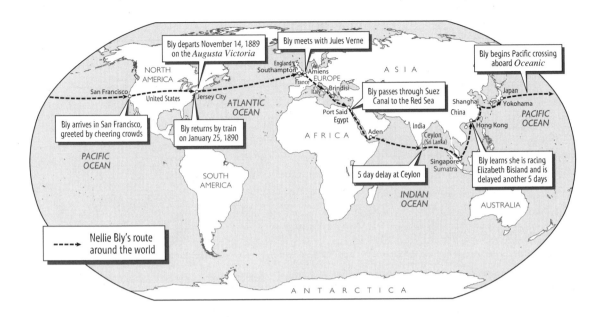

Bly departs November 14, 1889 on the *Augusta Victoria*

Bly meets with Jules Verne

Bly begins Pacific crossing aboard *Oceanic*

England
Southampton
Amiens
France
EUROPE
Italy
Brindisi

ASIA

Japan
Yokohama

Bly passes through Suez Canal to the Red Sea

Shanghai
China

PACIFIC
OCEAN

NORTH
AMERICA

San Francisco

United States
Jersey City

ATLANTIC
OCEAN

Port Said
Egypt

Hong Kong

Bly arrives in San Francisco, greeted by cheering crowds

Bly returns by train on January 25, 1890

AFRICA

Aden

India
Ceylon
(Sri Lanka)

PACIFIC
OCEAN

SOUTH
AMERICA

Singapore
Sumatra

Bly learns she is racing Elizabeth Bisland and is delayed another 5 days

5 day delay at Ceylon

INDIAN
OCEAN

AUSTRALIA

- - - - ▶ Nellie Bly's route around the world

ANTARCTICA

tors who were supposed to work to cure the patients did nothing at all. After a while, Bly was convinced that many of the patients were really as normal as she. For who wouldn't act crazy when forced to live that way?

Bly left the island after ten days. Her front-page story stunned New York and the rest of the country. It led to major reforms at Blackwell's Island and at other mental hospitals across the nation. Pulitzer gave Bly a permanent job as an investigative reporter. Over the next few years, she continued to write about other injustices.

Plans race around the globe

In 1889, Bly came up with an idea for a different kind of story. She would travel around the world, and try to beat the record of Phileas Fogg, the main character in *Around the World in Eighty Days,* a novel by French author Jules Vernes (1828–1905). At that time, there were no planes or cars and people traveled by train and boat. It would be quite a feat to circumnavigate (circle) the globe in eighty days or less. Bly's editors loved the idea, sure that their readers would be eager to read about the adventures of their favorite reporter. But women rarely traveled alone in those days, much less all the way around the world. They decided to send a man instead.

Bly was furious, and threatened to find another newspaper that would send her on the trip. Her editors finally agreed to let her go. She packed one small bag with clothes, thinking that too much luggage might slow her. Her journey would be a race against the clock. On November 14, 1889, she set off from Jersey City, New Jersey, on the *Augusta Victoria,* a ship headed for England.

Bly reached the English port city of Southampton in seven days. When she arrived she received a message from Verne, who wanted to visit with her in France. Would she have the time? She decided to meet with him at his home in the city of Amiens. Impressed by the adventurous reporter, the author wished her luck, but still did not think she would break the record of his fictional character. Bly hurried on to Italy, telegraphing her travel stories to *The World* and its anxious readers. Then she boarded another ship at the Italian port of Brindisi, heading south.

Bly sailed across the Mediterranean Sea to the Egyptian city of Port Said. She then passed through the Suez Canal to the Red Sea, stopping at the southern Arabian port of Aden. Next she traveled to Ceylon (now Sri Lanka), an island off the coast of India. There she had a five-day delay that caused her great concern. Would the delay keep her from making it to Hong Kong in time to catch her boat back to America?

When Bly's next ship finally arrived, she sailed on to Singapore and then to Hong Kong. But bad news awaited her there. Another female reporter, Elizabeth Bisland, was trying to beat Bly around the world, traveling in the opposite direction! Bisland had already passed through Hong Kong and was making swift progress. Who would win the race? When Bly learned that she would have to wait another five days for her ship to set sail, she was absolutely frantic.

Bly finally boarded the *Oceanic,* but it would take another five days and stops in Shanghai, China, and Yokohama, Japan, before the boat began its Pacific crossing. The ship's engineer promised the now-famous reporter that he would do his best to speed her along and posted this saying in his engine room: "For Nellie Bly, we'll win or die!" When Bly at last arrived in San Francisco, she was joyously greeted by crowds of people, for she had become a national heroine. She quickly boarded a special train that would take her across the United States; she had just one week left.

Breaks all circumnavigation records

Cheered at every train stop, Bly arrived back in Jersey City on January 25, 1890. Her trip around the world had taken 72 days, 6 hours, and 11 minutes and she had covered 21,740 miles. She had broken Fogg's record by a wide margin and, of course, had beaten the pace of any normal traveler. (Bisland completed her own trip four days later.) Verne sent Bly a telegram, warmly congratulating her.

For a time after the trip, Bly lived the life of a celebrity. She went on lecture tours, appeared in advertisements endorsing products, and wrote the best-selling *Nellie Bly's Book: Around the World in 72 Days*. In 1893, though, she returned to what she loved best, writing investigative stories for *The World*. When she married Robert L. Seaman—owner of one of America's largest hardware-producing companies—in 1895, she also became involved in business. Bly took over the company when her husband died nine years later, and made sure that her female and male workers received equal pay, along with family health care and other employee benefits.

In 1914, while Bly was traveling in Austria, World War I broke out and she was forced to remain there for the length of the conflict. She sent newspaper stories across the Atlantic, becoming America's first female war correspondent. Afterward, she continued her written crusades for social justice in the United States. Bly died from pneumonia on January 27, 1922.

Sources

Graves, Charles P. *Nellie Bly: Reporter for* The World. Champaign, IL: Garrard Publishing, 1971.

Kendall, Martha E. *Nellie Bly: Reporter for the World.* Brookfield, CT: Millbrook Press, 1992.

Kroeger, Brooke. *Nellie Bly: Daredevil, Reporter, Feminist.* New York: Random House, 1994.

Quackenbush, Robert. *Stop the Presses, Nellie's Got a Scoop: A Story of Nellie Bly.* New York: Simon & Schuster, 1992.

James Bruce

Born December 14, 1730, Stirlingshire, Scotland

Died April 27, 1794, Stirlingshire, Scotland

James Bruce was a Scottish traveler who journeyed to the highlands of Ethiopia in search of the source of the Blue Nile River.

Africa's Nile River was the site of numerous expeditions during the eighteenth and nineteenth centuries. Many European travelers to the little-known continent were determined to find the source of the river, which had remained a mystery for centuries. It was believed that the Nile was fed by two great southern rivers, one that coursed across east central Africa (the White Nile) and the other running through northern Ethiopia (the Blue Nile). But early attempts at river travel up these branches were not successful, and European adventurers intent on finding the Nile's source or sources planned overland expeditions to locate them. One such traveler was Scotsman James Bruce, who did find and map the springs that feed the Blue Nile in the highlands of Ethiopia. While he felt certain that he had discovered the great Nile's true source, later explorations of the White Nile—with its origins in Lake Victoria—would prove otherwise. Lake Victoria would come to be generally accepted as the main source of the Nile, and the Blue Nile would be designated, instead, as a great tributary.

Bruce was born on his family's grand estate, Kinnaird, in Stirlingshire, Scotland, on December 14, 1730. His mother died when he was very young and his father directed his education. After years of private schooling, James attended Edinburgh University, beginning in 1747. His father made him study law and medicine, although he was really interested in art and foreign languages. In 1752 he married the daughter of a wealthy Scottish wine merchant and entered his wife's family business. But within months of their marriage, his wife died tragically from tuberculosis. In an attempt to forget his sorrow he traveled abroad.

While in Spain, Bruce became especially interested in the Moors—the Arabic-speaking people who had conquered much of southwest Africa and Spain in the eighth century and had ruled the region for some five hundred years. He was inspired to study Arab history and language. When his father died in 1758, Bruce returned to London for a time. There he began studying Ge'ez and Amharic, the languages of Ethiopia (at that time called Abyssinia). His inheritance at his father's death meant that he no longer had to earn a living and could travel full-time. He journeyed to places such as Crete, Rhodes, and the Mediterranean coast of present-day Turkey. He began having thoughts of traveling to Ethiopia to look for the source of the Nile River.

Arrives in Africa

Bruce was appointed British consul general to the Moorish city of Algiers in northwest Africa in 1763. He remained in diplomatic service for two years. During that time he developed an interest in Roman antiquities in North Africa and, beginning in 1765, he visited Tunis and Tripoli, among other places, to study the ruins. He hired an Italian artist named Luigi Balugani to make drawings of the sites and to serve as his assistant. They journeyed along the Mediterranean coasts of North Africa and the Middle East. Instead of traveling luxuriously, like most wealthy Europeans of his day, Bruce lived and dressed like an Arab. His fluent Arabic made him a wel-

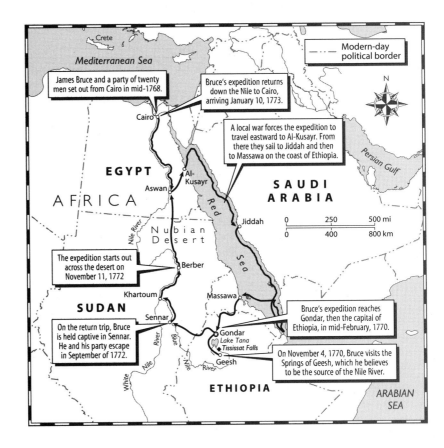

Modern-day political border

Crete

Mediterranean Sea

James Bruce and a party of twenty men set out from Cairo in mid-1768.

Bruce's expedition returns down the Nile to Cairo, arriving January 10, 1773.

Cairo

A local war forces the expedition to travel eastward to Al-Kusayr. From there they sail to Jiddah and then to Massawa on the coast of Ethiopia.

EGYPT

Al-Kusayr

AFRICA

Aswan

SAUDI ARABIA

Persian Gulf

N

Jiddah

0   250   500 mi
0   400   800 km

Nile River

N u b i a n
D e s e r t

Red Sea

The expedition starts out across the desert on November 11, 1772.

Berber

Khartoum

Massawa

SUDAN

Sennar

On the return trip, Bruce is held captive in Sennar. He and his party escape in September of 1772.

Bruce's expedition reaches Gondar, then the capital of Ethiopia, in mid-February, 1770.

Gondar
Lake Tana
Tississat Falls
Geesh

On November 4, 1770, Bruce visits the Springs of Geesh, which he believes to be the source of the Nile River.

White Nile River

Blue Nile River

ETHIOPIA

ARABIAN SEA

come visitor and his knowledge of medicine earned him a reputation as a healer.

While in Cairo, Bruce's medical skills brought him in contact with influential people. These included the Bey (local governor) of Cairo, who gave Bruce a letter allowing him to travel anywhere and practice his healing arts. The Patriarch (bishop) of Ethiopia was another acquaintance; he gave the Scotsman a letter of introduction to a group of Christians who lived in his country. Bruce felt that the time was right for him to attempt his great ambition—finding the source of the Nile River.

Nile expedition begins

In mid-1768 Bruce and Balugani and a party of about twenty men set out from Cairo by boat, sailing up the Nile

River as far as the Egyptian city of Aswan. However, a local war made it too dangerous to sail on, so the expedition traveled eastward overland, crossing the desert to the port of Al-Kusayr on the Red Sea coast. From there Bruce and his men sailed to the port of Jidda in Arabia, where they re-crossed the Red Sea south to Massawa, on the coast of Ethiopia. They arrived there in September 1769, but were detained by the Turks who had control of the port at that time. The expedition was finally allowed to resume its journey on November 15.

Travelers enter Ethiopia

Bruce was headed for Gondar, then the capital of Ethiopia, located in the highlands. Along the way he and his men encountered many unusual sights. They passed through immense flocks of antelopes that showed no alarm at their presence. They partook of the Ethiopian diet, which consisted of honey and millet bread and raw meat. The meat was obtained in an unusual way—from living animals. The first time Bruce witnessed the practice he watched in amazement as three natives captured a cow, cut two pieces of meat off its flanks, folded the skin back over the wound and secured it, and then sent the animal on its way!

Bruce and his expedition reached Gondar in mid-February 1770. Smallpox had broken out in the city and he was summoned to the palace of the Empress Iteghe to care for her sick grandchildren. By using Western methods of sanitation he kept the outbreak under control, and became a welcome member of the court, well-received by the fifteen-year old Emperor Tecla Haimanot (the son of Iteghe) and his advisor, Ras Michael of Tigre, who was the real ruler of the country. Ethiopia was in a state of civil war and Bruce took part in several military campaigns on behalf of the royal family. Although he was often shocked by the brutality with which Ras Michael dealt with his enemies (the ruler once had the eyes of captives torn out and he often left prisoners in the wild to be eaten by hyenas), Bruce also knew that such a powerful man could help him achieve his great goal. As a reward for his military efforts, the emperor named Bruce honorary governor of

Geesh, the province where the source of the Blue Nile was reportedly located.

Reaches source of Blue Nile

While on a military campaign with Ras Michael, Bruce got his first look at the Blue Nile. He came upon the magnificent Tississat Falls, which is near where the river exits Lake Tana, located some six thousand feet up in the mountains. Bruce used the scientific instruments he had brought from Europe to record the exact position of the falls. But he was forced to return to Gondar with the royal army before he could do any further exploration. In October 1770, however, he was granted permission to return to the area. As he, Balugani, and a small party of men approached the river, they climbed a steep mountain and surveyed its course. It appeared that the Blue Nile's source was the Little Abbai River, which flowed into Lake Tana. On November 4 Bruce arrived at the Springs of Geesh, underground streams that—in turn—feed the Little Abbai River. The Scotsman felt jubilant, sure that he was the first European to at last reach the source of the great Nile River, and that his achievement would go down in history. It would not be until his return to Europe that he would learn that Spanish missionary Pedro Paez (1564–1622) had been to the springs before him, in 1618.

With his goal accomplished, Bruce wanted to return to Europe. But the civil unrest that plagued Ethiopia continued, and he was forced by his royal patrons to remain there and take part in further military campaigns. During that time Bruce was able to visit large parts of northern Ethiopia and also the region that lies south of Lake Tana. He and Balugani kept detailed records and drawings of what they saw, and made scientific measurements to chart various locations. Bruce also collected many Ethiopian manuscripts, which he

This image shows the generosity of James Bruce, as he carries his own pack to spare one of his men and even a donkey.

took with him when he finally left the country. The valuable documents, now kept in the Bodleian Library of Oxford University in England, would become one of the main sources of European knowledge about Ethiopian history.

Begins return journey

Still in Ethiopia, Balugani died from dysentery and Bruce fell sick with malaria. In December 1771 the Scotsman was at last given permission to leave the country because of his poor health. This time he planned a different route to his destination—Cairo—which would prove to be a long and difficult one. He and his small traveling party headed for the Muslim town of Sennar in the Sudan. It was located on the Blue Nile, whose route he hoped to follow. Upon reaching Sennar, Bruce was welcomed into the royal court, but—as in Gondar—he was then denied permission to leave. After four months there he and his party escaped, in September 1772. They followed the Blue Nile to the spot where it meets the White Nile, at what would later be the site of the great city of Khartoum. Bruce noticed that the White Nile appeared to be a deeper river, but still thought that the Blue Nile was the more important of the two.

Barely survives desert passage

On November 11, 1772, near the Sudanese town of Berber, Bruce decided to stop following the Nile, which was beginning to curve away from his destination. He and his party struck out on a more direct route that was far more dangerous—a four-hundred-mile trek across the Nubian Desert to Aswan. It took eighteen days and the men suffered greatly. Their shoes wore out and they trudged over the burning sand barefoot, their feet becoming so swollen that they could barely walk. Swirling sandstorms threatened to suffocate them. They ran out of food and water, and in desperation killed their camels and drank the animals' bodily fluids. Without the camels to carry supplies, all of Bruce's scientific instruments and records from his four years of travel had to be left behind. The men lost all hope of survival.

James Bruce | 32

But on November 29 the group limped into Aswan. Bruce asked the governor there to send out a party to retrieve his baggage, which was found untouched and was returned to him. He then took a boat down the Nile to Cairo, arriving January 10, 1773.

Journey home ends in disappointment

Bruce traveled to France, where he received praise for his explorations. He went on to Italy before returning to London in June 1774. There he expected even greater recognition for his achievements. And at first people were impressed by his stories of Africa. England's King George III (1738–1820) received Bruce at court and accepted the traveler's gift of some of Balugani's drawings. The explorer was elected a fellow of the Royal Society of London for Improving Natural Knowledge.

But then London intellectuals began to doubt Bruce's rather tall tales of African adventure. His worst critic was the influential writer and scholar Dr. Samuel Johnson (1709–1784), who made it known that he thought that Bruce had not been to Ethiopia at all. With that harsh judgment, the Scotsman's reputation was ruined. Angry and disgusted that he had received none of the recognition and honors he expected, Bruce retired to his family estate in Scotland. He married a woman twenty-four years younger than he, had children, and happily lived the life of an upper-class landowner. Only after his wife died suddenly in 1788 did he again turn his attention to the notes and journals he had brought back from Africa. Perhaps in an attempt to regain his reputation, he spent a year in London working on a five-volume illustrated account of his explorations, titled *Travels to Discover the Source of the Nile*, published in 1790. Again the truth of Bruce's stories was questioned by serious readers, although the book did became popu-

Opposite page: The new Bodleian Library at Oxford University, which opened on October 24, 1946, houses valuable collections of books and manuscripts, including Bruce's Ethiopian texts.

lar as a work of romantic adventure. (Later African explorers would verify that much of what the Scotsman had reported was true, and his book became a valued scientific, geographical, and cultural record of North Africa in the late eighteenth century.)

Not having achieved the effect that he had hoped for with his book, Bruce retired once again to his estate. He died on April 27, 1794, after a fall down the stairs of his manor house while helping a lady into her carriage. While he was not the first European to locate the Blue Nile's source—nor correct in his thinking that it was the main branch of the great Nile—his contribution to the history of exploration is still of great value. Bruce was the first European to verify the source of the Blue Nile and map it, and he was the first to follow its course to the place where it joins the White Nile. He was one of the earliest Western explorers to undertake an expedition in search of the Nile's source, which would not be found until the discovery of Lake Victoria by Englishmen Sir Richard Burton (1821–1890) and John Hanning Speke (1827–1864) in the late 1850s.

Sources

Baker, Daniel B., ed. *Explorers and Discoverers of the World.* Detroit: Gale Research, 1993.

Bohlander, Richard E., ed. *World Explorers and Discoverers.* New York: Macmillan, 1992.

Marshall Cavendish Illustrated Encyclopedia of Exploration and Discovery, Volume 11: *The Challenge of Africa,* written by Elspeth Huxley. Freeport, NY: Marshall Cavendish, 1990.

Waldman, Carl and Alan Wexler. *Who Was Who in World Exploration.* New York: Facts on File, 1992.

Jean-Louis Burckhardt

Born November 24, 1784, Lausanne, Switzerland

Died October 15, 1817, Cairo, Egypt

In 1788 a group of twelve London gentlemen, led by scientist and explorer Sir Joseph Banks (1743–1820), formed the Association for Promoting the Discovery of the Interior Parts of Africa—also known as the African Association. Intent on sending explorers to investigate the little-known interior of the continent, the group was especially interested in opening up the Niger River region, which was believed to be an area of great wealth and the location of a rich trade center called Timbuktu. In 1796 Scottish physician Mungo Park (1771–1806) was the first Association-sponsored explorer to successfully reach the Niger, although he died during a second expedition there. In 1806 Swiss scholar Jean-Louis Burckhardt was hired for the same mission, but his route to the Niger was to begin in North Africa, from Cairo by way of caravan travel. While Burckhardt arrived in the Middle East in 1809, he was never able fulfill his plans. He did, however, travel extensively through Syria, Egypt, the Sudan, Palestine, and Arabia, and his detailed accounts became a valuable

Jean-Louis Burckhardt was a Swiss explorer who was hired by a British group to travel to Africa's Niger River. While he never reached his destination, he spent several years exploring the Middle East, even visiting the Muslim holy cities of Mecca and Medina.

source of information for Europeans about Muslim life during the early nineteenth century.

Hired by African Association to explore Niger River

Burckhardt was born on November 24, 1784, into a wealthy family in Lausanne, Switzerland. When the Bonapartists (followers of the French emperor Napoleon Bonaparte) came into power there, Burckhardt's family moved to Germany, where they had close ties. Burckhardt attended universities in the German cities of Leipzig and Göttingen, studying science and languages. Knowing that the young scholar was interested in traveling to exotic lands, one of his professors arranged for him to meet Joseph Banks in London in 1806. Already familiar with Arabic culture and history from his studies, Burckhardt was hired by the African Association to make a journey to the Niger River and Timbuktu by way of the Nile River and the Sahara Desert.

Because Burckhardt's route to the Niger would take him through mostly Arab territories, he would need to pose as a Muslim (a follower of Islam) and speak excellent Arabic. So he attended Cambridge University in England for a year to study the language and other subjects—such as astronomy, mineralogy, and medicine—that would help him in his travels. He also learned the teachings of the Islamic holy book, the Koran. Determined to make a success of his mission, Burckhardt's efforts to prepare himself bordered on the extreme: he wore Arab dress, slept outside, took long walks barefoot, and adopted the common Muslim diet of vegetables and water.

Changes identity in Middle East

Burckhardt left England on March 2, 1809, and arrived in Aleppo, Syria, in July. Possessing a scholar's meticulous nature, he stayed there for two and a half years, continuing to perfect his knowledge of Arabic and of Muslim customs. He took up a new identity as Sheikh Ibrahim ibn Abdullah—an Islamic convert—and made several trips into the Syrian interior. In the spring of 1810 he lived with a nomadic Turkish tribe; later that year he traveled to the ruins of the ancient city of Palmyra, north of the Syrian Desert. He is thought to be the first Westerner to have seen the city since ancient times.

Starting in June of 1812, Burckhardt began to make his way to Cairo, which would be the starting point of his intended trip to the Niger River. He traveled through the Jordan River valley and across the Sinai Peninsula to Egypt. Along the way he came upon ancient ruins, including the temple-tomb known as the Pharaoh's Treasure, which stands more than sixty feet high and was carved out of red rock. He also visited the city of Petra, the capital of the ancient Nabateans, now in southern Jordan. Cut into rock cliffs, Petra had been a settlement since the days of the Old Testament, and became a thriving city in Roman times. Burckhardt was the first European to visit there since the Crusaders (European Christians who tried to recover the Holy Land from Muslim rule) in the Middle Ages.

Discovers ancient Egyptian temple

Burckhardt arrived in Cairo on September 3, 1812. There he tried, without success, to arrange passage with one of the caravans that made regular trips west from Cairo across the Sahara into the Fezzan region of present-day Libya. Undisturbed by the delay, he decided to learn more about Arab culture by traveling through Egypt and the northern region of the Sudan, known as Nubia. He traveled south on the Nile River to the Egyptian town of Isna. From there he set out early in 1813, traveling by donkey south along the Nile. He covered more than one thousand miles—reaching Tinareh—before a group of hostile natives forced him to turn back. During his return trip to Isna, Burckhardt made one his most important discoveries: on March 22, in the village of Abu Simbel, he came upon the ancient Egyptian temple of King Ramses II, with its four 60-foot high statues of the pharaoh. Burckhardt was the first Westerner to see this great wonder of ancient Egypt, carved into the side of a cliff at some point during the thirteenth century B.C.

The colossal temple of Abu Simbel, built by King Ramses II, undergoes salvage work.

Back in Isna, Burckhardt hoped to at last catch a caravan traveling west across the desert to the Niger River. But a serious eye infection stalled his plans. When he realized that his mission would be on hold for yet another year, he wrote to the African Association and told them he would use the time to try to visit Mecca, the holy city of Islam to which thousands of devout Muslims made religious pilgrimages every year. The city was forbidden to non-Muslims, and if Burckhardt's true identity were discovered while he was there, it would mean certain death.

Begins trip to Mecca

On March 2, 1814, Burckhardt accompanied a caravan of African slave traders south along the Nile, heading for the great trading center of Shendi in northeastern Sudan. It was a miserable trip, for the Africans hated Muslims, and Burckhardt appeared to be a poor one at that. They mistreated him, forcing him to work in the blazing desert sun while they rested. In

Following a miserable 20-day crossing of the Red Sea, Burckhardt arrives in Cairo on June 24, 1815. While awaiting passage to the Niger, he develops a severe case of dysentery. He dies on October 15, 1817, at the age of thirty-two.

Jean-Louis Burckhardt arrives in Aleppo, Syria, in July, 1809. He remains here for two and a half years, perfecting his knowledge of Arabic and of Muslim culture.

1810: Burckhardt travels to the ruins of the ancient city of Palmyra.

Burckhardt arrives in Cairo on September 3, 1812.

Burckhardt makes a trip to Medina in January, 1815. While there, he falls desperately ill with malaria.

Burckhardt sets out from Isna in 1813, heading south along the Nile. He covers more than 1,000 miles before he is forced to turn back. On his return trip, he visits the Egyptian temple of Ramses II, becoming the first Westerner to see this great wonder.

Burckhardt sails across the Red Sea and arrives in Jidda on the Arabian coast. From there he travels to Mecca, arriving there on September 7, 1814.

— · — · — Modern-day political border

After Burckhardt's mission to the Niger is put on hold because of an eye infection, he decides to visit the holy city of Mecca. He heads south along the Nile to Shendi. From there he travels east to the port city of Suakin.

order to make the detailed notes (which he took wherever he went), Burckhardt had to ride ahead on his donkey and hide behind a rock, secretly writing, until the caravan caught up. On April 17, 1814, he reached Shendi, and joined another caravan that was heading east, to the Red Sea port of Suakin.

From Suakin, Burckhardt sailed on a boat filled with Muslim pilgrims from Africa to the port of Jidda on the Arabian Peninsula. It was located in the Muslim region known as the Hejaz (now western Saudi Arabia), whose forbidden capital city of Mecca lay only a short distance away. Disguised as an Egyptian, Burckhardt carried with him letters from the Turkish viceroy of Egypt claiming that Burckhardt was a faithful Muslim. This helped him in his passage to Mecca, where he arrived on September 7. Once in the holy city, Burckhardt performed the required Muslim rituals. He was one of the first Europeans to visit Mecca.

Visits holy city of Medina

Burckhardt returned to Jidda on September 15 to buy supplies and then returned to Mecca for a stay of several weeks. He was there during the pilgrimage season and wrote one of the earliest and most accurate accounts of the religious phenomenon. From Mecca he made a trip to Medina, leaving on January 15, 1815. It is another Muslim holy city, where the Islamic prophet Muhammad (570?–632) is entombed, and it, too, was forbidden to Westerners.

In Medina, Burckhardt fell desperately ill with malaria. When he became well enough to travel, he left the city on April 21, and headed to the port city of Yenbu. From there it took him twenty miserable days to cross the Red Sea to the Sinai Peninsula. Following his return to Cairo on June 24, 1815, he again searched for passage with a western-bound caravan, so that he could begin his long-standing mission for the African Association. Several years had already passed, and Burckhardt was no closer to its completion. While he waited in Cairo, he wrote about his observations and travels in Arabia. When a plague arose in Egypt and further delayed his trip to the Niger, he made a brief expedition east to explore the Sinai Peninsula. While there he studied the manuscripts kept in the monastery at Mount Sinai and traveled along the coast of the Gulf of Aqaba.

Burckhardt returned to Cairo in 1816 and continued his wait. After his years of impoverished living and harsh travel, his health was fragile, and frequent bouts of illness further delayed his departure for the Niger and Timbuktu. While preparing to at last join a caravan, he developed a severe case of dysentery, dying during the night of October 15, 1817, at the age of thirty-two. He was buried in a Muslim ceremony.

Travel accounts published after death

Ever the painstaking recordkeeper, Burckhardt had mailed his journals to his Association sponsors before he died. While he had not completed the mission for which the group had hired him—nor had he made any significant geographical discoveries—the Association members were nonetheless impressed with his travels and detailed observations. As well as recording the social and religious customs of the peoples he had encountered, Burckhardt had also noted facts about the terrain, weather, and wildlife in the regions in which he had traveled. Between 1819 and 1830, the African Association published his writings in four books; they earned Burckhardt the reputation as a great scholar-traveler. He had provided Europe with its most thorough account to date of the forbidden cities of Islam and their inhabitants, as well as of the little-known areas of the Sudan. His descriptions of Mecca and Medina would inspire future trips there by explorers including Sir Richard Burton (1821–1890).

Sources

Baker, Daniel B., ed. *Explorers and Discoverers of the World.* Detroit: Gale Research, 1993.

Bohlander, Richard E., ed. *World Explorers and Discoverers.* New York: Macmillan, 1992.

Marshall Cavendish Illustrated Encyclopedia of Discovery and Exploration, Volume 11: *The Challenge of Africa,* written by Elspeth Huxley. Freeport, NY: Marshall Cavendish, 1990.

Waldman, Carl and Alan Wexler. *Who Was Who in World Exploration.* New York: Facts on File, 1992.

Gaspar Corte-Real

Born c. 1455, Portugal

Died 1501

Miguel Corte-Real

Born c. 1450, Portugal

Died c. 1502

Brothers Gaspar and Miguel Corte-Real were Portuguese noblemen who sailed the Atlantic and explored the northern coast of North America.

Gaspar and Miguel Corte-Real were born in the Algarve region of southern Portugal in the mid-fifteenth century. They, along with older brother Vasco Annes, were the sons of Joäo Vaz Corte-Real, a nobleman and military officer who served as captain of Terceira, one of Portugal's Azore Islands, located about eight hundred miles west of that country's Atlantic coast. According to some historical sources, Joäo Vaz may have preceded his sons in exploring the North Atlantic, participating in a joint Portuguese-Danish expedition to Greenland and Newfoundland around 1472, well before Christopher Columbus (1451–1506) was credited with discovering the New World. For in 1474 the elder Corte-Real was given the title Discoverer of La Terra do Bacalhao—Land of the Codfish—which suggests that he had indeed sailed as far west as the rich cod-fishing grounds between Greenland and Newfoundland.

Gaspar and Miguel grew up on Terceira. But they were also favorites of the Portuguese king, Manuel I (1469–1521),

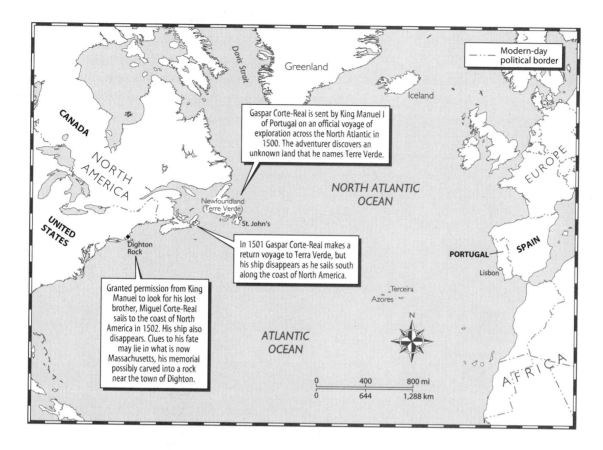

Gaspar Corte-Real is sent by King Manuel I of Portugal on an official voyage of exploration across the North Atlantic in 1500. The adventurer discovers an unknown land that he names Terre Verde.

In 1501 Gaspar Corte-Real makes a return voyage to Terra Verde, but his ship disappears as he sails south along the coast of North America.

Granted permission from King Manuel to look for his lost brother, Miguel Corte-Real sails to the coast of North America in 1502. His ship also disappears. Clues to his fate may lie in what is now Massachusetts, his memorial possibly carved into a rock near the town of Dighton.

and spent a great deal of time at the royal court in Lisbon. Following their father's death around 1496, the brothers returned to Terceira to oversee the island, with Miguel becoming its captain and Gaspar taking the post of deputy captain. In 1499 Gaspar may also have undertaken his first voyage across the Atlantic Ocean, at his own expense. Although the trip was undocumented, scholars believe that he may have traveled along the North American coast, from the Gulf of St. Lawrence in the north to the Gulf of Mexico in the south.

Gaspar makes first official voyage across north Atlantic

On May 12, 1500, King Manuel authorized Gaspar to make an official voyage of exploration across the North Atlantic. It is likely that the king was interested in learning more

A caravel.

about the territory (the North American mainland) recently discovered by explorer John Cabot (1450–1499) which was believed to be a far northeast part of Asia. At that time Europeans were looking for a shorter route to the Orient by way of the Atlantic Ocean, not realizing that two vast continents—the Americas—stood in their way. King Manuel granted Gaspar unusual privileges on his trip, guaranteeing him and his descendants all property and trading rights over the lands that he discovered.

The route of Gaspar's 1500 Atlantic trip is the subject of debate. He came upon a land that he named Terra Verde, which means "green land" in Portuguese. It is believed that this territory—located around latitude 50° N and described as "a land that was very cool and with big trees"—was the island of Newfoundland. But a second interpretation has Gaspar traveling north of Iceland, through the Denmark Strait, and on to the southwest tip of Greenland. He reportedly continued to navigate north around the island, traveling through the Davis Strait and almost to the Arctic Circle before masses of floating ice made further progress impossible. Regardless of his route, Gaspar returned to Lisbon in the fall of 1500.

Disappears on second expedition

Like Cabot, Gaspar believed that the land he had reached was the northeast coast of Asia, and that he had only to travel farther south along it to reach the Orient, with its exotic riches and spices. So in May 1501 he set off once more across the Atlantic. This time he headed an expedition of three caravels (small, sturdy ships with specially designed sails); it is believed that his brother, Miguel, commanded one of them. In October 1501 two of the ships returned to Portugal, but the one captained by Gaspar was not among them.

Those expedition members who returned reported that they had once again traveled to Terra Verde. Scholars believe that the explorers may have revisited the island of Newfoundland or sailed to the coast of what is now Labrador and headed south. The expedition members did capture fifty-seven Native Americans, whom they brought back with them and presented to the king, probably to prove that they had indeed reached Asia. It is believed that the Indians were members of the Beothuk tribe. King Manuel was pleased to learn that the new land, with it large forests and Indian inhabitants, would be a good source of timber for shipbuilding and a source of slaves.

Miguel sets sail to find lost brother

It was reported that Gaspar and his ship had continued to sail farther south along the coast, in order to reach China. Miguel obtained permission from the king to lead his own expedition across the ocean in search of his brother. He left Lisbon with two vessels in May 1502 and reached the site of the present-day seaport of St. John's in southern Newfoundland on June 24. The ships separated in order to look for Gaspar and his men, and were to reunite at St. John's in late August. But the flagship commanded by Miguel never appeared, and the remaining vessel returned to Portugal. King Manuel refused permission for the third Corte-Real son, Vasco Annes, to launch an expedition to look for his lost brothers.

No definite trace of either of the Corte-Real brothers has ever been found. But a large sandstone boulder located at the mouth of the Taunton River near present-day Dighton, Massachusetts, may hold a tantalizing clue. Covered with a mysterious jumble of Native American drawings and English inscriptions, the Dighton Rock—measuring about four by ten feet—has puzzled observers for centuries. Edmund B. Delabarre of Brown University made a detailed study of the rock early in the twentieth century, and was certain he could make out a Portuguese coat of arms among the letters and figures, as well as a memorial statement about Miguel, dated 1511. It supposedly read: "Miguel Cortereal by Will of God, here Chief of

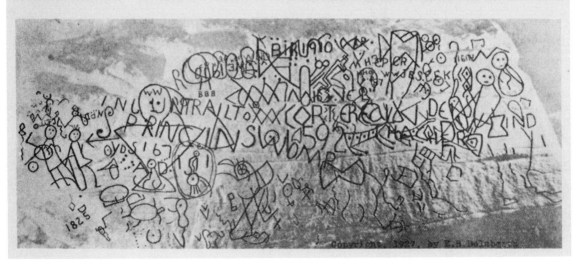

the Indians." It was Delabarre's theory that Miguel, shipwrecked somewhere near New England, had made his way to the mouth of the Taunton River, where he had became chief of the Wampanoag Indian tribe. His death in 1511 had then been recorded. While other scholars have found Delabarre's interpretation of the boulder's markings questionable, Portuguese-Americans are nonetheless proud of Dighton Rock, considering it proof that their ancestors were in New England more than a century before the pilgrims of the *Mayflower.*

While the Corte-Real brothers had failed in their attempts to find a new route to China, they had undertaken some of the first voyages across the North Atlantic Ocean since the days of the Vikings (from the ninth to eleventh centuries) and had reached the North American mainland. Although their ill-fated journeys discouraged the king of Portugal from planning more explorations of North America, Portuguese fishermen would later visit Newfoundland waters to catch codfish, which would become an important item in the national diet. Cod-fishing would also become an important industry for Portugal, contributing significantly to the nation's economy.

Sources

Baker, Daniel B., ed. *Explorers and Discoverers of the World.* Detroit: Gale Research, 1993.

Morison, Samuel Eliot. *The European Discovery of America: The Northern Voyages, A.D. 500-1600.* New York: Oxford University Press, 1971.

Waldman, Carl and Alan Wexler. *Who Was Who in World Exploration.* New York: Facts on File, 1992.

Opposite page: Three photos of Dighton Rock, with observer's interpretations of the inscriptions chalked or painted on. The top image was taken in 1875, the middle image in 1894, and the bottom image in 1928.

Sylvia Earle

Born August 30, 1935, Gibbstown, New Jersey

American marine biologist Sylvia Earle is one of the leading deep-sea explorers of our time. In 1979 she made a record-breaking dive to the ocean floor.

Scientist Sylvia Earle has devoted much of her life to making ocean exploration easier. Because the marine biologist believes that underwater plants and animals can best be studied in their natural environment, she has worked to develop new ways and tools to make the ocean depths into a working laboratory. In 1970 Earle led an all-woman team that spent two weeks in a habitat on the seafloor, studying the surrounding marine life. In 1979 she made a record-breaking dive in a specially designed "Jim suit" that allowed her to walk more deeply underwater than anyone had before. And since 1982 the scientist has been involved in developing small, easy-to-use submersibles (underwater craft) for deep-sea exploration. Earle believes that if more people know about the wonders of this "deep frontier," the more concerned they will be about protecting it.

Passion for sea begins with first dive

Earle was born August 30, 1935, in Gibbstown, New Jersey, the daughter of an electrician and a retired nurse.

When she was still very young her family moved to a farm in New Jersey, where Earle spent much of her childhood. The farm had a backyard pond and she spent hours there, watching its wild inhabitants and writing her observations in notebooks. When she was a teenager, her family moved again, this time to a small Florida town near Clearwater, on the Gulf of Mexico. At seventeen, Earle took scuba diving lessons and after her first dive in the Gulf she was hooked: her life-long love affair with the ocean and its inhabitants had begun.

Earle attended Florida State University, studying to be a marine biologist. Her speciality was underwater plants, especially algae. Unlike most marine botanists at that time, Earle insisted on gathering her specimens during dives, rather than through the usual method of dragging a large net or trawl from the back of a boat and studying the assortment of organisms it caught. Over the course of her many underwater trips (she would eventually log nearly six thousand diving hours), Earle encountered countless fascinating sea creatures. Once, when she spotted a small crab carrying a tiny bouquet of coral in its hind legs, she thought to herself, "If I hadn't been in that animal's own home, I would never have known that it does such a thing." This experience made Earle feel more strongly than ever that scientists should study underwater plants and animals in their habitat.

Leads all-woman scientific team in underwater habitat

Earle participated in several underwater expeditions as a student. These included studies of the Indian Ocean, and of the waters near the Galápagos and Juan Fernández Islands in the Pacific. In 1970 she had the chance to make an intensive study of marine plants when she took part in Tektite II, a government-sponsored project that had teams of scientists living for weeks at a time in a specially made underwater habitat that rested on the ocean floor, fifty feet below the surface. Earle led the first all-woman team of aquanauts, who spent two weeks in the coastal waters off the U.S. Virgin Islands. For several hours each day the scientists, using scuba gear,

left the habitat to explore the area's marine life. Of the 153 species of plants that Earle recorded, 26 had never been seen in the region before.

As the years passed, Earle became increasingly interested in the deep sea—the part of the ocean that was so difficult for humans to reach that it was nearly as unknown as outer space. What mysterious plants and animals lived in its dark depths? Could she find an easier way for scientists to study this last great frontier on Earth?

Makes record-breaking dive to ocean floor

On September 19, 1979, Earle made a historic dive to the bottom of the Pacific Ocean, six miles off the Hawaiian island of Oahu. She descended 1,250 feet to the seafloor in a specially designed "Jim suit," which allowed her to become the first person to walk underwater at such a depth without being connected to life support from a surface vessel. Named after the first diver to use it—Jim Jarrat—the half-ton suit had thick walls of metal armor that protected Earle from the intense pressure felt in such deep water. (On land, we experience about fourteen-and-a-half pounds of pressure on every square inch of our bodies from the earth's atmosphere; during her dive, Earle endured six hundred pounds of pressure per square inch. Any leak in the suit would have crushed her instantly.) Much like the suits worn by astronauts, the Jim suit also supplied Earle with air to breath and comfortable temperatures. At such depths, so far from the rays of the sun, the ocean is unbearably cold.

Although the Jim suit was originally designed to perform deep-sea work on oil rigs, Earle thought that it could be used for scientific exploration. She descended to the ocean floor strapped to a platform on the front of a small submarine named *Star II*. Then she freed herself and walked around, connected to the vessel only by an eighteen-foot communications cable that kept her in constant radio contact with the two

Opposite page: Sylvia Earle, helped by filmmaker Al Giddings, slips into the "Jim suit."

A look at deep-sea diving

Since ancient times man has tried to devise tools and methods to stay underwater longer than the length of time that human breath allows. As early as 360 B.C. Greek philosopher Aristotle (384–322 B.C.) described how sponge divers worked inside kettles that were lowered into the water, breathing the air trapped inside. By the seventeenth century A.D. various types of armored diving outfits were used, with fresh air supplied by a pipe from the surface, its end kept above the water by a float. The first real practical diving suit was created early in the nineteenth century in England by German inventor Augustus Siebe (1788–1872). It consisted of a helmet attached to a jacket made of waterproof material; air was pumped to the helmet through a pipe from the surface and exhaled air escaped through open vents at the jacket's bottom. Siebe's second, improved—or "closed"—suit used valves to let the air out instead. This prevented water from getting in should a diver lose his balance. Such a suit type is still in use today. Its disadvantage, however, is that a diver is restricted in his movements, as he is always

men who piloted the submarine. As she looked through the heavy plastic portholes of the Jim suit, she was thrilled to find the deep ocean teeming with life. Most of the plants and animals in the pitch dark world sparkled, flashed, or glowed with bioluminescence, the same organic chemicals that light up fireflies. One of Earle's favorite sights was that of a small brown lantern fish, whose row of lights along its sides made it look like a tiny passenger liner.

In the two and a half hours Earle spent on the ocean floor, she collected specimens (with the pincers at the ends of the Jim's mechanical arms), took notes (by withdrawing her arms into the huge body of the suit), and planted a United States flag attached by a supply line to the surface. Freedom of movement underwater was greatly improved with the introduction of the SCUBA (Self-Contained Underwater Breathing Apparatus) in 1943. Perfected by Frenchmen Jacques Cousteau (1910–1997) and Emile Gagnan, it delivers compressed air from a portable tank carried on a diver's back. The air is carried by a tube to the diver's mouth, and is usually exhaled into the water after breathing.

Other devices for underwater exploration include the bathysphere, a hollow, globe-shaped steel structure built to withstand heavy water pressure. Created by Otis Barton, the sphere was used by Barton and Charles William Beebe (1877–1962) for deep-sea observation during the 1930s. Its drawback was that it needed to be maneuvered by a heavy cable attached to a surface ship, and could only go as deep as the longest cable allowed. The first free and self-operating deep-sea diving craft was the bathyscaphe, invented by Swiss physicist Auguste Piccard (1884–1962). His submersible, the *Trieste,* descended to depths of more than thirty-five thousand feet in 1960.

on the seafloor. Then the *Star II* dragged her to the surface by the communications line and she was hoisted by a large crane onto the deck of the research ship the *Aloha.* Breaking all existing diving records, Earle's daring trip to the ocean bottom would earn her the nickname "Her Royal Deepness."

Still, Earle was not satisfied. She wanted to explore parts of the ocean that were even deeper. She began discussing her ideas with Graham Hawkes, the British engineer who had designed the Jim suit. Could they build a craft that made deep-sea exploration easier? At that time, most submersibles used in deep-sea exploration had poor devices for specimen collecting. Additionally, their portholes were small, making ob-

September 18, 1985. The Deep Rover *vessel is lifted out of the ocean after exploring a world of absolute darkness, two thousand feet below the surface of Monterey Bay, California.*

servation of marine life difficult. Further, they were large, heavy, and expensive to run and required large mother ships and crews to handle them at exploration sites.

Forms company to create new kinds of exploration submersibles

In 1982 Earle and Hawkes formed Deep Ocean Engineering, a company dedicated to designing and building small, easy-to-use submersibles. By 1984 they had created *Deep Rover,* a one-person underwater vehicle the size of a small car. Its "windshield" was a large transparent sphere that provided all-around views of sea life. It also had two mechan-

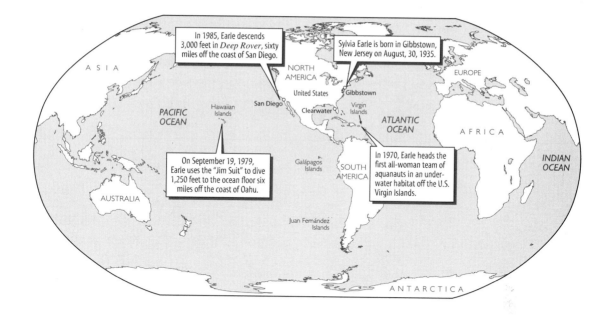

In 1985, Earle descends 3,000 feet in *Deep Rover*, sixty miles off the coast of San Diego.

Sylvia Earle is born in Gibbstown, New Jersey on August, 30, 1935.

On September 19, 1979, Earle uses the "Jim Suit" to dive 1,250 feet to the ocean floor six miles off the coast of Oahu.

In 1970, Earle heads the first all-woman team of aquanauts in an underwater habitat off the U.S. Virgin Islands.

ical arms—one with steel grabbers and the other with a large suction cup—for examining and collecting underwater finds. It had its own fresh air and temperature control systems.

Earle took *Deep Rover* on one of its test runs. Sixty miles off the coast of San Diego, California, the small vehicle took about an hour to descend to three thousand feet, its maximum depth. Earle was twice as far below the ocean's surface as she had been in the Jim suit off Oahu, breaking her own solo diving record. Once again she marveled at the bioluminescent parade of sea creatures that passed before her. She—and other marine biologists—would subsequently use *Deep Rover* to conduct frequent underwater expeditions.

But Earle still couldn't rest—for the deepest parts of the world's oceans remained unexplored. Some sea trenches—long, narrow underwater depressions in Earth's crust—reached depths of six-and-a-half miles! Was there life there, and how could scientists find out? In an attempt to answer these questions, Earle and Hawkes (who married in 1986) began work on a new kind of deep-ocean vehicle.

Called *Deep Flight*, the vessel is an underwater glider that moves very quickly for a deep-sea submersible (about fourteen miles per hour). Operating at the speed of the fastest whale, it can be used to study the swiftest of marine animals (such as whales, tuna, and squid), whose lives and habits have been difficult to follow. Able to descend to depths of around four thousand feet, *Deep Flight* will bring scientists closer yet to the ocean bottom. Earle sees it as another step toward the development of *Ocean Everest*, a submersible meant to operate at depths of up to 35,800 feet (almost seven miles), in the ocean's lowest-lying trenches.

Speaks out for protection of the environment

Earle wishes that nonscientists could take a ride in *Deep Flight*, and get to know the ocean "from the inside out." She is sure this would give people a greater appreciation for—and a concern about protecting—the ocean and its wondrous inhabitants. She knows that healthy oceans are vital to the health of the planet and are therefore essential to man's survival. Thus, throughout her career, Earle has been an outspoken environmentalist, advising governments and organizations on how to better care for the world's waters and wildlife. In 1989 she studied the effects of the *Exxon Valdez* oil spill in Alaska's Prince William Sound, and following the Persian Gulf War she visited the area to assess the damage done to the ecosystem by the destruction of hundreds of oil wells in Kuwait.

Earle has shared her passion for the ocean through her writings and lectures. She has also held posts in the government and at universities and museums. Frequently honored for her oceanic achievements and environmental efforts, Earle has had a species of marine plant named for her, *Pilina earli,* as well as the *Diadema sylvie,* a new kind of sea urchin.

Sources

Conley, Andrea. *Window on the Deep: The Adventures of Underwater Explorer Sylvia Earle.* New York: Franklin Watts, 1991.
Current Biography. New York: H. W. Wilson, 1992.

Dian Fossey

Born January 16, 1932, San Francisco, California

Died December 27, 1985, Rwanda

For nearly two decades scientist Dian Fossey lived in the wilds of the Virunga Mountain range in east central Africa, studying mountain gorillas. By copying their behavior, she was able to get close enough to the little-known animals to observe everything about them, and her findings revealed that their reputation as violent creatures was untrue—that they were really "gentle giants." Alarmed by their decreasing population, Fossey began an active campaign for protection of the gorillas from poachers (those who hunt animals illegally), and for preservation of their dwindling habitat. Her conservation efforts made many enemies, and she was murdered at her wilderness research camp in 1985.

Fossey was born January 16, 1932, in San Francisco, California. She loved animals as a child, and after high school graduation she enrolled at the University of California in a pre-veterinary medicine program. During that time she was also an award-winning horseback rider.

American zoologist Dian Fossey was the world's leading authority on the rare mountain gorillas of east central Africa. Her years of field research contributed enormously to a greater understanding of these "gentle giants."

Louis Leakey, Fossey's mentor.

Fossey never became a veterinarian, though, transferring to San Jose State College and completing a degree in occupational therapy instead. She moved to Kentucky in 1956 and became director of occupational therapy at the Kosair Crippled Children's Hospital in Louisville. Still, her interest in animals remained. She was especially drawn to the writings of American zoologist George B. Schaller, who in 1959 became the first scientist to observe Africa's mountain gorillas in the wild. Longing to travel to Africa, she took out a bank loan to finance a safari there in 1963.

Arrives in Africa

Fossey's first stop was the Olduvai Gorge in the east African country of Tanzania, where famed British anthropologist Louis S. B. Leakey (1903–1972) and his wife Mary Leakey (1913–1996) had been carrying out their long-term search for fossils of early man. Louis Leakey was intrigued by Fossey's determination to observe for herself the mountain gorillas that lived in the forests of the now dormant volcanic Virunga Mountains, located in Rwanda, the Democratic Republic of the Congo, and Uganda. Fossey did manage to see a group of these "greatest of the great apes" (males can reach six feet in height and weigh four hundred pounds) before her return to the United States—and was captivated.

When Leakey traveled to America on a lecture tour in 1966, he visited with Fossey and encouraged her to leave her job as an occupational therapist in order to become a field scientist and study the mountain gorilla. He was already a supporter of scientist Jane Goodall, who was making an extended study of chimpanzees at Tanzania's Gombe National Park. Leakey believed that learning more about the great apes might shed light on his own special interest, human evolution. He also feared that the mountain gorilla—recognized as a separate species in 1902—was bound for extinction before it even had a chance to be studied. Natives of the area needed farm and cattle-grazing land in order to meet the needs of their growing population, and had moved into the gorillas' already tiny habitat. Furthermore, poachers killed the creatures, selling their heads and hands as trophies. Leakey felt that Fossey had the qualities that would make her a good field observer and protector of these endangered animals, and went about getting her sponsorship from the National Geographic Society and other scientific organizations.

Tries new methods of field research

Returning to Africa in late 1966, Fossey visited Goodall to learn the best methods for fieldwork and data collection. She then set up a research camp of her own at Kabara, in the Congo's Parc National des Virungas, where Schaller had begun his pioneering studies. Observing the gorillas was difficult from the start, for they were shy creatures that ran away when they sensed Fossey's presence. The scientist began to imitate their behavior, so that they might think that she was one of them, or at least find her less disturbing. She tried knuckle-walking, announcing her approach by making contented gorilla noises, munching on their favorite foods (they were vegetarians), and copying their grooming behavior. This inventive method of field research worked, and the gorillas grew comfortable with Fossey among them. After seven months, though, the scientist was forced to leave the Congo as the country erupted with political unrest. Fossey was held by armed guards for two weeks until she escaped to Uganda.

Founds Karisoke Research Centre

With the help of Leakey and others, Fossey was able to set up a new scientific base in Rwanda in September 1967. Called the Karisoke Research Centre, the remote, tented camp would eventually become an international center for gorilla research. Four different groups of gorillas—about fifty animals in all—lived near the site. As she began to recognize individ-

Dian Fossey sits among her beloved mountain gorillas, copying their behavior.

ual apes, she gave them names, just as Goodall did with her chimpanzees. A favorite gorilla was Digit, a silverback (silverbacks are the large, mature males, with gray or white hair on their backs, who dominate each group). Over time, Fossey was able to observe gorilla behaviors that had never been seen before. She came to identify fifteen different sounds that the animals make: they chuckle when they play, for instance, and make belching noises when content. And the scientist found that, contrary to their popular image as violent, chest-beating creatures, the gorillas are peaceful beasts that only charge humans or other animals when startled or threatened. The gorillas have strong family ties and take care of one another almost tenderly, especially when a group member is ill or hurt. Fossey grew to love the gorillas she observed, often preferring them and their gentle ways to the company of humans.

Fossey ran her isolated research camp with the aid of African natives and occasional student volunteers from other countries. In 1981 they helped her conduct a widespread count of the mountain gorilla population, and the results were alarming. In the twenty-two years since Schaller's census, the number of gorillas had dropped almost 50 percent, to just 242. Fossey's desire to protect the animals and preserve their habitat became stronger than ever.

Increases efforts to protect gorilla population

Fossey got her students and some of the natives to join her in what she called "active conservation"—aggressive acts, like destroying poachers' traps and stealing their weapons. She did everything she could think of to stop hunters from capturing young gorillas for foreign zoos or selling their body parts for souvenirs. She also tried to keep cattle herders from bringing their animals to graze in protected park areas—where the gorillas roamed—for she did not trust Rwandan officials to do the job. (And the government made the situation worse by eventually turning over four thousand acres of its Parc National des Volcans to farmers.) Her interference caused hostile feelings among members of the local population and government, but Fossey didn't care. When her beloved Digit was killed by hunters in 1978 she decided to bring the plight of the endangered mountain gorilla to the attention of the world. She wrote magazine articles about her work, appeared on wildlife television programs, and created the Digit Fund to raise money for anti-poacher patrols and equipment.

Around 1970 Fossey left Africa for a while so that she could earn a Ph.D. in zoology from Cambridge University in England. And in 1980 she had to leave Africa again, this time because of failing health. During her years of living in the wild and worrying about the well-being of the gorillas, she had neglected to take good care of herself. She stayed in the United States for a time, teaching at Cornell University in New York while still serving as project coordinator for the Karisoke Research Centre. While in America she also completed the book *Gorillas in the Mist,* published in 1983, which lovingly tells of the many years she spent observing three generations of mountain gorillas. Written in a nontechnical

In 1966, Fossey sets up a research camp in Virunga National Park and after much effort, the gorillas grow accustomed to her presence. Political turmoil in early 1967 forces her to flee to Uganda.

In 1963, Fossey visits Olduvai Gorge and meets Louis and Mary Leakey. The Leakeys later encourage Fossey to become a field scientist and study the mountain gorilla.

In September 1967, Fossey establishes Karisoke Research Centre in Rwanda. She spends many years here studying, observing, and protecting the gorillas from poaching. On December 27, 1985, Dian Fossey is murdered.

way, the book is filled with stories about individual animals and family groups, making the gorillas seem almost human. The book became very popular, bringing more attention to Fossey and her fight to save the endangered animals. (After her death, the book was also made into a motion picture with the same title, starring Sigourney Weaver.)

Believed murdered by poachers

Fossey returned to her research camp in Rwanda, where she was murdered as she slept on December 27, 1985. She was buried near Karisoke Research Centre—as she had requested—in a cemetery she had built for gorillas killed by poachers. While her murder was never solved, it was believed to be an act of retaliation for her anti-poaching activities. Still, due largely to her research and international conservation efforts, the mountain gorilla now has a good chance of survival into the next century. It is currently protected by the government of Rwanda; during recent fighting there, in fact, both sides agreed not to harm the animals. While often resentful of Fossey and her activities during her lifetime, the country's inhabitants are now increasingly proud and protective of the magnificent animals that live in their mountain forests.

Sources

Current Biography. New York: H. W. Wilson, 1985.

"Slain in Central Africa: Dian Fossey, Who Studied the Mountain Gorilla, Is Killed at Her Camp in Rwanda." *The New York Times,* December 29, 1985: 12A.

"Slain U.S. Naturalist Buried in Gorilla Cemetery She Built." *The New York Times,* January 2, 1986: D15.

Simon Fraser

Born 1776, Bennington, Vermont
Died April 19, 1862, St. Andrew's, Ontario

Simon Fraser was an American-born Canadian who discovered the Fraser River and opened up British Columbia to European trade and settlement.

In the early nineteenth century both Great Britain and the United States competed for rights to the Pacific Northwest. In 1804, Americans Meriwether Lewis (1774–1809) and William Clark (1770–1838) claimed much of the Northwest for the United States in the first government-sponsored expedition across North America to the Pacific Ocean. British North American settlers hurried to establish their own claims in the area, the movement led by fur-trading companies. Simon Fraser, part-owner of the North West Company, set up fur-trading posts and settlements in what would become central British Columbia and explored west of the Rocky Mountains in an attempt to find an easy water route to the Pacific. In his unsuccessful attempts to find the Columbia—the largest North American river that flows into the Pacific Ocean—he discovered a great river of western Canada: the Fraser.

Enters fur trade

Fraser was born into a family of Roman Catholic Scottish

immigrants who settled in Vermont in 1774. His father fought with the British during the American Revolution (1775–1783), was captured, and died in a prison in Albany, New York, in 1778. Fraser's mother moved the family to British North America in 1784, settling in Cornwall, upper Canada (Ontario), where Simon grew up. At sixteen, he began an apprenticeship with the British North West Company, a major fur-trading business (furs comprised the main industry of upper North America) located in Montreal, Quebec. By 1802, at the age of twenty-five, Fraser was made a partner in the company.

In 1805 Fraser was given the task of establishing trading posts on the western side of the Rocky Mountains. Along with opening up new territories for fur-trapping, he was instructed to try to find an easy route to the Pacific Ocean. That way trade goods and supplies could go back and forth from inland to the coast, instead of along an expensive overland route to distant Montreal. The North West Company had been interested in the area ever since fur tradesman Alexander Mackenzie crossed the Rockies from the east in 1793. While Mackenzie had reached the Pacific Ocean, the route he had taken was such a difficult one that it was considered useless for future travelers. Members of the North West Company hoped that Fraser would have better luck on his expedition.

Sets out for western Canada

Fraser headed for Fort Chipewyan on Lake Athabasca, the North West Company's trading post in what is now northeastern Alberta. He then followed Mackenzie's route and explored the upper reaches of the Peace and Parsnip rivers into what is now central British Columbia. Fraser called the area New Caledonia (Caledonia was the ancient name for Scotland), because it reminded him of his mother's description of the land of his ancestors. For a time he explored the northern Rockies, developing the local fur trade there. He founded Fort McLeod, the first European settlement west of the Rockies.

But when news of Lewis and Clark's explorations in the Northwest reached him, Fraser was anxious to launch an expedition in search of a water route to the Pacific. During the winter of 1805–1806 he and his lieutenant—John Stuart—had heard from local inhabitants about a nearby lake (which would be called Stuart Lake) that emptied into a river flowing south. Hoping that the river might be the great Columbia, which flows into the Pacific Ocean near present-day Portland, Oregon, Fraser set off to find it on May 20, 1806. He and his party of twenty-four men reached Stuart Lake on July 26 and he founded a trading post there called Fort St. James. But because his supplies were very low, he had to stop traveling and wait for a shipment to come from the east in the fall of 1807. During the delay he and his men built two other posts in the area: Fort Fraser and Fort George (now the town of Prince George, British Columbia).

Expedition endures treacherous river travel

On May 28, 1808, the expedition finally left Fort George in four canoes and followed the great river—which would later be called the Fraser—south. The men were retracing Mackenzie's route; the earlier explorer had believed that he, too, was traveling on the Columbia. And, like Mackenzie, Fraser met with Native Americans along the way who gave him very discouraging reports about making much progress on the river. For it was full of rapids, whirlpools, and waterfalls, and the steep rocky cliffs on either side made portaging (carrying a boat around an obstacle) extremely dangerous. At one point the rock walls were more than three thousand feet high. But unlike Mackenzie, who had left the river's difficult course in favor of an overland route, Fraser was determined to follow it to its end.

But by June 10, even Fraser realized that the river was unnavigable. Near the present-day town of Lillooet (in British Columbia), he and his men abandoned their canoes, deciding to follow the river overland. Just as treacherous as the swirling rapids that threatened to swallow them, their land route was often comprised of narrow, slippery paths along high cliffs. As they approached the river's mouth, the water became calmer and looked more suitable for boat travel. Finally, on July 2, Fraser and his men reached the Strait of Georgia, where the river joins the Pacific. The newly discovered ocean outlet would become the site of the great city of Vancouver.

Journey ends in disappointment

When Fraser reached the river's mouth he took a latitude reading. It showed that he and his men had definitely not been traveling on the Columbia, which was known to empty into the Pacific Ocean much farther south. In addition, the river that they had traveled down had been so unnavigable that it would be of no use to inland fur traders trying to reach the coast. Fraser was disappointed with the results of his expedition.

Faced with hostile Native Americans on the coast and a shortage of supplies, Fraser and his men turned back at once. They recovered their hidden canoes and paddled upriver, following the same difficult route. Amazingly, the party arrived safely back at Fort George on August 6, 1808.

Sometime after 1811, Fraser was assigned to manage the North West Company's fur trading posts near the Red River in

The Fraser River, as it looks today, in British Columbia. The large rock in the middle of the river is known as Franklin Rock.

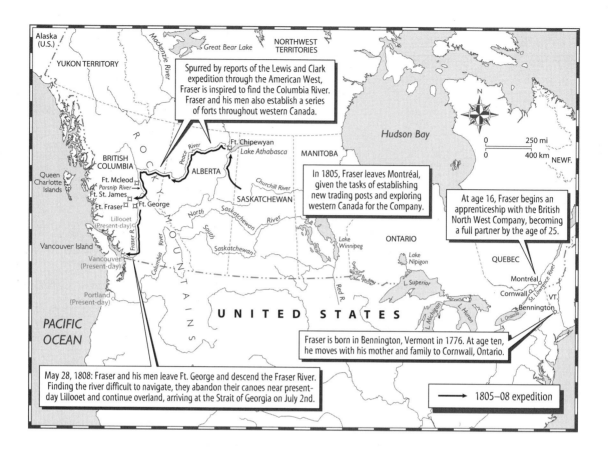

Spurred by reports of the Lewis and Clark expedition through the American West, Fraser is inspired to find the Columbia River. Fraser and his men also establish a series of forts throughout western Canada.

In 1805, Fraser leaves Montréal, given the tasks of establishing new trading posts and exploring western Canada for the Company.

At age 16, Fraser begins an apprenticeship with the British North West Company, becoming a full partner by the age of 25.

Fraser is born in Bennington, Vermont in 1776. At age ten, he moves with his mother and family to Cornwall, Ontario.

May 28, 1808: Fraser and his men leave Ft. George and descend the Fraser River. Finding the river difficult to navigate, they abandon their canoes near present-day Lillooet and continue overland, arriving at the Strait of Georgia on July 2nd.

⟶ 1805–08 expedition

what is now southern Manitoba. He became involved in disputes between fur traders and settlers there, and in 1816 he was accused of participating in an attack on a Hudson's Bay Company post. He was acquitted of all wrongdoing following a trial in Ontario. A few years later, in 1820, he retired to a farm in Stormont County in eastern Ontario. During the Canadian rebellion of 1837–1838 he served as a militia captain and was severely injured. His injuries prevented him from running his farm, and he lived out the last twenty-four years of his life in poverty, dying on April 19, 1862.

Sources

Baker, Daniel B., ed. *Explorers and Discoverers of the World*. Detroit: Gale Research, 1993.

Bohlander, Richard E., ed. *World Explorers and Discoverers*. New York: Macmillan, 1992.

Delpar, Helen, ed. *The Discoverers: An Encyclopedia of Explorers and Exploration.* New York: McGraw-Hill, 1980.

Waldman, Carl and Alan Wexler. *Who Was Who in World Exploration.* New York: Facts on File, 1992.

Johann Grüber

Born c. 1621, Linz, Austria

Died September 30, 1680, Saros Patak, Hungary

Austrian priest Johann Grüber and his Jesuit traveling companion Albert d'Orville were the first Europeans to reach the mountain kingdom of Tibet by traveling a western route from China.

Johann Grüber was born around 1621 in the Austrian city of Linz. He entered a Jesuit seminary where he studied mathematics before deciding to become a missionary priest. In 1656 he volunteered to travel to China to work with Roman Catholic missionaries. Accompanied by Father Bernard Diestel, he set sail from Italy.

Reaches Chinese mission

Arriving at the port of Izmir in Turkey, Grüber and Diestel traveled over land through parts of the Ottoman Empire (what is now Syria and Iraq), Armenia, and Persia (now Iran). When they reached the great port city of Ormuz on the Persian Gulf, they boarded a second ship that took them to the city of Surat on the west coast of India, north of Bombay. There they had a ten-month stay as they tried to find passage to China. Finally the travelers boarded an English ship that took them to the Portuguese colony of Macao, off China's southern coast. Then, in 1658, they journeyed to the capital city of Peking (now Beijing) in northern China, where the Jesuits had a large mission.

For the next few years, Grüber engaged in missionary work in Peking. But at that time it was nearly impossible for the Jesuits there to maintain contact with their headquarters in Rome. This was because armed Dutch vessels had begun blockading ports along China's coast in an attempt to break Portugal's monopoly on trade routes to Asia. Portuguese colonial officials told the Jesuits that it was too dangerous for them to make their way to Rome by ship. They needed to find an overland route back to India and Europe.

Chosen to chart new overland route

Because he was a mathematician and a trained geographer, Grüber was selected for the important and difficult task of finding the new overland route, and for transporting the paperwork and documents that needed to go with them to Rome. To assist him in these efforts, Grüber chose a Belgian Jesuit, Albert d'Orville (1622?–1662), who was also a skilled geographer and surveyor. The two set out from Peking on April 13, 1661. They followed an ancient caravan route that took them west along the Great Wall of China to the Yellow River and Hsi-ning (now Xining), at that time the westernmost city of China. They then headed southwest, across the Ordos Desert and beyond the great salt lake of Koko Nor. Encountering mountainous terrain, they crossed the Burkhan Buddha Range and Shuga Mountains—sometimes traveling at elevations of more than fifteen thousand feet—before reaching the Tibetan Plateau.

Visits little-known Tibet

Once in Tibet, Grüber and d'Orville endured three months of treacherous and lonely mountain travel before reaching Lhasa, its capital city, on October 8, 1661. Lhasa had last been visited by Europeans some three hundred years before. The Jesuits were awed when they first caught sight of the Potala, a great royal palace and Buddhist monastery built

into the side of a soaring mountain. It had been recently constructed by the Fifth Dalai Lama, who was the ruler of Tibet and head religious leader of the its Lamaist sect of Buddhism. Grüber sketched the Potala and when he returned to Europe his drawing would give the West its first look at this magnificent center of Tibetan Buddhism.

Grüber and d'Orville could not stay long in Lhasa because winter was approaching and snow would soon close the Himalayan mountain passes that they needed to cross to continue their journey. But for a few weeks they were able to observe Tibetan life. Grüber was impressed by the elegance of members of the royal court—and equally struck by the filth and poverty of the common people. He also noticed that Christianity and Tibetan Buddhism had similar practices: baptisms were performed and confessions heard; fasts were undertaken and mass-like ceremonies were conducted where food and wine were blessed. The high priests and lamas (monks) who performed these sacraments were much like Roman Catholic priests and brothers.

But the Tibetan Buddhism religion also had intriguing differences from Christianity. Grüber would be the first Westerner to describe the Tibetans's use of the prayer wheel. This small cylinder, usually mounted on a pole, held a printed prayer inside; spinning the wheel—by the wind, water, or hand—would send the prayer continuously up to heaven.

Grüber and d'Orville left Lhasa in November 1661, traveling with a caravan that was headed for India. This route required them to make a difficult passage through the Himalayas. Crossing the Bhotia River gorge was especially frightening, for at one point their path became a series of stones jutting out from the side of a cliff. It took the travelers eleven days to make their way across the 775 steps. Soon after, they entered the mountain kingdom of Nepal and visited its capital city of Katmandu.

Opposite page: A view of Lhasa, the capital of Tibet, as seen from a monastery.

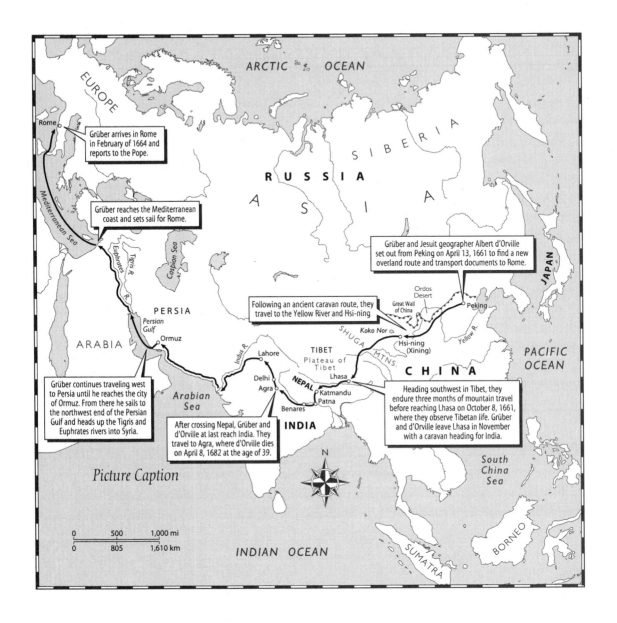

ARCTIC OCEAN

EUROPE

SIBERIA

RUSSIA

ASIA

Rome

Gruber arrives in Rome in February of 1664 and reports to the Pope.

Gruber reaches the Mediterranean coast and sets sail for Rome.

Mediterranean Sea

Euphrates R.

Tigris R.

Caspian Sea

PERSIA

Persian Gulf

Ormuz

ARABIA

Gruber continues traveling west to Persia until he reaches the city of Ormuz. From there he sails to the northwest end of the Persian Gulf and heads up the Tigris and Euphrates rivers into Syria.

Gruber and Jesuit geographer Albert d'Orville set out from Peking on April 13, 1661 to find a new overland route and transport documents to Rome.

Following an ancient caravan route, they travel to the Yellow River and Hsi-ning

Ordos Desert

Great Wall of China

Peking

Koko Nor

SHUGA MTNS.

Hsi-ning (Xining)

Yellow R.

PACIFIC OCEAN

JAPAN

Indus R.

Lahore

Delhi

Agra

TIBET
Plateau of Tibet

Lhasa

NEPAL

Katmandu

Patna

CHINA

Heading southwest in Tibet, they endure three months of mountain travel before reaching Lhasa on October 8, 1661, where they observe Tibetan life. Gruber and d'Orville leave Lhasa in November with a caravan heading for India.

Arabian Sea

Benares

INDIA

After crossing Nepal, Gruber and d'Orville at last reach India. They travel to Agra, where d'Orville dies on April 8, 1682 at the age of 39.

Picture Caption

N

South China Sea

0   500   1,000 mi
0   805   1,610 km

INDIAN OCEAN

SUMATRA

BORNEO

d'Orville dies in India

A month after leaving Tibet, Grüber and d'Orville at last reached India. Traveling south, they passed through the cities of Patna, Benares, and Agra, where d'Orville died on April 8, 1662. Just thirty-nine years old, the Jesuit had been weakened by the months of hard travel. Grüber continued on his journey to Rome alone.

Completes overland mission

Grüber traveled to the north Indian city of Delhi, then crossed into what is now Pakistan. From the city of Lahore, he descended the Indus River to its mouth on the Arabian Sea. He then headed west, entering Persia (present-day Iran) and making his way to Ormuz, where he boarded a ship and sailed to the northwest end of the Persian Gulf. From there, he followed the Tigris and Euphrates rivers north through what is now Iraq, and into Syria. Finally reaching the eastern Mediterranean coast, he set sail for Rome. He arrived there in February 1664, and reported to Pope Alexander VII.

Book about travel experiences published

Grüber intended to return to China to continue his missionary work, but never made it back. He did, however, tell his travel experiences to another Jesuit—the German scholar Athanasius Kircher (1601–1680)—who wrote about them in a book called *China Illustrata*. Published in 1667, the account of Grüber's journey provided valuable information about central Asia and the little-known religion and culture of Tibet.

Grüber became a chaplain in the Imperial Austrian army and served in Hungary's Transylvania region (in present-day Romania). He returned to Austria in 1669. Little is known about his life after that. He died in the Hungarian town of Saros Patak on September 30, 1680.

Sources

Baker, Daniel B., ed. *Explorers and Discoverers of the World*. Detroit: Gale Research, 1993.

Marshall Cavendish Illustrated Encyclopedia of Discovery and Exploration, Volume 12: *The Heartland of Asia,* by Nathalie Ettinger. Freeport, NY: Marshall Cavendish, 1990.

Waldman, Carl and Alan Wexler. *Who Was Who in World Exploration*. New York: Facts on File, 1992.

Hari Ram

Nineteenth century

Hari Ram was an Indian "pundit-explorer" who made four expeditions in the area of Mount Everest, on the Nepal-Tibet border. During his travels, the surveyor added new territory to Western maps.

In the middle of the eighteenth century Great Britain took possession of much of the Indian subcontinent. During the next several decades British surveyors set about making accurate maps of India and of the regions to the north, in the Himalayas. The British felt that in order to keep their Indian holdings safe from the powerful nearby empires of Russia and China, they needed to expand their geographic knowledge, especially of the remote mountain kingdoms of Nepal and Tibet.

Getting that information was difficult, for the mountainous terrain made traveling treacherous. British surveyors also encountered hostile native inhabitants and, after a while, some countries closed their borders to them. In order to continue their mapmaking, the British began training Indians to secretly carry out their surveys for them, disguised as merchants or pilgrims in order to enter forbidden areas.

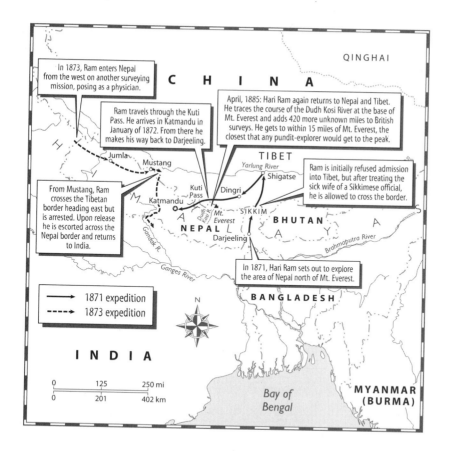

In 1873, Ram enters Nepal from the west on another surveying mission, posing as a physician.

Ram travels through the Kuti Pass. He arrives in Katmandu in January of 1872. From there he makes his way back to Darjeeling.

April, 1885: Hari Ram again returns to Nepal and Tibet. He traces the course of the Dudh Kosi River at the base of Mt. Everest and adds 420 more unknown miles to British surveys. He gets to within 15 miles of Mt. Everest, the closest that any pundit-explorer would get to the peak.

Ram is initially refused admission into Tibet, but after treating the sick wife of a Sikkimese official, he is allowed to cross the border.

From Mustang, Ram crosses the Tibetan border heading east but is arrested. Upon release he is escorted across the Nepal border and returns to India.

In 1871, Hari Ram sets out to explore the area of Nepal north of Mt. Everest.

→ 1871 expedition
--→ 1873 expedition

QINGHAI

C H I N A

TIBET

Jumla

Mustang

Yarlung River

Shigatse

Kuti Pass

Dingri

Katmandu

Mt. Everest

SIKKIM

B H U T A N

NEPAL

Darjeeling

Brahmaputra River

Ganges River

Gandak R.

Dudh Kosi R.

N

BANGLADESH

I N D I A

0   125   250 mi
0   201   402 km

Bay of Bengal

MYANMAR (BURMA)

India's "pundit-explorers"

The word "pundit" means "wise or learned man." Because the Indians chosen for these surveying jobs were well-trained, they were given the name "pundit-explorers." And because they were also British spies, they were taught a number of techniques to hide their true missions and identities. They were given code names, and dressed in clothes that had secret pockets in them. They learned to record information without drawing attention to themselves, perhaps using prayer beads as counting markers or measuring distances with their footsteps.

Hari Ram was one of these pundit-explorers. His code names were "M. H." and "No. 9." It is believed that he made his first expedition for the British government in 1868 to the area of Nepal north of Mount Everest, the world's highest mountain.

In 1871 Hari Ram was again sent to the region. He left the town of Darjeeling in the foothills of the Himalayas and traveled to the little mountain kingdom of Sikkim. From there he tried to cross into Tibet, but was refused admission by border officials, who thought he looked suspicious. Luckily though, he met a Sikkimese official and they became friends. The official's wife was sick, and Hari Ram used some of the Western medicines he had with him to treat her. The woman recovered, and her grateful husband used his influence to get Hari Ram over the border. The pundit-explorer reached the Tibetan city of Shigatse on September 17, 1871. He then traveled southwest to the town of Dingri, which was the main trading center between Tibet and Nepal.

Completes first recorded journey around Mount Everest

In order to get across the Himalayas before winter set in, Hari Ram traveled through the Kuti Pass, sixty miles west of Mount Everest. At some places the path he took—which ran along a mountainside—was only nine inches wide, with a drop of 1,500 feet at its edge. Hari Ram arrived in Nepal's capital city of Katmandu in January 1872. He then made his way back to Darjeeling. Thus, he made the first recorded trip completely around Mount Everest, and surveyed 844 miles that were totally unknown to Western geographers.

Hari Ram set out again on another surveying mission on July 1, 1873. He hid his identity by posing as a physician. This time he entered Nepal from the west and traveled to the city of Jumla and then on to the trading center of Mustang on the Tibetan border. He was able to cross the border and intended to head east to revisit the Mount Everest area when he was arrested and jailed at Tradom. Upon his release he was escorted back across the Nepal border. He then followed the Gandak River back to India.

Because Hari Ram was not able to complete his mission, he was laid off from his work for the British government. But other pundit-explorers assigned to his route also failed, and so

he was rehired in April 1885 for another try. He returned to Nepal and was stopped at the Tibetan border again. But his medical skills helped him once more: curing a Nepali governor's daughter of a thyroid condition, Hari Ram was allowed to travel with the governor's son on a caravan to Tibet. The caravan made its way through the Pangu La Pass at altitudes that reached twenty thousand feet. Hari Ram got within fifteen miles of Mount Everest, the closest that any pundit-explorer would get to the great peak.

Mount Everest, as seen from Darjeeling.

Adds more new territory to British maps

The caravan reached the town of Dingri in October 1885. Hari Ram was able to bribe his way back across the border into Nepal. During his journey he traced the course of the Dudh Kosi River at the base of Mount Everest, and added

420 more unknown miles to the surveys of the British government in India.

Sources

Baker, Daniel B., ed. *Explorers and Discoverers of the World.* Detroit: Gale Research, 1993.

Marshall Cavendish Illustrated Encyclopedia of Discovery and Exploration, Volume 12: *The Heartland of Asia,* written by Nathalie Ettinger. Freeport, NY: Marshall Cavendish, 1990.

Marguerite Baker Harrison

Born October 1879, Baltimore, Maryland

Died July 16, 1967, Baltimore, Maryland

Marguerite Baker Harrison was an adventurer whose restlessness for new experiences was inspired by the desire to learn more about other countries and peoples. At the conclusion of World War I (1914–1918), she traveled through Germany, Russia, Japan, Korea, and China to investigate the political changes that the worldwide conflict had brought. She hoped that by reporting what she saw she could create greater understanding between the United States and other nations. Through her many writings and lectures about her travels she also tried to increase the American public's interest in foreign affairs.

Marguerite was born in Baltimore, Maryland, in October 1879, the first daughter of Bernard Baker, the wealthy owner of a shipping company. During her childhood she traveled to Europe frequently, and learned to speak French and German well. Attending private schools in Baltimore, she liked to read in her spare time, and especially liked books on travel, exploration, history, and international politics.

Marguerite Baker Harrison was an American adventurer, journalist, and occasional government spy who traveled to Russia, Asia, and the Middle East.

In 1901 Marguerite married Thomas Bullitt Harrison, and the pair settled happily into family life in Baltimore. The couple had a son, whom they named after his father. Fourteen years later disaster struck, however, when Marguerite's husband was diagnosed with a brain tumor. He died in 1915, the illness leaving the young family in substantial debt.

Begins writing career

The widowed Harrison knew that she would have to make a living, but she had no professional training or job skills. She did know everyone in Baltimore high society, however, and managed to get a job as assistant society editor for the Baltimore *Sun*. She was such a good reporter that the newspaper made her its music and drama critic, and then a weekly columnist.

Her own natural curiosity about the world was sharpened by a newly acquired reporter's instinct for news. Harrison became determined to write more important stories. She wanted a first-hand look at the Europe she was so familiar with from her travels, and which was now engaged in a great world war. She especially wanted to see the changes in her beloved Germany, and knew that the only way she could enter the country was as a government agent. She contacted the Military Intelligence Division (MID) of the U.S. War Department and asked to serve her country. The government concluded that—with her fluent German—Harrison would make an excellent spy.

Does undercover work

Although the war ended before Harrison arrived in Germany, the MID asked her to secretly investigate new economic and political developments there and to relay the information to American peace negotiators while posing as a *Sun* reporter. After the Versailles Treaty (agreement ending World War I) was signed in June 1919, Harrison returned home. In 1920, however, she again approached the MID, this time to be sent to Russia to report on its recent communist revolution. It

Opposite page: Lubianka Prison in Moscow, where Harrison was held.

was a risky assignment, for communist leaders wished to keep their plans and methods for building the new Soviet Union secret from the rest of the world.

Imprisoned for spying

Harrison entered the Soviet Union illegally from Poland, and when she reached the Soviet capital city of Moscow, authorities confronted her with that fact. They did allow her to stay as a reporter, however, and for eight months she provided the Baltimore *Sun* with stories on Soviet life. She was even allowed to observe some activities of the Communist Party. The Soviet secret police arrested her, though, when they learned that she was smuggling other information out to the MID. She was thrown into the horrible Lubianka Prison, a place for political criminals and spies. The first American woman to know Soviet imprisonment, Harrison feared that she would spend the rest of her life there.

Conditions were so bad at Lubianka that Harrison's health deteriorated, and she was moved to a prison where the conditions were not as harsh. In the meantime, the U.S. government was trying to find a way to get her home. Because Russia's political turmoil had caused severe economic problems, the American Relief Administration offered to send food there in exchange for detained Americans. Thus, Harrison was released after ten months. Upon her return home she encouraged Washington officials—who were reluctant to do so—to recognize the new Soviet government. She lectured on her experiences in the Soviet Union and wrote a book about her imprisonment, called *Marooned in Moscow.*

Travels to Far East

Harrison embarked on her next trip in 1922, anxious to learn first-hand about the tremendous political and social changes that were taking place in the Far East. Crossing the Pacific Ocean by steamship, she arrived in Japan, where she interviewed government officials and observed the daily life of citizens. She did the same in Korea and Manchuria (northeastern China), reporting

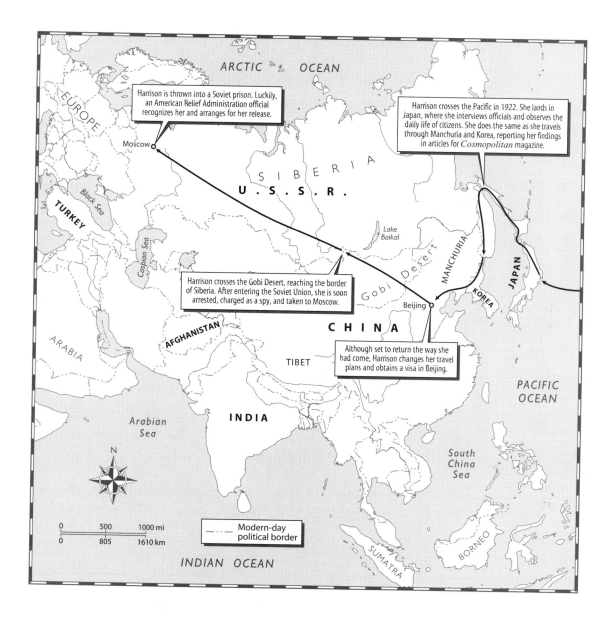

Harrison is thrown into a Soviet prison. Luckily, an American Relief Administration official recognizes her and arranges for her release.

Harrison crosses the Pacific in 1922. She lands in Japan, where she interviews officials and observes the daily life of citizens. She does the same as she travels through Manchuria and Korea, reporting her findings in articles for *Cosmopolitan* magazine.

Harrison crosses the Gobi Desert, reaching the border of Siberia. After entering the Soviet Union, she is soon arrested, charged as a spy, and taken to Moscow.

Although set to return the way she had come, Harrison changes her travel plans and obtains a visa in Beijing.

Modern-day political border

her findings in a series of articles for *Cosmopolitan* magazine. Although set to return home the same way she had come, Harrison unwisely decided to change her travel plans.

Again arrested as secret agent

Granted a visa from a Soviet official posted in Beijing, China, Harrison planned to revisit the Soviet Union to report on its continuing development. She crossed Mongolia's great Gobi Desert by way of a caravan route, reaching the border of Siberia. She entered the Soviet territory and was soon arrested, charged as a spy, and taken to Moscow. While innocent of the accusation this time, she was again thrown into a Soviet prison. She was pressured by the Soviet secret police to spy for them in the United States, and when she refused, her future looked grim. But in a lucky break, an American Relief Administration official saw her in the prison and recognized her, and arranged for her release. Her second imprisonment had lasted ten weeks.

Harrison arrived home in March 1923. While busy writing a book about Russia and Japan, a new opportunity for adventure presented itself. She ran into Merian Cooper (1893–1973), an American pilot she had met earlier in Soviet prison. Having escaped, he was now involved in the film industry, making travel documentaries. He and his cameraman, Ernest Schoedsack, had just returned from making a movie in Africa. They asked Harrison to join them in their next project: a film about a nomadic tribe that lived far from Western civilization.

Begins filmmaking adventure

As the film's financial backer, Harrison raised $10,000 for the project. The nomads chosen for the documentary were members of the Bakhtiari tribe, who lived in western Persia (now Iran). Every spring, Bakhtiari clans would pack up all their possessions and guide their huge livestock herds—goats, sheep, cattle, and horses—from winter grazing grounds in the lowland plains located along the Persian Gulf to summer grasslands in central Persia. It was a rough journey of more than two hundred miles, over several mountain ranges and rivers. In the fall they would repeat the journey, making their way back home.

Harrison, Cooper, and Schoedsack received permission from the Bakhtiari princes to accompany a clan just as the spring migration was about to began. They bought mules and donkeys to ride and to carry their supplies and equipment. On April 16, 1924, they set out with five thousand Bakhtiari men,

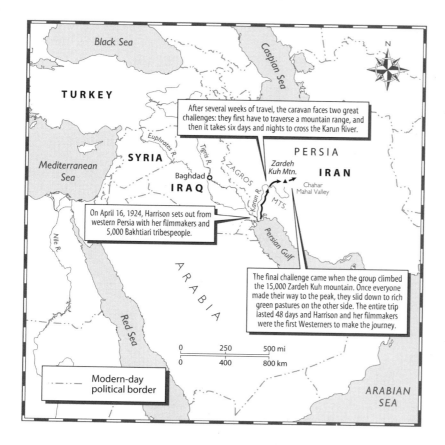

After several weeks of travel, the caravan faces two great challenges: they first have to traverse a mountain range, and then it takes six days and nights to cross the Karun River.

On April 16, 1924, Harrison sets out from western Persia with her filmmakers and 5,000 Bakhtiari tribespeople.

The final challenge came when the group climbed the 15,000 Zardeh Kuh mountain. Once everyone made their way to the peak, they slid down to rich green pastures on the other side. The entire trip lasted 48 days and Harrison and her filmmakers were the first Westerners to make the journey.

Modern-day political border

women, and children. While some of the tribespeople rode animals, most traveled on foot—and were barefoot besides.

After several weeks of travel, the huge procession reached the mountains. The men of the tribe went ahead, chopping a trail through the ice and snow; the group followed with feet bare, dressed in light clothing. Another challenge was crossing the swift, icy Karun River. The women and children rode on simple rafts, made of inflated goatskins, which were tied together. The men used the inflated skins like life-preservers, and swam across with the animals. It took six days and nights to get all of the clan and its livestock to the river-bank on the other side. Many animals drowned.

But the worst part of the journey was near the end of the trip, at the Zardeh Kuh. This was a mountain wall that rose nearly straight up into the clouds, to a height of fifteen thousand feet. For four days the clansmen chopped holes in the ice,

Blair Niles at a Society of Women Geographer's dinner in Washington, D.C. Niles was a co-founder of the society, along with Harrison.

making a slippery ladder; then everyone painstakingly made their way up the peak. Once there, they slid down the other side, to rich green pastures. The filmmakers were the first Westerners to make the incredible journey. It had taken forty-eight days.

Landmark documentary released

The resulting documentary, called *Grass,* was released by Hollywood in 1925. It was a disappointment to Harrison, for silly dialogue had been added using subtitles (films were still silent then). She felt that the subtitles ruined the documentary's natural drama and beauty. Movie audiences and critics also did not like the film, since it was different from the fictional romances and melodramas that they were used to. But scientists and geographers appreciated the documentary, which used new technology to record a distant people and culture for further study. *Grass* is considered a landmark achievement in the history of educational and documentary film.

Co-founds Society of Women Geographers

While Cooper and Schoedsack made more films together (including the giant-ape thriller *King Kong,* in 1933), Harrison returned to her writing and interest in foreign affairs. In 1925 she became a founder of the Society of Women Geographers, with Blair Niles (1887?–1959), Gertrude Emerson (1890–1982), and Gertrude Mathews Selby. Unhappy with the lack of respect women travelers and their projects often received, the four created a professional organization, based in Washington, D.C., for female scientists, explorers, and travel writers.

In 1926 Harrison was married for a second time, to Arthur Middleton Blake, an English actor living in Hollywood. She wrote an autobiography about her colorful life, *There's Always Tomorrow*. Published in 1935, it appeared a year later in England under the fitting title *Born for Trouble*. Widowed again in 1949, she continued to travel, visiting Australia and much of Africa. At the age of seventy-eight she sailed to South America on a freight boat. Harrison died on July 16, 1967.

Sources

Stefoff, Rebecca. *Women of the World: Women Travelers and Explorers*. New York: Oxford University Press, 1992.

Tinling, Marion. *Women into the Unknown: A Sourcebook on Women Explorers and Travelers*. Westport, CT: Greenwood Press, 1989.

Hatshepsut

Born c. 1520 B.C., Egypt

Died c. 1468 B.C., Egypt

Hatshepsut was an Egyptian queen who organized a great trading voyage to an east African kingdom called the Land of Punt around 1492 B.C.

Ancient Egypt was a civilization ruled by pharaohs: rulers who were believed to be half-men and half-gods. They lived in incredible luxury in palaces and temples that were filled with exotic goods from other lands. These precious possessions were also buried with the pharaohs in their grand tombs, to be enjoyed in the afterworld. Overseas voyages were necessary to bring such riches—ivory, gold and silver, feathers and animal skins, incense and spices—to the desert kingdom.

Records of ancient Egyptian sea journeys are scarce. It is known that shipbuilders had to bring in wood from other countries to make large, heavy, seagoing ships. (For their river boats, they used tightly woven reeds taken from the Nile's papyrus plant.) From ancient carvings, we know that the boats had flat hulls and square sails, which were used only when traveling with the direction of the wind. Otherwise, standing oarsmen—slaves—rowed the vessels along.

The Land of Punt

One place that Egyptian sailors visited often was the Land of Punt. Besides trading for gold and ivory there, they could obtain the incense and myrrh that were used to prepare the bodies of their dead. While scholars today are not exactly sure where the Land of Punt was located, most think that it was near what is now Somalia, the easternmost country on the African continent. The kingdom may also have included parts of southwestern Arabia and Ethiopia.

Hatshepsut takes the throne

Trading between Egypt and the Land of Punt stopped for some two hundred years when a people called the Hyksos overtook the land of the pharaohs. It resumed when the intruders were defeated and Hatshepsut became queen. The daughter of Thutmose I (c. 1525–c. 1512 B.C.), a pharaoh of the XVIII (18th) dynasty, she was the first woman to rule Egypt. She took the throne when her husband and half-brother, Thutmose II, died in 1504 B.C. She dressed herself in the traditional clothing of an Egyptian pharaoh.

Hatshepsut ruled Egypt for many years. During that time there were no wars, and the kingdom regained some of its wealth and power. The queen set about building new monuments and temples around the holy cities of Luxor, Karnak, and Thebes. In order to get the rich materials needed for these projects, she sent trade expeditions to far-off places.

Plans great trading voyage

Hatshepsut was especially interested in reopening trade relations with the Land of Punt. The queen reported that she had had a vision of the god Amon-Ra, who had told her to plant myrrh trees from Punt on the terraces of the temple she was building in his honor at Deir al-Bahri, in western Thebes. Egyptians believed in many deities (gods) and Amon-Ra was the greatest of these; it was through the pharaohs that deities communicated their wishes. Thus, Hatshepsut was spurred to organize an expedition at once, and to appoint her treasurer, a

Hieroglyphics adorn the walls of an Egyptian tomb.

nobleman named Nehsi, to lead it. Many large ships were loaded with Egyptian goods to trade: pottery, cosmetics, finely made linen, and cotton cloth. The boats may have been carried across the desert from the caravan town of Coptos (modern-day Kuft)—on the east bank of the Nile—to the Red Sea. But some scholars believe that the expedition reached the Red Sea by way of a canal connected with the Nile. Pharaoh Sesostris II (who died in 1878 B.C.) had created one four hundred years earlier, and it is possible that Hatshepsut had it re-excavated. The fleet set off in about 1492 B.C. It has been estimated that its voyage to the Land of Punt took between fourteen months and three years.

Details of the expedition were recorded, and later retold in the form of hieroglyphics (a pictorial system of writing) and colored reliefs (carvings on a flat surface) that were painted on the walls of the temple of Deir al-Bahri. One scene shows the Egyptian fleet anchored after reaching its destina-

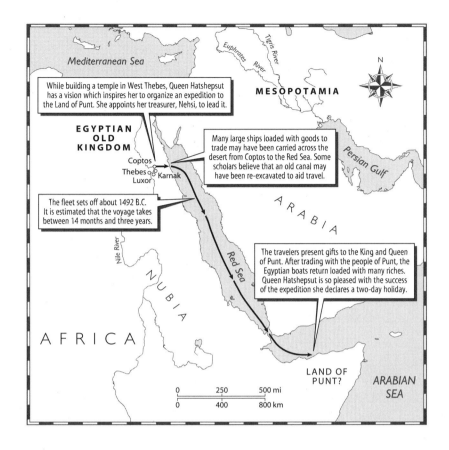

While building a temple in West Thebes, Queen Hatshepsut has a vision which inspires her to organize an expedition to the Land of Punt. She appoints her treasurer, Nehsi, to lead it.

Many large ships loaded with goods to trade may have been carried across the desert from Coptos to the Red Sea. Some scholars believe that an old canal may have been re-excavated to aid travel.

The fleet sets off about 1492 B.C. It is estimated that the voyage takes between 14 months and three years.

The travelers present gifts to the King and Queen of Punt. After trading with the people of Punt, the Egyptian boats return loaded with many riches. Queen Hatshepsut is so pleased with the success of the expedition she declares a two-day holiday.

Mediterranean Sea

MESOPOTAMIA

Euphrates River

Tigris River

N

EGYPTIAN
OLD
KINGDOM

Coptos
Thebes
Luxor
Karnak

Persian Gulf

A R A B I A

Nile River

NUBIA

Red Sea

AFRICA

LAND OF
PUNT?

ARABIAN
SEA

| 0 | 250 | 500 mi |
| 0 | 400 | 800 km |

tion, and another portrays the surprise of the natives, whose last contact with the Egyptians had been long ago. The travelers presented gifts to King Perehu and Queen Eti of Punt and a banquet was given in the Egyptians' honor. Then the trading of goods began.

The boats of the Egyptian fleet eventually became heavy with riches. The sailors returned with gold and silver, ivory and exotic woods, incenses and spices, and wild animals like baboons and a panther. They also brought back thirty-one young myrrh trees, each in a wooden tub. Some natives of Punt also made the journey back to Egypt.

Expedition's success celebrated

Nehsi and his crew were joyously welcomed when they returned. Hatshepsut was so pleased with the great success of the expedition that she declared a two-day holiday. Her sailors marched in a parade through the streets, showing off some of the riches from the Land of Punt. There were speeches and lavish banquets. It was later recorded on the temple wall that "such a treasure was never brought for any pharaoh who has ruled since the beginning."

Hatshepsut planted the fragrant myrrh trees on the terraces of the temple of Deir al-Bahri, which can still be visited today. The pictures that cover the temple walls are the first-known illustrated account of travel and exploration—and of a long sea journey—in history. During her reign, other overseas expeditions took place that restored the flow of trade into Egypt. This would stop, however, upon Hatshepsut's death in about 1468 B.C., when her stepson and successor, Thutmose III, would begin a series of military campaigns to expand the Egyptian empire into the Euphrates River valley. Nearly one thousand years would pass before Egyptian explorers would again travel the seas.

Sources

Marshall Cavendish Illustrated Encyclopedia of Discovery and Exploration, Volume 1: *The First Explorers,* written by Felix Barker and Anthea Barker. Freeport, NY: Marshall Cavendish, 1990.

Simon, Charnan. *The World's Great Explorers: Explorers of the Ancient World.* Chicago: Children's Press, 1990.

Waldman, Carl and Alan Wexler. *Who Was Who in World Exploration.* New York: Facts on File, 1992.

Louis Hennepin

Born May 12, 1626, Ath, Belgium

Died c. 1705

Louis Hennepin was born in the town of Ath, in what is now Belgium, the son of a butcher. After attending classical school there, he became a Franciscan novice (student priest) around the age of seventeen. He entered the priesthood and traveled to Rome in an effort to be assigned to a missionary post. But for the next several years he remained in Europe, preaching in Belgium and northern France. From 1672 to 1674 he cared for the sick and wounded during the war between France and the Netherlands.

Begins missionary work

In 1675, King Louis XIV (1638–1715) of France asked that the Franciscans send five missionaries to the North American colony of New France (Canada). Happily, Hennepin was among those chosen. At the end of May the missionaries left Europe on the same ship on which French explorer René-Robert Cavelier de La Salle (1643–1687) was

Belgian-born missionary priest Louis Hennepin accompanied French explorer René-Robert Cavelier de La Salle into the upper Mississippi River valley. He was the first European to visit two great North American waterfalls.

also traveling. After their arrival in Quebec, Hennepin set out at once on a preaching tour of the colony, through villages and the countryside. In the spring of 1676 he was called to serve at a mission at Fort Frontenac (now Kingston, Ontario), La Salle's headquarters at the eastern end of Lake Ontario.

Discovers Niagara Falls

La Salle had been newly authorized by King Louis to explore the western part of New France. He requested that Hennepin accompany him on his voyage of exploration to the Mississippi. The priest was a member of an advance party that set out by boat on November 18, 1678, to build a fort on the Niagara River. The group reached the river on December 6, and two days later came upon Niagara Falls. Hennepin was the first European to write a description of the natural wonder, describing it as "the most beautiful and altogether the most terrifying waterfall in the universe." In early 1679 the men set about building Fort Conti. They also constructed the *Griffon,* a ship on which to sail the Great Lakes.

Hennepin traveled with La Salle from August 7, 1679, to February 29, 1680. The expedition made its way on the *Griffon* from the Niagara River, through Lake Erie and Lake Huron, and on to the Straits of Mackinac (which separate Lake Huron from Lake Michigan). There the men left their ship and paddled south on Lake Michigan in canoes. In January 1860 they reached an Indian village on the Illinois River (near present-day Peoria, Illinois) and began to construct Fort Crèvecoeur.

Claims journey to mouth of Mississippi

On February 29 La Salle sent Hennepin and two others as advance scouts to the upper Mississippi region to see if they could find the river's source. Hennepin would later write that during the next several days—between February 29 and

Opposite page: Father Louis Hennepin celebrates mass for two Native Americans and a frontiersman.

March 25—the three men not only found their way to the Mississippi but canoed to its mouth, preceding La Salle to the destination by two years. Hennepin also claimed that the party returned to the upper Mississippi by April 10—making the journey one of more than three thousand miles! The feat seems an impossible one, and scholars since have tended to believe that Hennepin was either mistaken or lying. Still, the priest insisted that his account was true up until his death.

Captured by Indians

By April 11, 1680, Hennepin and his companions had traveled on the Mississippi to a place north of the Illinois River. There they were captured by a war party of Sioux Indians passing by their camp in thirty-three canoes. The Europeans' lives were spared because they offered the warriors the calumet (peace pipe) and gifts. (And the Indians also believed that Hennepin could use his magnetic compass to call upon supernatural forces). The Sioux forced the men to travel with them up the Mississippi River, toward their village. Along the way they came upon a great waterfall (near present-day St. Paul, Minnesota), which Hennepin named St. Anthony's Falls; he and his two companions were the first Europeans to see it. Then they went ashore and made a five-day march over marshes, lakes, and rivers to reach the Sioux village, located in what is now the Thousand Lakes area of Minnesota. They arrived there on April 21.

During his captivity, Hennepin studied the language and customs of the Sioux tribe. When hunting season arrived in the summer, he joined an Indian expedition headed for the Wisconsin River. On July 25 he had a chance meeting there with French explorer Daniel Greysolon Dulhut (1636–1710) and his party of five men, who had been sent by the colonial governor to visit the Sioux. They all returned to the Indian village on August 14, and by September its chief had granted them permission to leave, even giving them a map to follow. The Europeans made their way to the French post at Michilimackinac (on the Straits of Mackinac), where they spent the winter of 1680–1681. They left for Quebec in April of 1681.

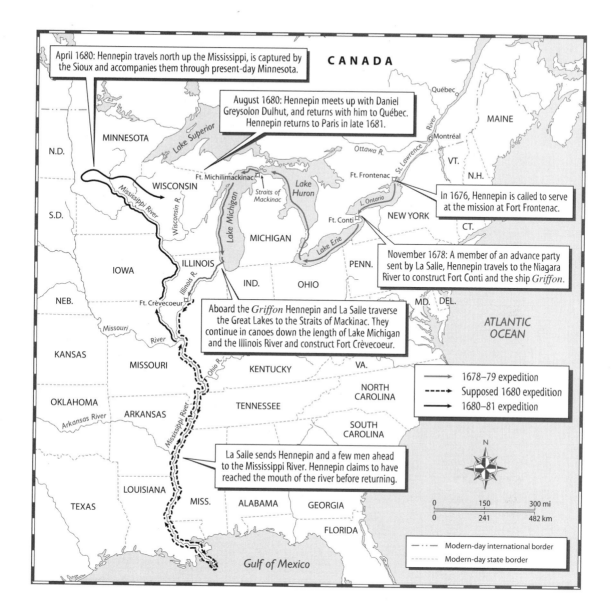

April 1680: Hennepin travels north up the Mississippi, is captured by the Sioux and accompanies them through present-day Minnesota.

August 1680: Hennepin meets up with Daniel Greysolon Dulhut, and returns with him to Québec. Hennepin returns to Paris in late 1681.

In 1676, Hennepin is called to serve at the mission at Fort Frontenac.

November 1678: A member of an advance party sent by La Salle, Hennepin travels to the Niagara River to construct Fort Conti and the ship *Griffon*.

Aboard the *Griffon* Hennepin and La Salle traverse the Great Lakes to the Straits of Mackinac. They continue in canoes down the length of Lake Michigan and the Illinois River and construct Fort Crèvecoeur.

La Salle sends Hennepin and a few men ahead to the Mississippi River. Hennepin claims to have reached the mouth of the river before returning.

CANADA

MAINE

MINNESOTA

N.D.

S.D.

IOWA

NEB.

KANSAS

OKLAHOMA

TEXAS

WISCONSIN

MICHIGAN

ILLINOIS

MISSOURI

ARKANSAS

LOUISIANA

Québec

Montréal

VT.

N.H.

NEW YORK

CT.

PENN.

IND.

OHIO

MD. DEL.

KENTUCKY

VA.

TENNESSEE

NORTH CAROLINA

SOUTH CAROLINA

MISS.

ALABAMA

GEORGIA

FLORIDA

ATLANTIC OCEAN

Lake Superior

Lake Michigan

Lake Huron

Ft. Michilimackinac

Straits of Mackinac

Ft. Frontenac

L. Ontario

Lake Erie

Ft. Conti

Ft. Crèvecoeur

Mississippi River

Wisconsin R.

Illinois R.

Missouri River

Ohio R.

Arkansas River

Mississippi River

St. Lawrence River

Ottawa R.

Gulf of Mexico

→ 1678–79 expedition
---- Supposed 1680 expedition
→ 1680–81 expedition

0   150   300 mi
0   241   482 km

N

-·-·- Modern-day international border
·····- Modern-day state border

From there Hennepin traveled on to Europe, and was in Paris by the end of the year.

Book of travels becomes bestseller

Upon his return to Europe, Hennepin retired to a monastery to write an account of his travels. His *Déscription de la Louisiane* was published in Paris on January 5, 1683, and became an immediate bestseller, reprinted forty-six times and translated into several languages. European readers delighted in his exotic and sometimes exaggerated accounts of the distant land he had visited, its unknown plants and animals, and the lives of its native inhabitants, with their strange customs and beliefs. As a result of his book's success, Hennepin's religious career flourished, and he was appointed to important posts. All that changed in 1687, however, when he was expelled from his monastery in France and forced to travel north to the Netherlands—for reasons unknown. Hennepin blamed his misfortunes on a plot by La Salle, who was supposedly provoked by the priest's claim of being the first European to sail down the Mississippi River.

From that point on, Hennepin's life was in turmoil. He became involved in different religious and political conflicts in the Netherlands, France, and Rome. He did manage to write two more books about his travels in North America, however: *Nouvelle découverte* (1697) and *Nouveau voyage* (1698) recounted more details about his alleged trip down the Mississippi. He was last heard of in the Netherlands in 1702, and it is not known how or where he died.

Sources

Baker, Daniel B., ed. *Explorers and Discoverers of the World*. Detroit: Gale Research, 1993.

Bohlander, Richard E., ed. *World Explorers and Discoverers*. New York: Macmillan, 1992.

Dictionary of Canadian Biography, Volume II: 1701-1740. Toronto: University of Toronto Press, 1969.

Saari, Peggy and Daniel B. Baker, "René-Robert Cavelier de La Salle." *Explorers and Discoverers*. Detroit: U•X•L, 1995.

Daniel Houghton

Born 1740

Died 1791, West Africa

I n the late eighteenth century, the West knew little about the interior of Africa, although Europeans had trading settlements along the African coast. In 1788, a group of twelve London gentlemen, led by scientist and explorer Sir Joseph Banks (1743–1820), formed the Association for Promoting the Discovery of the Interior Parts of Africa—also known as the African Association. The group was especially interested in sending explorers to Africa's Niger River region. They had heard rumors about the area's great wealth and of a rich trade center there, the city of Timbuktu.

In 1788, the African Association assigned two men to explore the Niger River. It was a challenging mission, because no Westerner had actually seen the river, and nothing was known about where it originated, in which direction it flowed, or if it emptied into the sea. Simon Lucas set out from the port of Tripoli on Africa's northern coast and traveled five hundred miles into the desert on his quest before turning back. American John Ledyard (1751–1789) planned to reach the Niger by

Daniel Houghton was an Irish explorer who searched for Africa's Niger River. Although he died before reaching his destination, he pushed further into West Africa than any European before him.

On October 16, 1790, Houghton sails from England to the mouth of the Gambia River. He ascends the river until he reaches the British trading post of Pisania.

Houghton makes his way as far as the town of Sinbing, about 500 miles into Africa. It is believed he perished near the town of Nioro, just 200 miles from the Niger.

After further travel on the Gambia, Houghton begins an overland journey to the Niger River. Along the way he narrowly escapes assassination, and after reaching Medina, his possessions are destroyed by fire and his guide steals his horse and three donkeys. Houghton is not able to leave Medina until May 8, 1791.

sailing south from Cairo along the Nile River, but he died in Egypt before he got started.

African Association hires Houghton

The African Association then hired Irishman Daniel Houghton, a retired major in the British Army. He had become a soldier in 1758, at the age of eighteen, and fought in the Caribbean during the Seven Years' War. In 1772 he had been stationed in Gibraltar on the southern coast of Spain and later served at the British consulate in Morocco. In 1778 he was made commander of a fort on Gorée, an island off the coast of Africa's Senegal. While there he learned Mandingo, one of the major languages used in trading in western Africa.

Houghton retired from the army and returned to England, married, and began a large family. In serious need of money, he offered his services to the African Association. He was hired on July 5, 1790, and given instructions to explore the Niger River and the territories that bordered it. Unlike his predecessors, Houghton planned to find the river by traveling inland from the west coast of Africa; once he reached Timbuktu he would then return by way of the Sahara Desert.

Begins search for Niger River

Houghton sailed from England on October 16, 1790, and arrived at the mouth of the Gambia River on the west coast of Africa in November. He began ascending the river until he reached the small British trading post of Pisania, located about halfway up the Gambia. There he met John Laidley, a British doctor who ran the post and who would later relay Houghton's expedition reports back to England.

After further travel on the Gambia, Houghton prepared for a long overland journey that he hoped would bring him to the Niger. He hired a guide and bought a horse and five donkeys to carry his supplies and the goods he had brought with him to give to the native inhabitants he would meet along the way. Houghton was well-received by the rulers of the small kingdoms through which he passed as he traveled east. But then his luck changed, and the explorer experienced a series of catastrophes.

Disasters slow expedition

First Houghton managed to escape an assassination attempt by a group of protective native merchants who feared that the success of his expedition would bring more English traders to the area. His life was saved by chance, because he had learned enough Mandingo to understand a conversation he overheard in which his murder was being plotted. Next, when he reached Medina, the capital of the Woolli kingdom, a fire struck the city and many of his supplies were destroyed, including his gun. The gun he bought as a replacement exploded in his hands, wounding him very badly. While he was recovering, his guide fled the city, taking Houghton's horse,

Mungo Park, who followed Houghton's route to the Niger.

three of the donkeys, and some equipment with him. Houghton was not able to leave Medina until May 8, 1791.

Reports new discoveries

Despite his great difficulties, Houghton pressed on. He made his way as far as the town of Sinbing, about five hundred miles into the African interior. It was from there that he sent a letter to Pisania—dated September 1, 1791—reporting that, although he had not yet reached the Niger, he had learned that it flowed eastward and was navigable (suited for boat travel). Houghton began to make plans to sail along the Niger to Timbuktu. In his letter the explorer also related that the land through which he had recently passed was rich with "gold, ivory, wax, and slaves," which could be easily traded for.

That letter would be the last word from Houghton. It was later learned that he had joined a trade caravan of Moors (North African Muslims) who were headed to the Niger. The traders soon stole the explorer's last few possessions and fled, abandoning him—perhaps to die of possible wounds they inflicted or from starvation. It is believed that he perished near the town of Nioro in what is now western Mali, just two hundred miles short of the Niger. His body was never found.

Still, the encouraging reports that Houghton sent back to his African Association sponsors led them to continue expeditions to the Niger River region. Although unable to reach his destination, Houghton had managed to travel farther into West Africa than any European before him; he had also been the first to accurately report on the eastward flow of the river. In 1795 the African Association would send Scottish explorer Mungo Park (1771–1806) on a subsequent expedition to find the Niger, following the route that had been pioneered by Houghton. Park would successfully reach the river.

Sources

Baker, Daniel B., ed. *Explorers and Discoverers of the World*. Detroit: Gale Research, 1993.

Bohlander, Richard E., ed. *World Explorers and Discoverers*. New York: Macmillan, 1992.

Marshall Cavendish Illustrated Encyclopedia of Discovery and Exploration, Volume 10: *Seas of Sand*, written by Paul Hamilton. Freeport, NY: Marshall Cavendish, 1990.

Waldman, Carl and Alan Wexler. *Who Was Who in World Exploration*. New York: Facts on File, 1992.

I-Ching

Born 634

Died c. 712

I-Ching was a Chinese Buddhist monk who traveled to India by way of Indonesia to study and collect religious texts. He provided valuable written accounts of both places.

I-Ching was one of a large number of Chinese Buddhist monks who traveled to India—the birthplace of Buddhism—to visit holy sites and study original religious texts there. One early Buddhist traveler was the Chinese priest Fa-Hsien (399–414), who began his journey in 399. Traveling by land and sea, he showed future Chinese pilgrims how to make their way to and from India. Beginning in 629, another Chinese monk, Hsüan-Tsang (602–664), made an epic sixteen-year journey through much of central Asia and the Indian subcontinent. He recorded all he saw and brought back many Buddhist relics and texts. This inspired I-Ching to undertake his own religious journey to India.

I-Ching set out in 671. Unlike most pilgrims before him, he could not take the usual land route to India across central Asia and the Himalayas. There was political turmoil in Tibet and Afghanistan and their surrounding areas, making overland travel dangerous. So the Buddhist monk would

have to make his way to India by a more southerly route, most of it by sea.

Begins voyage to India

At the southern Chinese port of Canton, I-Ching boarded a Persian boat headed for the islands of the East Indies, what we now call Indonesia. His first stop was at the city of Palembang—a center of Buddhist studies in southeast Asia—located on the southeast coast of the island of Sumatra. There I-Ching remained for six months learning Sanskrit, the ancient holy language of India. He then headed through the Strait of Malacca to the island's northwest tip, where he boarded a Sumatran ship going to the Nicobar Islands. From there he traveled across the Bay of Bengal to the great port of Tamralipti in the delta of the Ganges River, not far from India's present-day city of Calcutta.

This example of Chinese Buddhist Sanskrit, known as the Diamond Sutra, was printed in A.D. 868. It is the earliest dated specimen of blockprinting. I-Ching mastered Sanskrit before heading to India.

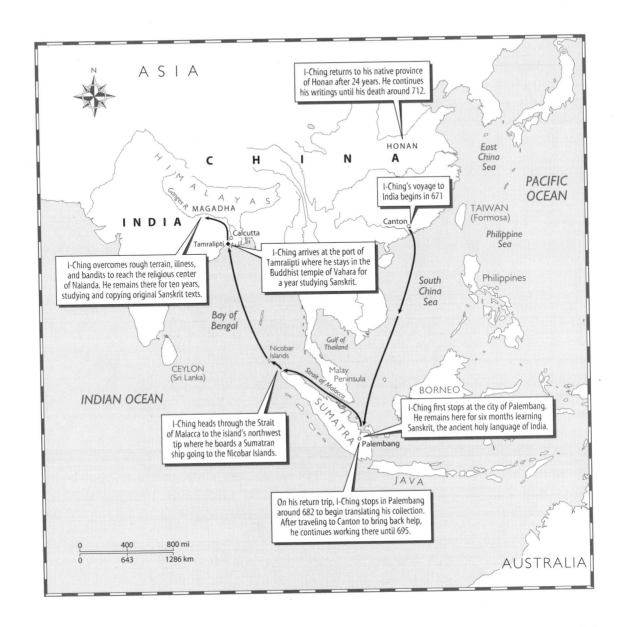

I-Ching returns to his native province of Honan after 24 years. He continues his writings until his death around 712.

I-Ching's voyage to India begins in 671

I-Ching arrives at the port of Tamralipti where he stays in the Buddhist temple of Vahara for a year studying Sanskrit.

I-Ching overcomes rough terrain, illness, and bandits to reach the religious center of Nalanda. He remains there for ten years, studying and copying original Sanskrit texts.

I-Ching heads through the Strait of Malacca to the island's northwest tip where he boards a Sumatran ship going to the Nicobar Islands.

I-Ching first stops at the city of Palembang. He remains here for six months learning Sanskrit, the ancient holy language of India.

On his return trip, I-Ching stops in Palembang around 682 to begin translating his collection. After traveling to Canton to bring back help, he continues working there until 695.

At Tamralipti, I-Ching stayed in the Buddhist temple of Vahara for another year, continuing his study of Sanskrit. He then wished to tour sacred Buddhist sites, located in the lower Ganges River valley. He was especially interested in visiting Magadha, an area where Buddhism first developed, and where the religious center of Nalanda was located. I-Ching had a difficult time making his way there, however, encountering mountains, woods, and swamps; illness and bandits further slowed his progress.

Collects Buddhist texts

At last arriving in Nalanda, I-Ching set about studying and copying original Sanskrit texts of Buddhist religious writings. He remained there for ten years, collecting some five hundred thousand Sanskrit stanzas (sections of verse) that he believed would fill one thousand volumes when translated into Chinese. While in India, I-Ching visited nearly thirty different kingdoms or principalities (regions ruled by princes).

Writes account of travels

Making his way home the same way he had come, I-Ching again stopped in Palembang around 682, where he decided to stay and begin the enormous task of translating his collection. He hoped to finish the job in about ten years. But finding that he had underestimated the project, he made a trip to Canton in 689 to recruit help and return to Palembang. I-Ching and his staff of Buddhist monks remained there until 695, working on the translations. I-Ching also worked on a detailed geographic account of his travels through India, and through the East Indies islands and along the Malay Peninsula. Considered I-Ching's most valuable contribution to world exploration, this written account—which still survives—is a rare record of the early history, culture, and religions of the peoples of Indonesia.

I-Ching returned to his native province of Honan in China after an absence of twenty-four years. Until his death around 712 he continued his scholarly writings and worked on his Buddhist translations. He also wrote books on the religious practices of the people of India and Sumatra, and about other Buddhist monks and pilgrims who had made the long voyage to India.

Sources

Baker, Daniel B., ed. *Explorers and Discoverers of the World.* Detroit: Gale Research, 1993.

Delpar, Helen, ed. *The Discoverers: An Encyclopedia of Explorers and Exploration.* New York: McGraw-Hill, 1980.

Waldman, Carl and Alan Wexler. *Who Was Who in World Exploration.* New York: Facts on File, 1992.

Jordanus of Séverac

Born 1290

Died 1354

Jordanus of Séverac was a French Catholic missionary who traveled to India in the fourteenth century. His Mirabilia (Book of Marvels) contains what is considered the best description of medieval India by a Westerner.

t is unclear how Christianity arrived in India. It is thought that St. Thomas, one of the twelve disciples of Jesus, traveled to India as a missionary. According to legend, he preached, performed miracles, and was martyred in India, and his tomb is located near the present-day port city of Madras.

It is certain that Christian communities existed on the Malabar (southwestern) and Coromandel (southeastern) coasts of India from at least the third century A.D. But it was not until the late Middle Ages that Christian missionaries from Europe traveled to the East. At that time the establishment of Mongol rule over much of Asia opened it to diplomatic, business, and religious contacts with the West.

Franciscan John of Monte Corvino (1247–1328) was the first Roman Catholic missionary who was known to have worked among the Christians of south India. He spent a year on the Malabar and Coromandel coasts before departing in 1292 to continue on to China. It appears that there was no further missionary activity in the area until 1321, when Jordanus of Séverac, a French Dominican friar, arrived with four others (three young Italian seminarians and a Franciscan brother) at the port of Thana on Salsette Island, just north of India's present-day city of Bombay.

Tragedy strikes soon after arrival

Sailing from Ormuz in Persia (now Iran), Jordanus and his group had intended to land farther south on the Malabar coast, at a place where the St. Thomas Christians (who claimed St. Thomas as their community's founder) were located. But a storm had blown them off course. When they landed in Thana a group of Nestorian Christians (who had different beliefs) persuaded Jordanus to travel north to visit one of their communities located near the city of Broach. During his absence, extremist Muslims attacked and killed the rest of the missionary group on April 7, 1321.

Jordanus gathered the remains of his murdered companions and took them to Suali, located near the present-day west Indian city of Surat. That was where St. Thomas was supposed to have landed at the start of his mission in India. Jordanus continued his own missionary activities, even after the tragedy. But he did so with a heavy heart. In two letters to fellow missionaries in Tabriz, Persia, Jordanus wrote of his unhappiness and loneliness, and of the challenge of living with poverty, illness, and people whom he did not trust.

Writes *Book of Marvels*

Nonetheless, Jordanus carried on, and in 1330 Pope John XXII named him bishop of Columbum (now Quilon), located near the southern tip of India. In the years that followed—probably between 1329 and 1338—he wrote *Mirabilia*, translated as *Book of Marvels* or *Description of Marvels*. In it Jordanus describes Armenia and Persia. He also gives a detailed account of the many parts of India he visited, and includes customs, principal products, and plants and animals native to each region. Considered the best description of medieval

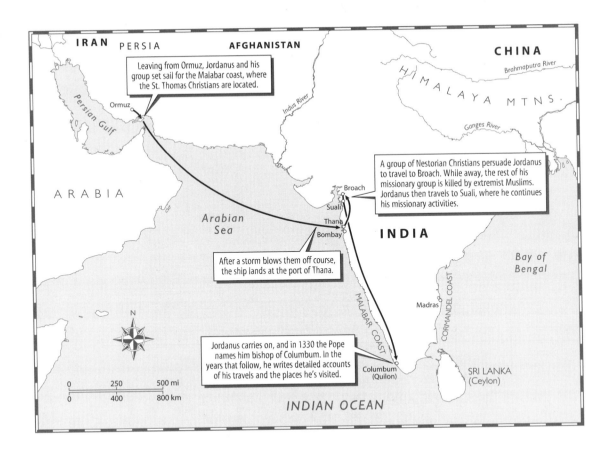

IRAN PERSIA   AFGHANISTAN   CHINA

Leaving from Ormuz, Jordanus and his
group set sail for the Malabar coast, where
the St. Thomas Christians are located.

Ormuz

Persian Gulf

ARABIA

Arabian
Sea

A group of Nestorian Christians persuade Jordanus
to travel to Broach. While away, the rest of his
missionary group is killed by extremist Muslims.
Jordanus then travels to Suali, where he continues
his missionary activities.

Broach
Suali
Thana
Bombay   INDIA

After a storm blows them off course,
the ship lands at the port of Thana.

Bay of
Bengal

Madras

Jordanus carries on, and in 1330 the Pope
names him bishop of Columbum. In the
years that follow, he writes detailed accounts
of his travels and the places he's visited.

Columbum
(Quilon)

SRI LANKA
(Ceylon)

0   250   500 mi
0   400   800 km

INDIAN OCEAN

India written by a Westerner, *Mirabilia* is Jordanus's most important contribution to world exploration.

In his book, Jordanus also includes descriptions of marvels of the East Indies and Indochina, but it is clear that he never visited those places. These tales—some true and some not—came from other travelers. One story, about a Christian kingdom in the mountains of northeastern Africa, led Jordanus to believe that he had finally solved the mystery of Prester John, a Christian priest who was thought to rule a vast, wealthy empire in Asia or Africa in the Middle Ages (fifth to fifteenth century). Christian visitors to the East had long wondered if Prester John really existed and where his kingdom was located. Jordanus was the first writer to connect reports of a Christian king in Abyssinia (now Ethiopia, in northeast Africa) to the legendary Prester John.

Sources

Baker, Daniel B., ed. *Explorers and Discoverers of the World*. Detroit: Gale Research, 1993.

Delpar, Helen, ed. *The Discoverers: An Encyclopedia of Explorers and Exploration*. New York: McGraw-Hill, 1980.

Kathleen M. Kenyon

Born January 5, 1906, England
Died August 24, 1978

Kathleen M. Kenyon was a British archaeologist who spent many years excavating Jordan's ancient city of Jericho. Her findings revealed that it was the oldest city in the world.

The site of the ancient city of Jericho (located in what is now Jordan) has long intrigued modern archaeologists. Frequently mentioned in the Bible's Old Testament, the city was an important cultural center and travel destination in the ancient world because it held a commanding position in the lower Jordan River valley—between the Sea of Galilee (now Bahr Tabariya) and the Dead Sea—and also because it had a steady supply of spring water.

The best-known Biblical incident involving Jericho is in the Book of Joshua. Joshua was a leader of the Israelites sometime between 1400 and 1250 B.C. Held as slaves in Egypt, the Israelites had crossed the desert to Canaan or Palestine, which God had told them was their Promised Land. Not allowed into Jericho by the Canaanites, the Israelites marched around the fortified city, blowing their horns. They then let out a mighty shout, and the walls of the city are said to have come tumbling down.

Kathleen Kenyon was born January 5, 1906, in England, the daughter of Sir Frederic Kenyon, who was director of the British Museum. Sharing his interest in history, she received degrees from Oxford University, specializing in archaeology. Between 1929 and 1935 she took part in excavations in southern Rhodesia, at historical sites in England (such as Verulamium, Samaria, Leicester, and Viroconium-Bath), and in Palestine (now Israel and Jordan).

In 1951, as the new director of the British School of Archaeology in Jerusalem, Kenyon planned an expedition to Jericho. There she would use the newest methods of excavation to reexamine findings made by earlier scientists and conduct diggings of her own. She was especially interested in any discoveries that dated around the "Joshua era" (c. 1400–1250). Excavations of the site had begun in the eighteenth century and continued at different times throughout the nineteenth and twentieth centuries. The last full-scale exploration of Jericho had been conducted by Professor John Garstang (1876–1956) of Liverpool University during the mid-1920s.

Begins Jericho excavations

Kenyon arrived at Jericho in the spring of 1952. The period of her excavation work would be brief—between February and April—for the intense summer heat of the desert would later make digging impossible. Her site was called Old Jericho, lying on the outskirts of the modern town of Jericho. It consisted of a seventy-foot high, oval-shaped heap that spread over about eight acres. A road was cut through part of the site. Kenyon hoped that it had not ruined too many artifacts. She was also concerned about the damage done by past excavations, when archeological methods were less careful and systematic. Often diggers worked their way straight down to a treasure, mixing together soil and other artifacts from different levels and time periods as they went. At a site as old as Jericho, it was important to carefully keep track of the different eras. Therefore, Kenyon's first job was to sift through the pile of rubble left behind by past digs.

Kenyon worked with an international team of archaeology experts and students. She also hired between 120 and 250 Arab workers to do the most difficult digging. In addition, an artist and a photographer made visual records of each new discovery. The team lived and worked in an old mill building or in tents set up in a nearby banana grove. Conditions were primitive and cramped.

New discoveries about Joshua era

In her first excavation season at Jericho, Kenyon made some important discoveries about the Joshua era. During the time period that scholars believed Joshua and the Israelites had collapsed the city's walls, the archaeologist found that the walls had already been destroyed, probably by earthquake and fire. It appeared that the bricks had fallen in an outward direction, and had been badly burned on their inner face. Thus the Joshua era was pushed back by at least a century. Kenyon also found that the city walls had been built upon layers of other ruined walls, suggesting that Jericho's history reached far into the past.

Surprising finds about Jericho's history

Kenyon had found evidence of Jericho's distant past in the pottery and figurines that she had come upon at the site— they appeared to be incredibly old. At the end of the 1952 digging season she made an exciting discovery that provided even more evidence: an ancient shrine located on a lower level. The large rectangular room held a skillfully made basin that was slightly burned. Kenyon believed that the vessel had been used for religious sacrifice, since the charred remains of humans and animals were found nearby. Ceremonial figurines were also discovered in the room. Using a scientific method called carbon-14 dating (which measures carbon's atomic decay over time), Kenyon's team traced the finds back to the Neolithic (New Stone Age) period, when prehistoric man progressed from hunting and gathering food to settling in villages and raising plants and animals. No one had imagined that Jericho could be that old.

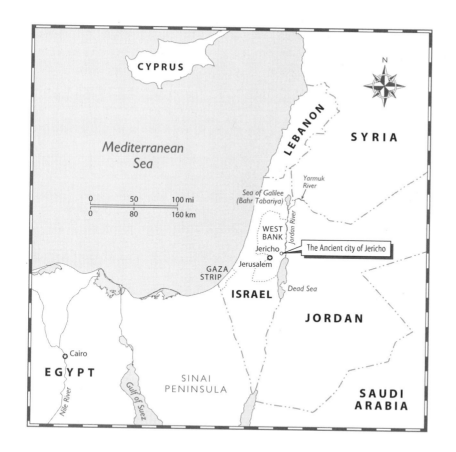

Tomb excavations

For the next five years excavations continued at Jericho. Kenyon and her team discovered many tombs, from different centuries B.C. Often, heavy granite stones and doors guarded their entries. In one such burial site, from around 1500 B.C., Kenyon entered on her hands and knees because the chamber had such a low roof. With generator-run lights illuminating the dark, she found the remains of a richly dressed man, laid on a platform of mud bricks with his head raised on a stone pillow. The bodies of earlier burials had been swept aside to make way for him, indicating that he had been of some importance. Buried with him were a woman, a young boy, and two little children. The group had been supplied with food and drink, for large storage jars with dippers were in the tomb, as well as baskets and plates that held sheep bones. They were also buried with jewelry, combs, and other personal items. It all reminded Kenyon of an Egyptian burial, and she wondered if—as was the practice in Egypt—the woman and children had been killed to accompany the man to the afterworld.

Other tombs suggested tribal groups with different customs, for some burial sites revealed bodies laid out in rows. It was clear that Jericho was a city built upon settlement after settlement. Kenyon painstakingly preserved and transferred all the burial finds—pottery, beads, pins, wooden bowls and furniture, and skeletons (even a shriveled brain encased in a skull)—to the camp headquarters for further cataloging and study. Other artifacts and building structures painted a picture of town life in Jericho. Kenyon was especially interested in the outside walls that protected the city from invaders. They had been rebuilt many times—twenty-nine in all.

Uncovers Neolithic settlement

In 1953 Kenyon made still more astonishing discoveries. While following a lower-level town wall, she came upon the ruins of a small group of rectangular houses that seemed to date from the same time period as the Neolithic shrine she had found in her first year at Jericho. They had the same plaster floors and mud brick walls. Near them lay cutting and grinding tools for grain, figurines, and painted plaster skull heads. Kenyon was amazed at the skill with which these items were created. Further excavation revealed that the houses covered the entire eight-acre mound of Old Jericho. Comparing her finds with discoveries at other nearby ancient archeological sites like Yarmuk and Ros Sharsba, it was clear to Kenyon that Jericho's first inhabitants lived at a time well before all other Neolithic peoples.

Other amazing finds

Further discoveries by Kenyon and her team would reveal just how advanced these Neolithic Jericho dwellers were. Attached to an even older town wall than the one that had led her to the houses was a great tower that must have been used in defending the city from outsiders. Inside it was a wide flight of stairs. The tower had been built thousands of years before the Egyptian pyramids. An irrigation ditch was also discovered at the base of the wall, lined with crushed and broken rocks. This sophisticated method of bringing water to the town would not be seen at other locations until much later.

By 1956 Kenyon had discovered yet another type of Neolithic house at Jericho, even older than the first. These were crudely built, domed and curved, and had rooms that were almost round. Could a more advanced Neolithic people have overthrown this more primitive tribe at Jericho? Kenyon dated the oldest houses to somewhere around 7800 B.C. That was two thousand years earlier than any other Neolithic settlement found in the Middle East.

Jericho discoveries capture world's imagination

Western newspapers had been following the work of Kenyon and her team with great interest. Not since the discovery of the tomb of Egyptian King Tutankhamen (c. 1370–1352 B.C.) during the 1920s had the public been so interested in archaeology. While Kenyon did not unearth fabulous riches, like those that had been found in the Egyptian pharaoh's crypt, she did dig through unimagined layers of human history to discover the oldest settlement in the world.

Kenyon completed her excavations at Jericho in 1957. She returned to England for a time, lecturing and writing about her discoveries in *Digging up Jericho* and in *Excavations at Jericho*. Still serving as director of the British School of Archaeology in Jerusalem (until 1966), her next excavation project centered around the old city of Jerusalem. There she unearthed parts of an ancient wall, dating from around 1800 B.C. Along with her field work, Kenyon continued to write books on archaeology. She also taught at universities in England and the United States, training a new generation of scientists. Much honored for her outstanding work, she died on August 24, 1978.

Sources

Charles-Picard, Gilbert, ed. *Larousse Encyclopedia of Archaeology.* New York: Putnam, 1972.

Contemporary Authors, New Revision Series, Volume 1-4. Detroit: Gale Research, 1963.

Rittenhouse, Mignon. *Seven Women Explorers.* Philadelphia: Lippincott, 1964.

Yerofey Pavlovich Khabarov

Born c. 1610, Ustyug, Russia

Died c. 1670

During the 1630s, inhabitants of Russia's eastern frontier heard rumors of a great river that was located in southeastern Siberia. It was said that the people who lived in that river valley possessed great wealth, for their land was rich with precious metals, especially silver. Russian expeditions were soon launched to find the Amur River valley. In 1644, for instance, cossack Vasily Danilovich Poyarkov (?–1668) and his party of men located the river and descended to its mouth near the Pacific Ocean. Yerofey Pavlovich Khabarov was another such explorer, who made two expeditions into the Amur region. He built several forts there during his second trip, establishing Russian claims to the area.

Khabarov was born around 1610 in the town of Ustyug in the northern part of European Russia. Sometime around 1636 he joined other pioneers in Siberia, Russia's eastern frontier. There he established a successful farm on the Yenisei River and became involved with fur trading at Yakutsk, a fort that was a center of Russian activity in the Far East. It was from there that

Yerofey Pavlovich Khabarov was a Russian farmer and fur trader who pioneered an overland route to the Amur River. He also established the first Russian settlements in the Amur River valley.

he launched an expedition in 1649—at his own expense—to travel south and east to the still-unexplored Amur River valley.

Pioneers new route to Amur River

With a force of 150 men, Khabarov traveled south along the Lena, Olekma, and Tungir rivers. He then crossed southeastern Siberia's Yablonovy Mountain Range before descending the Amazar River, a small tributary (branch) leading to the great Amur. This route proved easier than those taken by earlier explorers, and the party reached its destination in January 1650. Khabarov's way to the Amur River would be used by many future Russian expeditions.

Khabarov found the Daurians—the native inhabitants of the Amur River valley—very unfriendly. He did not wish to risk a conflict with them, because China considered the region a part of its domain and therefore Russian aggression in the area might bring a war with China. To avoid an international incident, Khabarov decided to return to Yakutsk, arriving there in May 1650.

Upon his return, Khabarov reported his findings to local government officials. He believed that Russia should undertake a military campaign to conquer the Amur region. He estimated that although it might take as many as six thousand soldiers to control the area, it would be well worth the effort. Khabarov's report was sent to Russia's capital city of Moscow. While military action to subdue the Amur River valley was subsequently planned, it was never carried out.

Frequent fighting during second expedition

In the meantime, Khabarov made a return expedition to the Amur region in the fall of 1650. This time the Daurians were openly hostile and Khabarov and his men were forced to fight. The Russians conquered the town of Albaza, where the Daur prince lived. They made the village into a fort, renaming it Albazin, and used it as their headquarters during the winter of 1650–1651. When spring arrived, Khabarov and his men continued their travels down the Amur, fighting local inhabi-

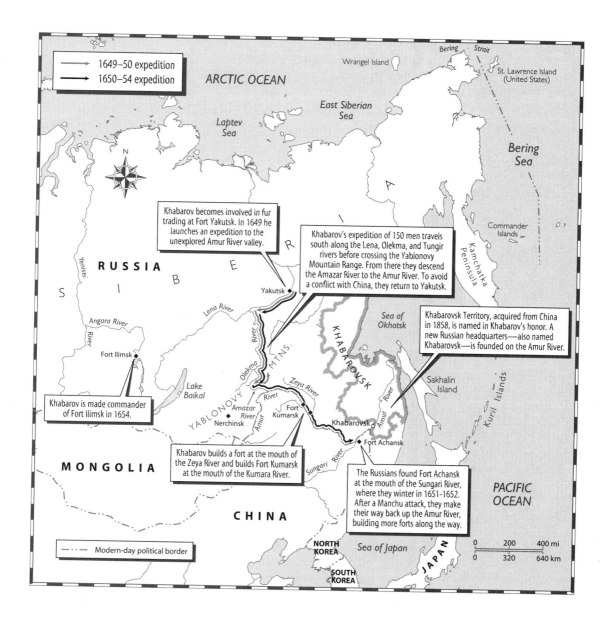

Khabarov becomes involved in fur trading at Fort Yakutsk. In 1649 he launches an expedition to the unexplored Amur River valley.

Khabarov's expedition of 150 men travels south along the Lena, Olekma, and Tungir rivers before crossing the Yablonovy Mountain Range. From there they descend the Amazar River to the Amur River. To avoid a conflict with China, they return to Yakutsk.

Khabarovsk Territory, acquired from China in 1858, is named in Khabarov's honor. A new Russian headquarters—also named Khabarovsk—is founded on the Amur River.

Khabarov is made commander of Fort Ilimsk in 1654.

Khabarov builds a fort at the mouth of the Zeya River and builds Fort Kumarsk at the mouth of the Kumara River.

The Russians found Fort Achansk at the mouth of the Sungari River, where they winter in 1651-1652. After a Manchu attack, they make their way back up the Amur River, building more forts along the way.

tants as they went. They founded a fort called Achansk at the mouth of the Sungari River, a tributary about halfway down the Amur. They wintered there in 1651–1652. In March 1652, Manchu soldiers from northern China launched an attack against them. While the Russians were able to drive them away, Khabarov knew that more battles with the Chinese would follow. So the expedition made its way back up the Amur River, founding more forts along the way.

Khabarov built a fort at the mouth of the Zeya River, site of the present-day Russian city of Blagoveshchensk. At the mouth of the Kumara River he built the Fort of Kumarsk, which is today located in Chinese territory. In the years following Khabarov's expeditions, Russia and China engaged in a serious struggle over control of the Amur River valley, with dominance in the area shifting from one country to another. But because neither nation wanted a full-scale war, a treaty was negotiated between them at the Russian post of Nerchinsk in 1689. Russia agreed to withdraw from the region, returning it to the Chinese.

Explorer later honored

In 1654 Khabarov was called to Moscow to face charges of cruelty to his men. His accuser was a Russian government official—newly sent to the frontier—who wanted control of the expedition's forces. After a full trial, Khabarov was cleared of any wrongdoing and was made commander of the Fort of Ilimsk, located west of Siberia's Lake Baikal. There he remained for the rest of his life.

In the 1850s, when China's internal political and social problems became so great that they weakened its military strength, Russia again took control of much of the Amur River valley. Russia's Khabarovsk Territory, acquired from China in 1858, was named in Khabarov's honor. A new Russian headquarters located on the Amur River—also named Khabarovsk—was founded that same year. It is now the largest city in the Russian Far East.

Sources

Baker, Daniel B., ed. *Explorers and Discoverers of the World*. Detroit: Gale Research, 1993.

Delpar, Helen, ed. *The Discoverers: An Encyclopedia of Explorers and Exploration*. New York: McGraw-Hill, 1980.

Waldman, Carl and Alan Wexler. *Who Was Who in World Exploration*. New York: Facts on File, 1992.

Christa McAuliffe

Born September 2, 1948, Boston, Massachusetts

Died January 28, 1986, over Cape Canaveral, Florida

In 1981 America's National Aeronautics and Space Administration (NASA) began its space shuttle program. Over the next three years, two dozen successful shuttle missions were launched. But more money was needed for space projects, and the U.S. government wanted to increase public support for the program. Thus, in 1984, NASA introduced its "citizens in space" project, which would send journalists, teachers, and other non-astronauts and non-scientists into space as shuttle passengers.

The first citizen passenger in space would be—in the words of then President Ronald Reagan—"one of America's finest, a teacher." Christa McAuliffe was chosen from among more than eleven thousand applicants. As NASA had hoped, the public was charmed by this enthusiastic young educator, who planned to teach students across the nation from space. She became a celebrity in the months leading up to her mission. But when the space shuttle *Challenger* exploded shortly after takeoff on January 28, 1986, killing all crew members

Schoolteacher Christa McAuliffe was chosen to become America's first private citizen in space. She was a crew member of the space shuttle Challenger, which exploded just after takeoff on January 28, 1986, killing all aboard.

aboard, Americans felt the loss especially deeply. The disaster had taken the life of an ordinary citizen they had come to know, someone like themselves.

She was born Sharon Christa Corrigan on September 2, 1948, in Boston, Massachusetts—but was called Christa. Her family moved to a Boston suburb, Framingham, when she was still young. It was a happy, busy childhood; Christa was a good student, took piano and dance lessons, became a Girl Scout, and was active in church and athletics. She had four younger brothers and sisters.

Watches as first U.S. astronaut is launched into space

At the time Christa was born, there was no space program. But by 1958 NASA had been created. On May 5, 1961, the first U.S. astronaut, Alan Shepard (1923–), was launched into space. Christa, then a junior high school student, watched the liftoff on television in her classroom. She was captivated by what she saw and told a classmate that she, too, wanted to ride in space someday.

With great interest, Christa followed the many, rapid successes of the U.S. space program over the next several years. In 1962 astronaut John Glenn (1921–) was the first American to orbit the earth; in 1965 Ed White (1930–1967) became the first U.S. astronaut to maneuver in space outside a spacecraft. On July 20, 1969, the American space program had done the unimaginable when astronaut Neil Armstrong (1930–) stepped out of the lunar module from *Apollo 11* and walked on the moon! Armstrong, who was joined by astronaut Edwin "Buzz" Aldrin (1930–), uttered the famous words, "That's one small step for [a] man, one giant leap for mankind." Christa collected magazine articles about the historic walk on the lunar surface.

Begins teaching career

By then Christa was a college student at Framingham State College, studying to become a history teacher. She was also planning her wedding to her high school sweetheart,

Steve McAuliffe, which would take place after their college graduations. The two married on August 23, 1970, and they moved to Washington, D.C., where Steve attended law school. Christa began her first teaching job at a junior high school in nearby Maryland.

The McAuliffes moved to Concord, the capital of New Hampshire, after Steve completed law school (and Christa earned a master's degree in school administration from Bowie State College in Maryland). By then they had a son, Scott, who was born in 1976. Three years later they had a daughter, Caroline.

For a while Christa stayed home and raised her young children. But she missed teaching, and in 1982 became a social studies instructor at Concord High School. She was an enthusiastic teacher, well-liked by her students. McAuliffe tried to get them involved in the learning process. Thus, when she taught about the law she sometimes had them participate in mock trials, and for special history lessons she had the students dress in period costumes. She also taught her history students that studying the lives of ordinary people was just as important as learning about the rulers and politicians of the past. In addition, McAuliffe always encouraged her pupils to try new things, to dream big dreams, and to "reach for the stars."

Competes to become first "teacher in space"

In 1984, after McAuliffe heard President Reagan's invitation to teachers to participate in a shuttle mission, she knew that it was her chance to fulfill her own lifelong dream. She filled out the eleven-page application, thinking that—with more than eleven thousand competitors—her chances for acceptance were very slim. But in April 1985 McAuliffe learned that she was one of 114 finalists. In June she traveled to Washington, D.C., where she was interviewed by government and NASA officials. She was asked what special project she would like to participate in if chosen. McAuliffe said she would like "to keep a space journal, an ordinary person's diary just as the earlier American pioneers did when they traveled West."

Christa McAuliffe, left, and her "teacher in space" backup, Barbara Morgan, try out the pilot's seats on the flight deck of a shuttle simulator at the Johnson Space Center.

When ten finalists were picked to go to the Johnson Space Center in Houston, Texas, McAuliffe was among them. There the candidates would undergo more interviews and tests. McAuliffe was a little worried about one test in particular, riding in the KC-135. This was a machine called the "vomit comet" because it simulated the changes in gravity experienced in spaceflight and often gave its riders motion sickness. As a girl, McAuliffe could not go on amusement park rides because they made her throw up. But she managed in the KC-135 just fine.

On July 19, 1985, NASA announced its decision. By unanimous vote, McAuliffe was chosen to become the first private American citizen to travel into space. She became an instant celebrity, appearing on television shows and becoming the subject of newspaper and magazine articles. The story of her happy, ordinary life was told. But soon her life would be anything but ordinary as she began serious training in Houston, getting ready for space shuttle *Challenger* Flight 51-L, a six-day mission scheduled for takeoff on January 23, 1986.

Begins astronaut training

In September 1985 McAuliffe began training with the other *Challenger* astronauts, as well as with Barbara Morgan (see box on page 130), an elementary schoolteacher from Idaho who came in second in the "teacher in space" contest. If for any reason McAuliffe could not take the flight, Morgan was her replacement. The *Challenger* would carry a crew of seven. Francis R. (Dick) Scobee would serve as flight commander and Michael J. Smith would pilot the shuttle. Mission specialists (astronaut/scientists) Judith A. Resnick, Ellison S. Onizuka, and Ronald E. McNair would also be aboard, as well as engineer Gregory B. Jarvis.

Over the next few months, McAuliffe spent long hours training with the crew. She had to get used to performing basic human functions—like eating, sleeping, and going to the bathroom—in an environment of weightlessness. The astronauts practiced moving around together in the crowded cabin of the shuttle. They also learned what to do in different emergency situations.

Prepares shuttle teaching sessions

McAuliffe also prepared the series of fifteen-minute-long teaching sessions she would transmit from space. Students across the United States would be able to watch her on television in their classrooms. She was very excited about the opportunity, believing that—as a teacher—she could explain space travel to young people better than could astronauts or scientists. McAuliffe called her first lesson "The Ultimate Field Trip," and planned to give a tour of the space shuttle. In her second lesson, "Where We've Been, Where We're Going,

Another teacher in space?

On January 16, 1998, Barbara Morgan—the backup "teacher in space" for Christa McAuliffe—learned that she would, at last, travel into space. NASA had chosen the Idaho elementary schoolteacher to become a mission specialist in the next group of astronauts it trains.

In the twelve years since her original astronaut training, Morgan has continued her connection with NASA. Until recently she has traveled one week each month for the space agency, doing educational and public relations work. And every year she has undergone—and passed—her astronaut physical.

NASA's "citizens in space" program was discontinued after the *Challenger* disaster in 1986. Morgan's participation in a shuttle mission will not be a revival of the program, for she will be trained as a regular astronaut. She will carry out routine flight duties in addition to her special educational projects. Like McAuliffe, Morgan sees her selection as "wonderful for education."

Morgan—who is married and the mother of two young boys—was in the crowd that watched the *Challenger* explode overhead. She was asked if she feared what could happen on her flight. "Living in a risk-free world is a big mistake," she replied. "If we are not willing as a society to take some risk for learning, for our future, then we are not doing enough."

Why," she would discuss present and future uses for the space shuttle.

The launch of the *Challenger* was originally set for January 23, 1986, from the Kennedy Space Center on Cape Canaveral, Florida. Delays postponed the flight schedule to

January 24 and then to January 25. A forecast of bad weather then held up the mission until Monday the 27th. On this date, a problem with a hatch bolt developed and by the time the problem was corrected, dangerous crosswinds had developed. Liftoff was rescheduled for Tuesday morning, January 28. On that day the sky was clear but the air was very cold; the space shuttle had never been launched in such cold temperatures. Space Center scientists were worried because icicles covered the outside of the spacecraft. They were also concerned about the rubber O-rings that held the steel panels of the two rocket boosters—located on either side of the huge fuel tank—together. Would the cold weather cause them to gap and break their tight seals? The scientists couldn't agree. As the icicles on the spacecraft were removed and the day's temperatures began to warm, the *Challenger* crew—who by this time had been strapped into their seats on the shuttle for nearly three hours—were told that the mission would proceed.

Challenger launches

Before a crowd of more than three thousand people, the *Challenger* took off at 11:38 A.M. McAuliffe's excited husband and children were there, as were her proud parents. The launch was also watched by millions of Americans on television. A minute into its flight, the *Challenger* was already traveling at more than one thousand miles per hour and had climbed above thirty-five thousand feet. Everything looked good.

But when mission control ordered Scobee and Smith to begin the next stage of their launch and open the *Challenger*'s engines to full power, tragedy followed. A small flame escaped from one of the rocket boosters and, in a flash, the entire spacecraft exploded in a huge fireball. The crew was killed instantly, seventy-three seconds into their flight, at an altitude of about fifty thousand feet. What remained of the spacecraft fell out of the sky and into the Atlantic Ocean. Later investigations would show that the cold weather had, indeed, caused one of the O-rings to fail. They have since been redesigned.

The remains of the space shuttle Challenger *drop to Earth in plumes of smoke, high above the Atlantic.*

Dead astronauts mourned

The *Challenger* explosion was the worst disaster in the history of the U.S. space program. The nation was in shock, and the tragedy was especially hard on schoolchildren, who had followed McAuliffe's experiences and looked forward to her lessons from space. President Reagan spoke to Americans about the disaster in a speech from the White House and later at a memorial service at the Johnson Space Center in Houston, where the astronauts had trained. He called the *Challenger* crew members "heroes" who had not been afraid to face the great risks that are a "part of the process of exploration and discovery."

McAuliffe's remains were buried in Concord, Massachusetts. Yet her extraordinary dedication to education has not been forgotten. To honor her, the city opened the Christa

McAuliffe Center, which holds workshops for teachers and has a planetarium for children to visit and learn about space. Other important programs supporting teachers and learning have also been created in her memory across the nation. Among them is the Christa McAuliffe Fellowship, awarded each year to a teacher in every state. Financing up to twelve months of study or work, the fellowship encourages outstanding teachers to continue their own education or to develop new learning projects and programs.

Sources

Naden, Corinne J. and Rose Blue. *Christa McAuliffe: Teacher in Space*. Brookfield, CT: Millbrook Press, 1991.

"Twelve-Year Wait Ends Happily for a Teacher-Astronaut." *New York Times,* January 17, 1998: A8.

Warbis, Mark. "NASA Tells Teacher to Start Training for Shuttle Flight." *Detroit Free Press,* January 17, 1998: 9A.

S.S. *Meteor*

German Atlantic Expedition, 1925–1927

The S.S. Meteor *was a German scientific research ship that made the first systematic survey of one part of the world's oceans.*

The 1919 Peace Treaty of Versailles that ended World War I (1914–1918) required Germany to take the blame for the war and to pay "reparations"—a large sum of money for the damages suffered by some of the nations it had fought against. These payments were hard for the Germans to make, for economic conditions were difficult in their country following the war. Alfred Merz, a geologist at the University of Heidelberg, thought that he might have a solution to Germany's debt problems. After studying samples of water taken from the South Atlantic Ocean, he felt that gold and silver might exist there in amounts large enough to extract and use. With the support of the German government a research steamer ship, the *Meteor,* was prepared to go to the South Atlantic to investigate Professor Merz's theories. It set sail from Hamburg on April 13, 1925.

Merz died on board the *Meteor* in August 1925 and its captain, Wilhelm Spiess, took over the mission. Although the professor's theories turned out to be wrong, the expedition still made many valuable contributions to the study of the ocean.

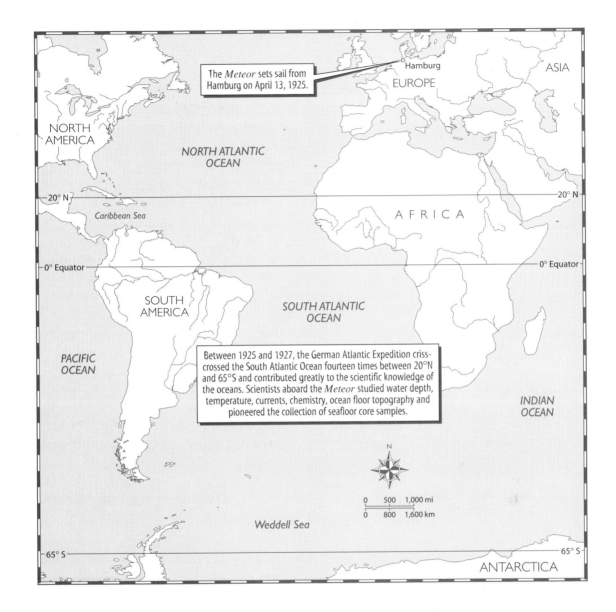

The *Meteor* sets sail from Hamburg on April 13, 1925.

Hamburg

ASIA

EUROPE

NORTH
AMERICA

NORTH ATLANTIC
OCEAN

20° N

Caribbean Sea

AFRICA

0° Equator

SOUTH
AMERICA

SOUTH ATLANTIC
OCEAN

PACIFIC
OCEAN

Between 1925 and 1927, the German Atlantic Expedition criss-crossed the South Atlantic Ocean fourteen times between 20°N and 65°S and contributed greatly to the scientific knowledge of the oceans. Scientists aboard the *Meteor* studied water depth, temperature, currents, chemistry, ocean floor topography and pioneered the collection of seafloor core samples.

INDIAN
OCEAN

N

0   500   1,000 mi
0   800   1,600 km

Weddell Sea

65° S

ANTARCTICA

Sets out with most advanced scientific equipment

The *Meteor* was carrying the most sophisticated new equipment for ocean research, including water current meters, echo sounders (sonar), and coring tubes to take samples of the ocean floor. Its crew of some 120 men included 5 oceanographers, 2 meteorologists, a chemist, a geologist, and a biologist. During the two years of the German Atlantic Expedition the ship crisscrossed the South Atlantic off the west coast of Africa from latitudes 20° N to 65° S. Research was restricted to one area of the ocean because data had to be collected from closely related points in order for water patterns to be discovered, and it had to be collected repeatedly so that changes could be recorded over time. The scientists made detailed studies of water depth, temperature, layers, and currents. They examined the chemical composition and properties of seawater and collected plankton—the microscopic plant and animal life that floats in the ocean. Physical features of the ocean floor and the sediments that settled on it were also studied. The scientific work of the *Meteor* crew contributed more to a basic understanding of the ocean than any expedition had done before. Not until the 1950s—during the International Geophysical Year when scientists from sixty-six nations joined to study the earth and its cosmic environment—would a similar comprehensive study of the ocean take place.

Records surprising features of ocean floor

One of the most important discoveries made by *Meteor* scientists was that the ocean floor is not smooth, but has mountains, valleys, and plains, just like the surface of Earth. This had been largely unsuspected until the research ship systematically began running lines of echo soundings across the ocean floor. Although sonar had been developed during World War I to guide submarines, it had been used only for military purposes and not for detailed mapping. Further improvements in sonar technology—following World War II (1939–1945)—would eventually give scientists an even more accurate picture of the ocean bottom, which would lead them to revise their ideas about how Earth's crust was formed.

Another practice that the scientific crew of the *Meteor* pioneered was the collecting of core samples from the ocean floor. The cores were only about a foot long and hardly penetrated the upper layers of the sea bottom beneath accumulated sediment. The scientific information that they revealed was not particularly useful and interest in core sampling remained slight during the next few decades. But after World War II, new technology was developed that did not depend on gravity and the force of heavy weights to punch into the ocean floor. Deep core samples were then possible, providing valuable geological information about Earth and its oceans.

Sets new standard for ocean research

By the end of its voyage in 1927, the *Meteor* had traveled more than sixty-seven thousand miles and had crossed the South Atlantic fourteen times. Its scientific crew had collected some nine thousand temperature and chemical readings of the ocean and had made more than thirty-three thousand echo soundings of its floor, mapping underwater terrain. The extent and accuracy of the information gathered on the *Meteor* expedition established a new scientific standard for all future oceanographic explorations to follow.

Sources

Baker, Daniel B., ed. *Explorers and Discoverers of the World*. Detroit: Gale Research, 1993.

Delpar, Helen, ed. *The Discoverers: An Encyclopedia of Explorers and Explorations*. New York: McGraw-Hill, 1980.

Muhammed ibn-Ahmad al-Muqaddasi

Born 945, Jerusalem

Died 1000

Muhammed ibn-Ahmad al-Muqaddasi traveled through much of the Muslim world during the tenth century. The book he wrote describing the countries he visited is considered one of the most accurate accounts of Islamic territories during the Middle Ages.

During much of the Middle Ages, the Muslim world—those territories that embraced Islam as their religion—stretched over a vast area. It reached from the Iberian Peninsula in southern Europe, across the north coast of Africa, through the Middle East, and into central Asia and the East Indies (present-day Indonesia).

One of the duties of a devout Muslim was, at least once in his life, to make a pilgrimage or *hajj* to the holy city of Mecca (now located in Saudi Arabia). That was the birthplace of Muhammad (570?–632), who was believed to be the prophet to whom Allah (God) had revealed his laws, which Muhammad wrote down in the holy book of Islam, the Koran. Thus, during the Middle Ages, dedicated Muslims traveled from near and far to make their way to the sacred site.

Undertakes pilgrimages to Mecca

One such Muslim traveler was Muhammed ibn-Ahmad al-Muqaddasi. He was born in Jerusalem in the middle of the

tenth century. Both of his grandfathers were important architects and builders who were responsible for several famous constructions, including the fortifications of the Syrian port city of Acre. In 966 al-Muqaddasi undertook his first pilgrimage to Mecca. In 977 and 987 he would make subsequent pilgrimages, each time using the opportunity to visit other Muslim lands. Thus, over the course of twenty years, he traveled through much of the Islamic realm of his time.

It is not known in what order al-Muqaddasi made his trips. But what is known is that he sailed all around the Arabian Peninsula, from the Red Sea to Abadan on the southwest coast of Persia (now Iran). He went to places like Shiraz, Khorasan, Bukhara, and Gurgan—located in Persia and central Asia. He said that he spent a year in what is now Yemen on the southern coast of Arabia. He also reported that he spent seventy days crossing Persia and that he traveled across the

The long pilgrimage to Mecca is a religious obligation for all Muslims—something they must do at least once in their lives.

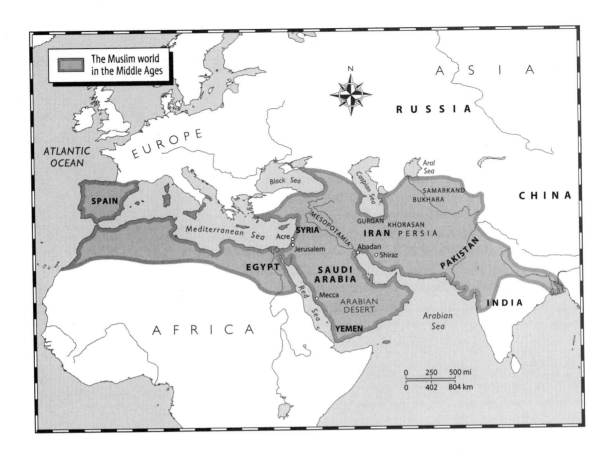

The Muslim world
in the Middle Ages

Arabian Desert several times, approaching it from the north, south, east, and west. He wrote that he visited every Muslim country except "al-Sind" (what is now Pakistan) and "al-An-dalus" (southern Spain).

A variety of adventures

Throughout his journeys, al-Muqaddasi took great care in gathering information about the climate, physical characteristics, native products, state of trade, and monetary systems of the countries he visited. He also reported on the languages and customs of their inhabitants. He wrote that he mixed with every class of people, sometimes enjoying lavish visits with grand rulers, at other times selling wares in the marketplace or laboring as a simple bookbinder in order to earn enough money to eat. He also worked as a messenger, teacher, doctor, lawyer, preacher, and *muezzin* (the man who calls the Muslim faithful to prayer). At one point he was accused of being a spy and thrown into prison, and at different times on his journeys he was robbed by highwaymen and other thieves. Once, in his travels, he almost drowned. Occasionally attaching himself to military expeditions, he observed battles on land and at sea. When he could afford it, he traveled in a palanquin (a covered, curtained couch carried by poles on the shoulders of others); other times he made his way on foot, sometimes through desert sands and mountain snows.

Records travel observations

In 985, al-Muqaddasi began to write a book about all he had observed and experienced during his wide travels. Called the *Ahsan at-takasim fi ma'rifat al-Akalim* (*Best Division for Knowing the Provinces*), his description of the Islamic world during the Middle Ages is considered by scholars to be one of the most complete and reliable geographical accounts written—during a time when countless Muslim travelers recorded their journeys as they made pilgrimages to Mecca. Al-Muqaddasi's reports on Mesopotamia (now Iraq), Syria, and Samarkand and Bukhara (now Uzbekistan) are especially appreciated for their accuracy.

Sources

Baker, Daniel B., ed. *Explorers and Discoverers of the World.* Detroit: Gale Research, 1993.

Delpar, Helen, ed. *The Discoverers: An Encyclopedia of Explorers and Exploration.* New York: McGraw-Hill, 1980.

Newton, Arthur Percival, ed. *Travel and Travellers of the Middle Ages.* "Arab Travelers and Merchants, A.D. 1000-1500," written by T. W. Arnold. New York: Knopf, 1930, reprint, Freeport, NY: Books for Libraries Press, 1967.

José Celestino Mutis

Born 1732, Spain

Died 1808, Spain

Spanish priest José Celestino Mutis spent many years studying the plant life of Colombia and discovered numerous valuable species.

During the eighteenth century, European rulers and governments—influenced by the ideas of the Enlightenment—sponsored studies of the natural sciences. Charles III (1716–1788) of Spain was one such ruler, who founded the Royal Botanical Garden in Madrid in 1774. Two years later a museum of natural history was also established, which housed the royal collection. Officials of Spanish colonies in the New World were advised to make studies of unknown native plants—especially those with medicinal uses—and send samples of them back to Spain.

Charles III had enlarged his botanical collection significantly by sending out three expeditions to American colonies: Peru, New Spain (Mexico), and New Granada (Colombia). Spanish priest and physician José Celestino Mutis was chosen to lead the Colombian study. The priest had become interested in botany—the study of plants—while in Madrid in 1757 and had spent several years expanding his knowledge in the field. When he was appointed physician to Pedro Mesía de la

Cerda, the newly chosen viceroy (governor) of New Granada, Mutis was excited—for he would be able to study the little-known vegetation of the distant colony.

Arrives in New Granada

Mutis set sail from Cádiz, Spain—aboard the *Castilla*—on September 7, 1760. After an uneventful voyage that included stops in the Canary Islands and Curaçao in the Caribbean, the ship arrived at the Colombian port of Cartagena on October 29. Following a brief stay, Mutis and his small party boarded a boat that took them up the great Magdalena River to the capital city of Bogotá, located on a plateau near the Andes Mountains. Along the way Mutis attended to the medical needs of the boat's crew and was able to observe native plants and animals and collect specimens. He was especially pleased when he came upon an *Aristoloquia* plant, which was valued as a remedy for snakebite. The travelers arrived in Bogotá on February 18, 1761.

Studies vegetation around capital city

Mutis spent the rest of 1761 and 1762 in the area around Bogotá, collecting specimens and making extensive scientific notes in his diaries. The location proved to be lush with interesting vegetation, including the American cinnamon plant. Mutis hoped not only to add to the king's collection, but to think up new uses for known species. Thus he was especially interested in hearing the local medical lore, to see if he could learn anything of real scientific use. While in Bogotá, the scientist also investigated other natural phenomena; in February of 1762, for instance, he climbed a nearby mountain—Cerro de Guadalupe—to take barometer readings, spending several rugged nights there. In addition, Mutis started a correspondence with the famous Swedish botanist Carolus Linnaeus (1707–1778), who was working on a scientific system for classifying plants and animals.

Makes first expedition into interior

Mutis was also busy performing his duties as the local doctor. So it was not until 1777 that he was finally able to make a lengthy trip away from Bogotá. On October 1 he set out for the settlement of Minas del Sapo—in the colony's interior—where he spent more than a year collecting and cataloging plant specimens. He observed the area's fascinating animal life as well, writing about flying ants, termites, flesh-eating flies, armadillos, and anteaters. He was excited when he saw a rubber tree, whose existence had first been reported in Europe in 1745 by French scientist Charles-Marie de La Condamine (1701–1774) following his trip to the Amazon. Mutis was careful to record the method used to extract latex from the tree and transform it into rubber. Another happy find occurred on January 2, 1778, when the scientist came upon a saffron plant, a species he had looked for for years. But on September 9 Mutis wrote in his diary about "the saddest news I have received in my entire life," referring to the death of the

Swedish naturalist Linnaeus some months earlier. He had just learned of it in a letter from his brother. For nearly eighteen years Mutis had corresponded with Linnaeus and had even sent him cases of specimens.

Returning to Bogotá and resuming his official duties, Mutis again struggled to find the time to pursue his botanical work. His expedition to Minas del Sapo had made him eager to do more extensive field studies in the interior, but it was not until 1782 that he could get royal support for another expedition. He received permission for such a trip from the new viceroy of New Granada—Archbishop Antonio Caballero y Góngora—but had to wait a year before royal approval came from Spain. During the wait, Mutis visited Colombia's Llano-grande region (an area of vast plains), where he collected more plant specimens.

More significant botanical finds

On April 29, 1782, Mutis and his small expedition (which included the well-known naturalist Eloy Valenzuela) left Bogotá and headed down the mountains to the Magdalena River valley. Their destination was the village of Honda, located on the Magdalena River. The way was challenging, and they traveled by horse, mule, or even on foot when the terrain demanded it. The party was delighted to come upon a *chinchona* tree, whose bark was the source of quinine—which, for the next two centuries, would serve as the main medication for treating malaria. The expedition spent a month gathering specimens at Mesa de Juan Díaz. In June they set up a new headquarters at Mariquita, and passed a few months there, finding an abundance of new plants and flowers; Mutis filled up some sixty pages of his diary with their descriptions. When the expedition at last reached Honda, it remained there for the rest of the year.

Alexander von Humboldt. He considered Mutis to be the "Patriarch of Botany in the New World."

Mutis and his group returned to Bogotá, but during the following years the botanist spent most of his time doing field work in the Magdalena River valley, using Mariquita as his base of operation. Assistants helped him preserve and document his collections, and they made illustrations. While Mutis spent much of his time identifying and classifying his plant samples, he also conducted studies of birds and insects. In his later years, trees would become the focus of his scientific work.

In 1792 Mutis resettled permanently in Bogotá. Some time later he returned to Spain, where he died in 1808. Most of his work remains unpublished, kept in archives in places like Madrid, Bogotá, and London. But naturalists Aimé Bonpland (1773–1858) and Alexander von Humboldt (1769–1859) brought his studies to the attention of the world when, in 1805, they dedicated their book *Equinoctial Plants* to Mutis, whom they called the "Patriarch of Botany in the New World."

Sources

Baker, Daniel B., ed. *Explorers and Discovers of the World*. Detroit: Gale Research, 1993.

Goodman, Edward J. *The Explorers of South America*. New York: Macmillan, 1972.

Jean Nicollet

Born c. 1598, Cherbourg, France
Died October 27, 1642, Sillery, Quebec

During the seventeenth century, the colony of Quebec was the center of French fur trading in North America. Its first governor was Samuel de Champlain (1567–1635), who spent much of his time trying to establish friendly relations with local Native American tribes, upon whose work the success of the fur-trading business depended. He had in his service a new type of adventurer called a *coureur de bois* or "forest runner." These were solitary young men who worked in the forests, and lived like the Indians from whom they gathered furs. Jean Nicollet was one such *coureur,* whose knowledge of Native American languages and customs helped the French make important alliances with Indian tribes in the Great Lakes area at a time when British and Dutch companies were also trying to take control of the fur trade in upper North America. In a 1634 expedition, Nicollet ventured farther west than any European had before, discovering Lake Michigan.

Jean Nicollet served as an interpreter and agent between French fur-trading companies and Native American tribes in what is now Ontario. He was also the first European to travel to Lake Michigan and explore its western shores.

Samuel de Champlain, governor of the colony of Quebec.

Travels to New France

Jean Nicollet was born in the port city of Cherbourg, in the French province of Normandy, around 1598. His father was a postal carrier who worked for the royal court. In 1618 Jean traveled to New France (Canada) as an agent for merchants in Rouen and Saint-Malo, France, who were hoping to develop a fur-trading business with Native Americans. Nicollet intended to live among the Indians he would deal with in order to learn their language and customs and serve as an interpreter for his employers.

Begins life among Native American tribes

Champlain had just begun to establish relations with the Algonquin tribe in the upper reaches of the Ottawa River (which now marks the southern border between Ontario and Quebec). It is believed that he instructed Nicollet—soon after he arrived in Quebec—to go and spend the winter on Allumette Island, located in the middle of the Ottawa River and which was a strategic spot on the fur-trade route. Nicollet stayed there for two years and learned the Huron and Algonquin languages from his Native American hosts. He shared their way of life and they accepted him into their society, making him a chief and allowing him to attend their councils. Nicollet served as a negotiator in their dealings with the French, and even with the Iroquois tribes, who were their enemies.

In 1620 Nicollet returned to Quebec and reported what he had learned about his Indian hosts and the land that they inhabited. He was then sent out to stay among the Nipissing tribe, who lived near a lake by the same name, which is situated between the Ottawa River and the Georgian Bay of Lake Huron. It was especially important to build an alliance with this Native American group, for they often acted as agents between European traders and other Indian tribes to the west and in the Hudson Bay area. (Hudson Bay is in east-central Canada, bounded by the Northwest Territories, Manitoba, Ontario, and Quebec.) Nicollet's mission was to ensure that the Indians directed all trade toward the French, and shared none with the English who had settled north around Hudson Bay.

Nicollet lived among the Nipissing for nine years. He had his own lodge and ran a small trading post. When Indians from different tribes stopped on their way to the shores of Lake Nipissing, he would question them about their land and write down what he had learned. While these records have since been lost, we know of them through the writings of missionary priest Paul Le Jeune, who consulted them when describing the customs of the Indians in that region.

Agrees to last diplomatic mission and search for China Sea

When Quebec was captured briefly by the English in 1629, Nicollet traveled farther west and took refuge with his friends the Hurons. He made sure that the Indians did not trade with the English. In 1633, after Quebec was returned to the French, Nicollet made his way to the colonial city of Trois-Rivières on the St. Lawrence River, where he requested a clerkship with the French fur-trading Compagnie des Cent-Associés (Company of One Hundred Associates). After his years of excellent service to the French fur-trading industry, he was readily granted the post; but it is believed that Champlain asked Nicollet to first undertake one last trip to build Native American alliances. This time he wanted the *coureur de bois* to visit the Winnebagoes, who lived at the far end of Green Bay (on the northwest side of Lake Michigan). Although surrounded by Algonquin tribes who were allied with the French, the Winnebagoes appeared close to establishing trade relations with the Dutch who had settled in the Hudson River region (in what is now New York). It was vital that the French develop an alliance with the Winnebagoes to keep peace in the area.

This painting by E. W. Deming depicts Jean Nicollet arriving in what is now Wisconsin, being greeted by the Winnebago Indians.

Nicollet was also asked to find out more about a great sea that reportedly lay beyond Lake Huron. At that time many Europeans thought that the Great Lakes waterway led to Asia, and that by sailing west through it they would come upon the China Sea. For that reason Nicollet brought with him a ceremonial robe of "China damask, all strewn with flowers and birds of many colors" so that he would be wearing the proper clothing when he greeted the Chinese officials he expected to encounter.

Discovers Lake Michigan and opens new fur-trading route

Nicollet set out from Quebec in mid-July 1634. He took the usual trading route up the Ottawa before heading to Lake Nipissing. He then went down the French River to Lake

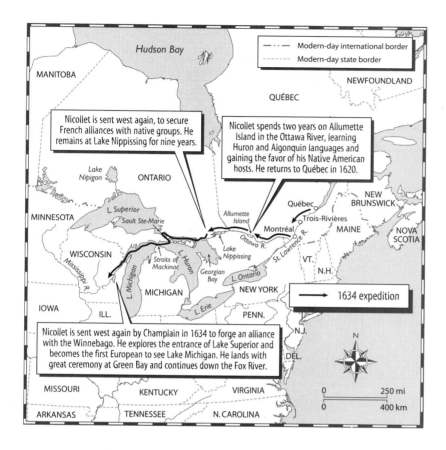

Hudson Bay

MANITOBA

NEWFOUNDLAND

QUÉBEC

Modern-day international border
Modern-day state border

Nicollet is sent west again, to secure French alliances with native groups. He remains at Lake Nippising for nine years.

Nicollet spends two years on Allumette Island in the Ottawa River, learning Huron and Algonquin languages and gaining the favor of his Native American hosts. He returns to Québec in 1620.

Lake Nipigon

ONTARIO

NEW BRUNSWICK

L. Superior
Sault Ste-Marie

Allumette Island

Québec
Trois-Rivières
Montréal

MAINE

NOVA SCOTIA

MINNESOTA

WISCONSIN

Mississippi R.

Straits of Mackinac

L. Huron

Lake Nippising

Ottawa R.

St. Lawrence R.

VT.

N.H.

Georgian Bay

L. Ontario

NEW YORK

1634 expedition

L. Michigan

MICHIGAN

L. Erie

PENN.

IOWA

ILL.

N.J.

Nicollet is sent west again by Champlain in 1634 to forge an alliance with the Winnebago. He explores the entrance of Lake Superior and becomes the first European to see Lake Michigan. He lands with great ceremony at Green Bay and continues down the Fox River.

DEL.

N

MISSOURI

KENTUCKY

VIRGINIA

0   250 mi
0   400 km

ARKANSAS

TENNESSEE

N. CAROLINA

Huron, delivering a group of Jesuit missionaries to Huron Indian settlements on Georgian Bay. From there he set out by canoe accompanied by seven Huron braves, and they traveled to the site of what is now Sault Sainte Marie. They explored the entrance to Lake Superior, located the Straits of Mackinac, and entered Lake Michigan, traveling along its northern coast to Green Bay. Nicollet was the first European to follow this course, which would become the main route for French fur traders traveling to the west. When he arrived at Green Bay, he put on his fancy attire, believing he had reached the Orient. One of the great images of North American exploration is that of Nicollet coming ashore dressed in his flowery Chinese robe.

Nicollet was disappointed when the Winnebagoes greeted him and he realized that he had not made it to China. But his grand appearance did immediately gain the respect of the Indians, who treated him royally and signed a peace treaty with the French. Still intent on finding the China Sea, Nicollet explored the area, first traveling down the Fox River as far as the village of Mascoutens. This was a mere three days' journey from the Wisconsin River, a branch of the Mississippi. Nicollet then traveled south toward the Illinois River. He was the first European to explore the region. But frustrated by what he found, he returned to Quebec in the autumn of 1635.

Settling into Trois-Rivières and his clerkship at last, Nicollet became a leading figure in the town, respected for his knowledge of Native American culture and for his service to Quebec. In 1637 he married, and later had a son and a daughter. A devoted Catholic, he served as an interpreter for missionaries as often as he could, and even taught religion to the Indians himself. He died in 1642—heroically—on his way to save an Iroquois prisoner that the Hurons were preparing to torture. The boat in which he was traveling overturned in rough waters, and he drowned near the town of Sillery, now a suburb of Quebec City.

Sources

Baker, Daniel B., ed. *Explorers and Discoverers of the World.* Detroit: Gale Research, 1993.

Bohlander, Richard E., ed. *World Explorers and Discoverers.* New York: Macmillan, 1992.

Dictionary of Canadian Biography, Volume 1: 1000-1700. Toronto: University of Toronto Press, 1966.

Waldman, Carl and Alan Wexler. *Who Was Who in World Exploration.* New York: Facts on File, 1992.

Cândido Rondón

Born May 5, 1865, Mato Grosso, Brazil

Died January 19, 1958, Rio de Janeiro, Brazil

B y the mid-nineteenth century Brazil's Amazon River valley had become settled with plantations that produced rubber and other natural products. But there were still vast areas to the river's south that had not been explored or developed, except for a few settlements along prominent rivers. Cândido Rondón, a Brazilian army engineer, was chosen by the government to help build a telegraph line across northwestern Brazil, through what would become the state of Mato Grosso into the Amazon valley. Between 1906 and 1909 he explored 193,000 square miles of little-known territory, charted the course of fifteen rivers, and discovered the River of Doubt (later renamed the Roosevelt River). In 1913–1914, he would return to map that river—accompanied by former U.S. president and adventurer Theodore Roosevelt (1858–1919)—in a famous scientific expedition.

Rondón was born in the Brazilian territory of Mato Grosso on May 5, 1865. His father was of Portuguese descent and his mother was a Native American. Orphaned at the age

Cândido Rondón was a Brazilian army engineer who spent many years exploring the little-known forests and rivers of northwestern Brazil.

of one, Rondón was raised by an uncle on a cattle ranch near Cuiabá, Mato Grosso's capital city. After completing his schooling there, he went to Rio de Janeiro—the capital of Brazil—and joined the army. He entered the Brazilian military academy in 1883, and graduated with honors in 1888. For a brief time afterward he taught mathematics there while training to become an officer. He was one of several army officers who united to overthrow the Emperor of Brazil (Pedro II, the only monarch in the Americas) in 1889. In a bloodless revolution, the country became a republic.

Conducts first explorations as army engineer

In 1890 Rondón began his career as an army engineer by helping to build a telegraph line across Mato Grosso. When it was completed in 1895, he then turned to constructing a road between Rio de Janeiro and Cuiabá. (Until it was completed, the only way between the two cities was by river travel through Argentina.) From 1900 to 1906 he was in charge of building telegraph lines across Brazil to Bolivia and Paraguay. During this time he opened up new territory, collected important biological specimens for Brazil's national museum, and served as a kind of diplomat between the government and the warlike Bororo tribe of western Brazil.

Encounters little-known rivers and native tribes

As a result of his successes, Rondón was put in charge of extending the telegraph line from Mato Grosso into the Amazon River valley in 1906. In the course of doing this, he explored vast unknown areas, accompanied by army personnel and civilian scientists. The explorers had their share of difficulties in the dense jungles; several members of their party died of beriberi (a nutritional-deficiency disease) and others were killed or wounded by hostile native tribes. Nonetheless, Rondón carried on with his mission, eventually making peace with the Indians—even with members of the Nambikwara tribe, who had a reputation for killing all Europeans they met, without exception. The engineer mapped the courses of several little-known rivers in the region, and discovered the Juruena in northern Mato Grosso. It is an important branch of the Tapajós, one of the main rivers that flow into the Amazon.

Discovers River of Doubt

On May 3, 1909, Rondón began one of his longest and most important expeditions. He left the tiny settlement of Tapirapuã in northern Mato Grosso and headed for the Jiparaná River, intending to descend it to the Madeira, a major branch of the Amazon. By August his party had eaten all of its food supplies, and for the next four months had to live on game (wild animals), fruit, and wild honey found in the forest. By the time they reached the Jiparaná River, Rondón's men were so weak that they had abandoned their baggage, and many of them crawled because they could no longer walk. Fighting illness, starvation, and exhaustion, they managed to build canoes and float down the river to the Madeira, which they reached on Christmas Day, 1909. Despite the grueling hardships of the trip, Rondón had made one important discovery during the expedition: he had come upon a large river flowing northwest between the Juruena and the Jiparaná that was totally unknown. He named it the River of Doubt, since it was unexplored.

Following Rondón's arrival in the Amazon city of Manaus in early 1910, he was stricken with a bad case of malaria. He was forced to return to Rio de Janeiro, where he was warmly received. He became an instant celebrity, in fact, for the people there had assumed that he had disappeared in the dense jungle forever.

In June 1910 the Brazilian government created an agency to protect its native population from exploitation and harmful treatment by Brazilian settlers and businessmen. Rondón became the first director of the National Service for the Protection of Indians. In March 1911 he resolved a dispute between the Caingangue tribe and settlers in Brazil's São Paulo region, and the following year he helped the Parintin Indians in Amazonas territory.

Heads Roosevelt-Rondón scientific expedition

After his years of explorations, Rondón was considered an expert on the geography, plants, animals, and Indians of the Brazilian interior. When former U.S. president and adventurer Theodore Roosevelt decided to make a trip into the interior of Brazil in 1913, Rondón was asked to lead the expedition. Because the River of Doubt was unexplored, it was suggested to Roosevelt that it be his destination. The mission appealed to the former president's strong spirit of adventure, and preparations were made for the Roosevelt-Rondón Scientific Expedition, one of the most famous expeditions of the century.

After a lecture tour in South America, Roosevelt traveled to Brazil in December 1913, where he was joined by Rondón. While the former president and his traveling party worried about encountering exotic jungle threats like piranhas and pumas, Rondón knew that real danger would come from insects and disease. The joint expedition left Tapirapuã in January 1914 and headed toward the River of Doubt. Along the way, Roosevelt—who was an avid hunter—managed to shoot a jaguar and a tapir, and to kill a peccary (a wild pig-like animal) with a spear. The group endured soaking downpours, mosquitos, fire-ants, and intense heat. But more challenges lay ahead.

Theodore Roosevelt—president and great adventurer. He accompanied Rondón on a trip to Brazil's interior in 1913.

Explorers endure numerous hardships

The Roosevelt-Rondón Scientific Expedition reached the River of Doubt on February 27, ready to map it, gather biological specimens along its route, and venture to its mouth. Travel was far more difficult than the men expected, however; the river was full of rapids and whirlpools, which swallowed

Between 1915–19, Rondón completes a thorough mapping of the interior of Mato Grosso. Later (from 1927–30), he performs a complete boundary survey of Brazil.

Rondón discovers vast unknown territories while in charge of extending telegraph lines from Mato Grosso territory to the Amazon from 1906–09.

→ Rondón's 1909 expedition
---→ Roosevelt-Rondón Scientific Expedition, 1914

canoes and supplies and—on a few unhappy occasions—people. (Roosevelt and his son Kermit were nearly drowned in a whirlpool.) Fever and dysentery weakened the men, and food ran short, forcing them to eat wildlife. Portaging (carrying one's boat) around rapids compelled the explorers to reduce their baggage to the barest necessities, and the added effort of land travel (once it took them three days to make their way to the bottom of a treacherous gorge) further robbed their strength. By a stroke of luck they came upon rubber harvesters, who had a house on the river where the men could recover. It was not a moment too soon, for Roosevelt was hobbled by a cut on his leg that had become infected and Kermit had a very high fever.

Thanks to the assistance and generosity of the rubber harvesters, the physical condition of the expedition members improved. The settlers told the travelers that they called the

River of Doubt the Castanho, and that it was a west branch of the Aripuanã, which flows into the Madeira. (Rondón had already renamed the River of Doubt the Roosevelt.) The expedition continued on its way, with the route much easier this time, for the harvesters had already cut portage paths around the rapids ahead. On April 26 the Roosevelt-Rondón Scientific Expedition reached the mouth of the river at last.

Expedition judged great success

Roosevelt and his party continued on to the Amazon. Rondón and his group remained behind to finish up the scientific work they had begun on the journey. Despite its many ordeals, the trip was considered a great success. Hundreds of bird, reptile, and mammal specimens had been collected—many never before seen. And, while not starting at the River of Doubt's source, the expedition had explored and mapped 750 kilometers of the river, and had determined its connection with other rivers in the region.

In the following years Rondón continued to serve his country. Between 1915 and 1919 he worked on mapping Mato Grosso, tracing the courses of several more unknown rivers and establishing first contact with a number of Native American tribes. In 1919 he became chief of Brazil's army engineering corps as well as head of its telegraph commission. In 1924 and 1925 he led army forces against a rebellion in São Paulo.

From 1927 to 1930 Rondón surveyed the boundaries between Brazil and all neighboring countries. During this work, he encountered and wrote about many native tribes that had had little or no contact with Brazilians: the Wapixana, Yanomami, Maku, Mayongong, Pianokotó, Tiriyó, and Wayaná. From 1934 to 1938 he was in charge of a commission to solve a dispute between Peru and Colombia over the Amazon River town of Leticia, which was eventually awarded to Colombia. In recognition of his diplomatic work, the Brazilian composer Heitor Villa-Lobos (1887–1959) composed a symphony in Rondón's honor.

Years of service honored

Rondón was responsible for increasing the power and re-
sources of the Native American protection service in Brazil.
He also established the National Indian Museum as well as
Brazil's first national park, along the Xingu River. His efforts
to promote harmony between the nations of South America—
and especially between its European and native populations—
earned him a nomination for the 1952 Nobel Peace Prize.
Rondón received many other honors and tributes during his
long life. These included having a territory (now a state)
named after him: in 1956 Guaporé became Rondônia. Rondón
died in Rio de Janeiro on January 19, 1958, at the age of
ninety-three.

*Famed Brazilian composer
Heitor Villa-Lobos. He wrote a
symphony to honor Rondón´s
diplomatic work.*

Sources

Baker, Daniel B., ed. *Explorers and Discoverers of the World*. Detroit: Gale Research, 1993.

Bohlander, Richard E., ed. *World Explorers and Discovers*. New York: Macmillan, 1992.

Goodman, Edward J. *The Explorers of South America*. New York: Macmillan, 1972.

Sacagawea

Born c. 1788, Lemhi River valley
(in what is now Idaho)

Believed to have died April 9, 1884,
Wyoming territory

I n 1803 President Thomas Jefferson purchased the Louisiana Territory from France, doubling the land area of the United States. The new nation now included all territories from the Mississippi River to the Rocky Mountains, from the Gulf of Mexico to the Canadian border. A short time later, Jefferson requested funds from Congress to send an exploring party to the West in search of an overland route to the Pacific Ocean. Captained by Meriwether Lewis (1774–1809) and William Clark (1770–1838), the party was called the Corps of Discovery, and consisted of forty-five men in three boats. They set out from St. Louis, Missouri, on May 14, 1804. About halfway through their journey, a number of the men would return to St. Louis with expedition reports. Twenty-nine members would continue on to the Pacific.

The first part of the journey was through well-traveled country, up the Missouri River. The expedition met Native American tribes along the way, and told them that their territory was now a part of the United States. As they pushed

Sacagawea was a Native American woman who served as an interpreter and guide during the first official United States expedition across North America to the Pacific Ocean, led by Meriwether Lewis and William Clark in 1804–1806.

deeper into the West, into what would later become North Dakota, they encounted lands and tribes that no Americans had ever visited before. Lewis and Clark needed guides and interpreters for the territories that lay ahead.

Lewis and Clark hire translator

Some months after they had started out, Lewis and Clark reached a small cluster of Mandan Indian villages and decided to build a fort there, spending the winter preparing for the next part of their journey. It would not be long before the men would have to abandon their boats and travel overland, for the Rocky Mountains lay ahead. They would need to trade their boats for packhorses from a Native American tribe called the Shoshone, who bred horses. As luck would have it, the interpreter they hired— French-Canadian trader Toussaint Charbonneau—was married to a Shoshone Indian named Sacagawea.

Meriwether Lewis.

Sacagawea's early life

Sacagawea was born sometime during the 1780s in the Lemhi River valley in what would later become Idaho. The daughter of a Shoshone chief, she was given the name of Bo-i-naiv at birth, which means "Grass Maiden." As a young girl, she was captured by a band of Hidatsa warriors who raided the Shoshone camp. She was taken from her home in the plateau region of the Rocky Mountains to a Hidatsa village on the Knife River in the Great Plains, the site of the future city of Bismarck, North Dakota. Renamed Sacagawea, which means "Bird Woman," she was made to work in the fields by her captor, the warrior Red Arrow. A few years later she was the prize in a gambling game between Red Arrow and the French-Canadian fur trader Charbonneau. The trader won, making Sacagawea one of his three wives. While she was awaiting the birth of their first child, Lewis and Clark and the Corps of Discovery arrived at their village.

When Lewis and Clark hired Charbonneau as their guide and interpreter, the trader insisted on taking Sacagawea on the journey. The captains were worried about taking a woman along, especially one who had just given birth. (On February 11, 1805, her son, Jean Baptiste—nicknamed "Pomp" —was born.) Sacagawea would be carrying her baby along on a cradle-board on her back. They feared that the length and hardships of the journey would be too much for the pair.

William Clark.

Native American skills help expedition

But on April 7, 1805, twenty-seven soldiers, two interpreters, Sacagawea, and the baby Pomp set out in several small boats for the American northwest. Unable to pronounce her name, Clark took to calling the small Indian woman "Janey." Sacagawea soon proved herself a valuable member of the party. She gathered wild food such as berries, carrots, and potatoes, which added nutrition and variety to the men's diet of salt fish, dried meat, and bread. She mended the men's clothes with needles made from small bird bones, and made them moccasins when their shoes wore out. Because Native American war parties never took women and children on raids, the presence of Sacagawea and her son eased the fears of the tribes that the expedition met along the way, assuring that the white travelers had come in peace.

Sacagawea prevents disaster

Countless times throughout the long journey—as noted by Clark in his expedition journal—it was Sacagawea's skills

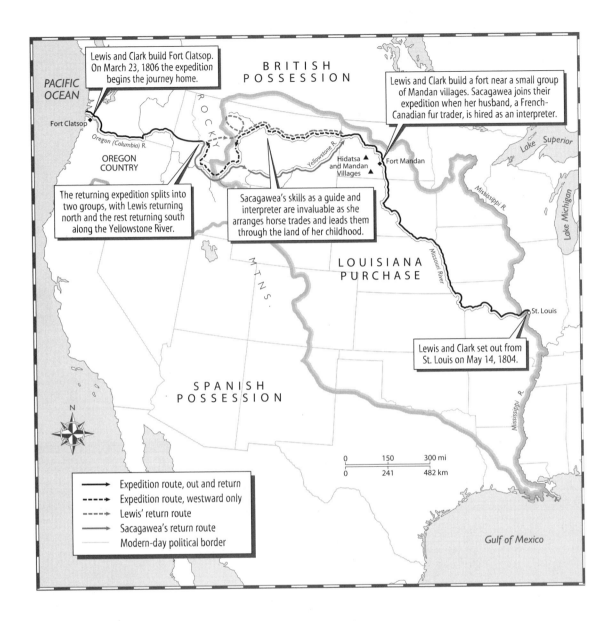

Lewis and Clark build Fort Clatsop. On March 23, 1806 the expedition begins the journey home.

Lewis and Clark build a fort near a small group of Mandan villages. Sacagawea joins their expedition when her husband, a French-Canadian fur trader, is hired as an interpreter.

PACIFIC OCEAN

BRITISH POSSESSION

Fort Clatsop

Oregon (Columbia) R.

OREGON COUNTRY

ROCKY

Yellowstone R.

Hidatsa and Mandan Villages

Fort Mandan

Lake Superior

Lake Michigan

Mississippi R.

The returning expedition splits into two groups, with Lewis returning north and the rest returning south along the Yellowstone River.

Sacagawea's skills as a guide and interpreter are invaluable as she arranges horse trades and leads them through the land of her childhood.

MTNS.

LOUISIANA PURCHASE

Missouri River

St. Louis

Lewis and Clark set out from St. Louis on May 14, 1804.

SPANISH POSSESSION

N

Mississippi R.

| 0 | 150 | 300 mi |
| 0 | 241 | 482 km |

Expedition route, out and return
Expedition route, westward only
Lewis' return route
Sacagawea's return route
Modern-day political border

Gulf of Mexico

as a guide and interpreter, as well as her courage and quick thinking, that made her invaluable. A few weeks after the Corps of Discovery set out, for instance, a strong wind tipped the lead boat on its side, spilling its contents into the Missouri River. While its passengers frantically paddled to shore, Sacagawea calmly retrieved the floating bundles. They contained the expedition's surveying instruments, maps, medicine, and other essential supplies. Had she not saved them, Clark wrote that night, the expedition would have had to turn back (they were already 2,200 miles from home). They would have had to begin the journey all over again, the delay perhaps giving Great Britain the chance to explore and lay claim to the Pacific Northwest. A few days after the incident, Lewis and Clark named a waterway in Sacagawea's honor: Bird Woman's River, now known as Crooked Creek.

Lewis and Clark were especially glad to have Sacagawea with them as they approached the Rocky Mountains and Shoshone territory. She remembered the land of her childhood, and easily guided them as the Missouri River narrowed and the landscape steepened. Because Charbonneau did not know the Shoshone language, Sacagawea would be essential in dealing with the tribe and getting the horses that would allow the expedition to continue.

A lucky, surprise meeting

The first group of Shoshone that the expedition met with seemed hostile, however, and the travelers' futures looked bleak. That is, until Sacagawea recognized among them a girl-friend from long ago. These were her people! Their chief, Cameahwait, was her older brother. After a tearful reunion, he welcomed his sister's traveling companions. Cameahwait sold Lewis and Clark twenty-nine packhorses, and he and his tribesmen postponed their annual buffalo-hunting trip so that they could lead the travelers partway through the Rocky Mountains, a passage that would prove to be one of the most difficult parts of expedition.

The Corps of Discovery trudged through knee-deep snow as it crossed the mountainous Great Divide. Now the rivers that the travelers encountered were flowing from east to west—to the Pacific Ocean. If they could find their way to the great Columbia River (then called the Oregon), they knew they could sail it to the sea. With the help of the Nez Percé Indians, they made dugout canoes. Leaving their horses and extra supplies behind with the tribe, they set off downriver.

Lewis and Clark and their party reached the Columbia River on October 16, 1805. But instead of a smooth and swift

What became of Sacagawea after Lewis and Clark?

Some historians believe that Sacagawea died in 1812. John Luttig, a member of a work crew that was building a fort in South Dakota that year, wrote that he worked with Charbonneau, and that the trader's young Indian wife died from fever there on the night of December 20. He did not record the name of the woman, but most assumed that it was Sacagawea.

Many decades later, however, the U.S. Bureau of Indian Affairs sent writer Charles Eastman (1858–1939) to investigate the fate of Sacagawea. Along with historian Grace Hebard, he talked to people who claimed that they had known her and that she had lived another seventy-two years. Sacagawea had left Charbonneau, they reported, and married a Comanche, giving birth to five more children. When her second husband died in battle, she left the Comanche to rejoin her own people, the Shoshone in the Rocky Mountains. It was rumored that along the way she joined the second expedition of surveyor John Charles Fremont (1813–1890). Other rumors had her traveling in Canada, Arizona, and California. But by the 1860s she was back in Wyoming and with the Shoshone, it was said, where government agents used her as an interpreter for many years. Because whites showed her respect, she was revered by her people, and the tribal councils listened to her advice carefully. Upon her death in 1884, a small wooden marker was placed at her burial site. It has since been replaced with a grand granite tombstone that commemorates her part in the Lewis and Clark expedition.

journey to the ocean, they had a difficult time. Its many rapids and waterfalls often forced them to carry their boats and equipment overland. Their supplies ran low and food was scarce. As they approached the mouth of the Columbia, where it joined the Pacific, the waters were so rough and the expedition members so seasick that Lewis and Clark set up camp some miles from the ocean. They would winter there, exploring the coast, and begin their journey home in the spring.

Sacagawea sees the Pacific Ocean

The expedition built Fort Clatsop, named for the local Indian tribe that brought them much needed food, and endured a rainy, sunless Northwest winter. On Christmas Day, when the homesick travelers exchanged gifts, Sacagawea presented to Clark—who was her favorite—two dozen beautiful white weasel tails. She had carried them hidden under her clothes for hundreds of miles. Later that long winter, when members of the party reported that a whale had washed up along the ocean coast, Sacagawea asked to go along to see it, for she had not yet seen the Pacific. With Pomp in her arms, she finally got to see the "great water," and marveled at the giant fish stranded on its shore. It measured 105 feet.

On March 23, 1806, Lewis and Clark and their party began their journey home. As before, travel was difficult and finding food was a constant problem. As they approached the mountains, Sacagawea again helped the expedition obtain horses, this time from the Walla Walla tribe. After crossing the Rockies, the travelers split into two groups, with Lewis turning north to try to find a shorter route. Clark, Charbonneau, Sacagawea, and others continued along the way they had come. Once again in the territory she had known as a child, Sacagawea guided the group with great skill; "[she] has been of great service to me as a pilot through this country," Clark wrote. On a great rock near the Yellowstone River in what would become Montana, the captain carved his name and the date, July 25, 1806, and named it Pompy's Rock in honor of Sacagawea's little boy. Lewis and Clark and their parties reunited two weeks later on the Missouri River.

The expedition soon reached the Mandan village that Charbonneau and Sacagawea called home. Clark paid the trapper $500.33 for his months of service as a translator and guide. Sacagawea received no payment, but had earned the respect and gratitude of the men of the Corps of Discovery. She had bravely traveled through what would become the states of Montana, Idaho, Washington, Oregon, Kansas, Iowa, Nebraska, South Dakota, North Dakota, and Wyoming. Before heading back with Lewis to Washington, D.C., Clark offered to take Pomp—whom he had grown to love—with him to raise in "such a manner as I thought proper." While the boy was too little for such a move at the time, Clark would later act as Pomp's guardian when he attended school in St. Louis.

Sacagawea's contribution recognized

Lewis and Clark and their party were celebrated for their great achievement when they reached Washington, D.C. The two captains were awarded large land grants, and given important government posts. Recognition of Sacagawea's role in the opening of the American West, however, did not come until many decades later. In 1905 in Portland, Oregon, at the one-hundred-year anniversary celebration of the landing of Lewis and Clark on the Pacific Coast, a statue of the young Indian woman was at last unveiled. It was the first of many markers and monuments that would eventually be erected in her honor. And places like Sacagawea Peak and Washington's Lake Sacajawea and Sacajawea State Park have since been named for this Native American hero.

Sources

Brown, Marion Marsh. *Sacagawea: Indian Interpreter to Lewis and Clark*. Chicago: Children's Press, 1988.

Ross, Nancy Wilson. *Heroines of the Early West*. New York: Random House, 1960.

Saari, Peggy and Daniel B. Baker. "Meriwether Lewis and William Clark." *Explorers and Discoverers*. Detroit: U•X•L, 1995.

Sanford, William R. and Carl R. Green. *Sacagawea: Native American Hero*. Springfield, NJ: Enslow Publishers, 1997.

Robert Hermann Schomburgk

Born June 5, 1804, Freiburg, Germany

Died 1865, Berlin, Germany

Beginning in the seventeenth century, the region on the northeast coast of South America known as Guiana was colonized by the French, the British, and the Dutch. In 1815 Great Britain was granted official possession of the settlements of Berbice, Demerara, and Essequibo, which were united as British Guiana (now Guyana) in 1831. At that time the three settlements were actually thin strips of plantations along the coast, and little was known about the region's interior. Britain wanted to further develop the area, and its Royal Geographical Society sent an expedition there in 1835 led by German-born Robert Hermann Schomburgk. The explorer and naturalist investigated the interior of British Guiana from 1835 to 1837. In 1841 he conducted further explorations that helped establish the northwestern boundary of British Guiana, guarding against future territory disputes with its neighbors.

Schomburgk was born in the town of Freiburg in Prussia (now eastern Germany) on June 5, 1804, the son of a minister. His education included studies in geology and the natural sci-

German-born Robert Hermann Schomburgk was employed by the British government to explore Guyana and its surrounding areas.

ences, although he became a businessman in Germany following his schooling. Restless to see more of the world, he moved to the United States and had a brief career as a Virginia tobacco merchant that ended when a fire destroyed his business. He then moved to the West Indies in 1830, and was able to pursue his interest in natural history when he surveyed the coast of Anegada—one of the British Virgin Islands—the following year. His work helped navigators avoid dangerous shallows and reefs around the island.

Hired to lead expedition for Great Britain

Schomburgk published his survey findings in Britain's *Journal of the Royal Geographical Society*. His article was well-received and in 1834 the society hired him to explore British Guiana's potential for future settlement by venturing into its interior, investigating its great rivers, and collecting botanical and geological specimens. Schomburgk began the expedition on October 1, 1835, with a party of twenty-two men in canoes, heading up the colony's longest river—the Essequibo. Like all the rivers in Guiana, the Essequibo is full of rapids and waterfalls, making travel difficult. As the first European to reach many of the Essequibo's falls, Schomburgk named several of them. The explorer pushed on, and by late February 1836 had reached the spot where the Essequibo is joined by the Rupununi River—its largest branch. He and his men continued traveling on the Essequibo until March 5, when they came upon one of its greatest waterfalls, a twenty-four-foot-high wonder that was named King William's Cataract, after the king of England. Because the travelers could only proceed if they constructed a path around the obstacle, Schomburgk decided to turn back, unwilling to undertake the enormous task. The expedition headed back to the coast, to British Guiana's capital city of Georgetown. Misfortune struck along the way when one of the expedition canoes overturned and all the biological and geographical specimens that Schomburgk had collected were lost.

In September 1836 Schomburgk made a second trip into the colony's interior, this time by traveling up the Courantyne,

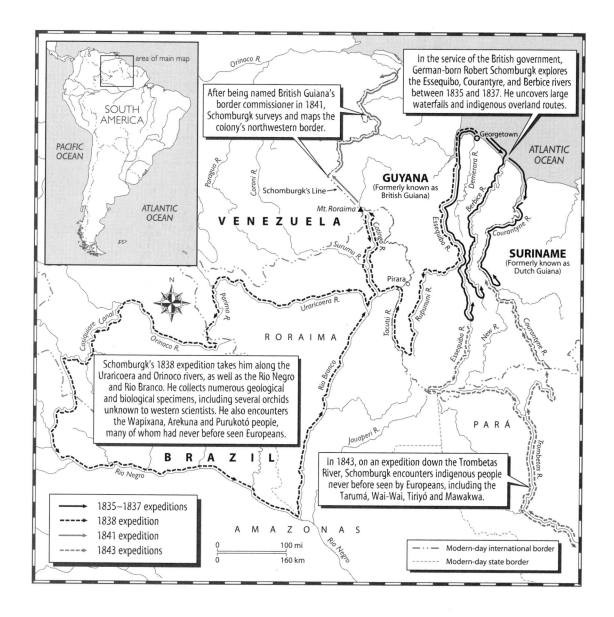

In the service of the British government, German-born Robert Schomburgk explores the Essequibo, Courantyre, and Berbice rivers between 1835 and 1837. He uncovers large waterfalls and indigenous overland routes.

After being named British Guiana's border commissioner in 1841, Schomburgk surveys and maps the colony's northwestern border.

Schomburgk's 1838 expedition takes him along the Uraricoera and Orinoco rivers, as well as the Rio Negro and Rio Branco. He collects numerous geological and biological specimens, including several orchids unknown to western scientists. He also encounters the Wapixana, Arekuna and Purukotó people, many of whom had never before seen Europeans.

In 1843, on an expedition down the Trombetas River, Schomburgk encounters indigenous people never before seen by Europeans, including the Tarumá, Wai-Wai, Tiriyó and Mawakwa.

SOUTH AMERICA

PACIFIC OCEAN

ATLANTIC OCEAN

area of main map

Orinoco R.

VENEZUELA

Paragua R.

Coroni R.

Schomburgk's Line

Mt. Roraima

Catirgo R.

Surumu R.

Pirara

Parima R.

Casiquiare Canal

Orinoco R.

RORAIMA

Uraricoera R.

Rio Branco

GUYANA
(Formerly known as British Guiana)

Georgetown

ATLANTIC OCEAN

Demerara R.

Berbice R.

Essequibo R.

Courantyne R.

SURINAME
(Formerly known as Dutch Guiana)

Rupununi R.

Tacutu R.

Essequibo R.

New R.

Courantyne R.

PARÁ

Jauaperi R.

Trombetas R.

B R A Z I L

Rio Negro

A M A Z O N A S

Rio Negro

	1835–1837 expeditions
	1838 expedition
	1841 expedition
	1843 expeditions

0   100 mi
0   160 km

| | Modern-day international border |
| | Modern-day state border |

the easternmost river of British Guiana (which now marks its boundary with Suriname). He and his small party reached the largest waterfall of that river on October 18 and, just as before, could find no way around it. He estimated that cutting a path through the dense jungle would take almost two months; faced with that prospect, the expedition headed back toward the coast. The brief venture had at least proven that the Courantyne was a major river, and was far longer than expected.

Completes survey of British Guiana's great rivers

Undaunted by his expedition difficulties, Schomburgk set out again on November 25, 1836, to explore the colony's third great river, the Berbice. But the explorer and his men would encounter even more hardships than before. Their native guides deserted them; they narrowly escaped being attacked by thousands of ants; and wild hogs charged them, forcing them to seek safety in the trees. In addition, dense jungle growth slowed their progress on the river and their supplies ran low, with fresh food hard to find. But on January 28, 1837, Schomburgk accidentally found a path used by the local inhabitants that took him through the forest to the Essequibo River. Not long after that he found a second overland route to the Courantyne (which went around its great waterfall) and was able to continue his exploration of that river. By the end of this third expedition Schomburgk had met his objective of mapping the courses of the three great rivers of British Guiana.

Visits unknown places and peoples

Still, Schomburgk was eager to explore more of the region. In 1838 he traveled into what is now the Brazilian territory of Roraima, making his way down the Tacutœ River (which forms part of the present-day border between Guyana and Brazil). As he headed toward the main post in the area—Fort São Joaquim—he came upon Brazilian slave traders who raided local native villages and stole their inhabitants to sell as laborers. The explorer sadly reported that "they brought away little children of five and six years old, and showed us that even *they* had been tied with their hands to their backs." From the outpost Schomburgk traveled up the Surumu River to Mount Roraima, a flat peak that rises far above its surrounding forest and is now the point where Guyana, Brazil, and Venezuela meet; he was the first Westerner to visit it. Along the way he encountered members of Native American tribes such as the Wapixana, Arekuna, and Purukotó—many of whom had never seen a European before.

From Mount Roraima, Schomburgk traveled back down the Surumu and Tacutœ rivers to the Uraricoera and Parima rivers, which eventually took him to the great Orinoco River, which runs through what is now Venezuela. He nearly made his way to the river's source before coming upon the Casiquiare Canal—a unique natural canal that runs through the forests between the two river systems of the Orinoco and the Amazon. It was first discovered by German scientist Alexander von Humboldt (1769–1859) in 1800, and Schomburgk was the second European to visit it. Schomburgk followed the Rio Negro—a tributary of the Amazon River—to the Rio Branco, which took him back to Fort São Joaquim. He finally made his way to Georgetown by way of the Essequibo, his journey at last complete.

Rehired for border expedition

Schomburgk returned to England in 1840 and for his work was awarded a gold medal from the Royal Geographical Society. He brought back many geological and botanical specimens, including a lily that he named Victoria Regia, after the new queen; it quickly became a favorite among European gardeners. He also returned with a number of unknown orchid plants, one of which would later be named the Shomburgkia in his honor. In meetings with members of the British government, the explorer recommended further development of British Guiana and suggested that its borders be mapped as soon as possible. Schomburgk was named British Guiana's border commissioner at once, and set out on a new expedition to the colony in 1841.

During that year, Schomburgk surveyed and marked British Guiana's northwestern border. He established the "Schomburgk Line" between British Guiana and Venezuela, which would prove significant in resolving the border dispute that would arise between the two colonies later in the century. He traveled to the outpost of Pirara on the Tacutœ River, which was claimed by both Britain and Brazil. He also revisited places he had been to in his earlier travels, like Fort São Joaquim and Mount Roraima. The explorer reinvestigated the

Essequibo and its tributaries, and followed the main river to its source on the Brazilian border. Then in June and August of 1843 he explored the Trombetas River and its branches, which flow into the Amazon. There he met native tribes never before encountered by Europeans: the Tarumá, the Wai-Wai, the Tiriyó, and the Mawakwa. He completed his expedition by a second examination of the Courantyne River and its surrounding areas, from its upper reaches on the Brazilian border all the way to the coast.

Receives knighthood

Schomburgk returned to England in 1844 and became a naturalized British subject. He was also knighted that same year, in recognition of his service to Great Britain. In 1848 he entered the diplomatic service with an appointment as British consul to Santo Domingo (now the Dominican Republic). From 1857 to 1864 he served as British consul in Bangkok, Thailand, and during that time explored the northern part of the kingdom as far as Chiengmai. He also traveled south and surveyed the Isthmus of Kra, to determine whether it was practical to dig a canal there for boat travel through the Malay Peninsula. He returned to Germany when he retired in 1864, and settled in Berlin, where he died the following year.

Sources

Baker, Daniel B., ed. *Explorers and Discoverers of the World.* Detroit: Gale Research, 1993.

Bohlander, Richard E., ed. *World Explorers and Discoverers.* New York: Macmillan, 1992.

Goodman, Edward J. *The Explorers of South America.* New York: Macmillan, 1972.

Waldman, Carl and Alan Wexler. *Who Was Who in World Exploration.* New York: Facts on File, 1992.

Willem Corneliszoon Schouten

Born c. 1567, Hoorn, the Netherlands

Died 1625

Since the 1494 Treaty of Tordesillas, Portugal had controlled European commerce in the Far East, including the rich spice trade of the East Indies. But after the Netherlands declared its independence from Spain in 1581, the rising young nation—with its large population of merchants and seaman—decided to challenge Portugal's declining position in the Orient. By the beginning of the seventeenth century, the Netherlands had displaced Portugal as the major maritime and trading power in southeast Asia. In 1602 the Dutch East India Company was formed to establish trade policy and control in the area. The Dutch government granted the company exclusive rights to trade in the Indies. The company was allowed its own armed forces on land and sea, and could wage war against Spain and Portugal. It could also establish trading posts and colonies, make treaties, and had legal authority over the territories it managed.

Independent Dutch businessmen didn't think that the trade monopoly of the Dutch East India Company was fair. It

Willem Schouten was a Dutch navigator who piloted an expedition meant to break the trade monopoly of the Dutch East India Company in the western Pacific. He also discovered a new route between the Atlantic and Pacific oceans near the tip of South America.

had control of trade going to and from the East, either around Africa's Cape of Good Hope or through the Strait of Magellan at the tip of South America—the only known southern routes used by European traders. One merchant from Amsterdam, Isaac Le Maire, tried to end the company's Eastern monopoly by bringing a case before the Dutch parliament. His attempt was unsuccessful.

Schouten contacted to pilot expedition

But Le Maire thought that he might get around the company's trade restrictions by finding another route to the Pacific. He consulted with well-known Dutch navigator Willem Corneliszoon Schouten, who had already made three voyages to the East Indies while working for the Dutch East India Company. The two suspected that another passage between the Atlantic and Pacific oceans might exist south of the Strait of Magellan. For while many Europeans at that time believed that Tierra del Fuego—the land that lay south of the strait—was the tip of a great southern continent, Le Maire and Schouten thought that it was a large island, and that a clear sailing route lay to its south.

Le Maire and Schouten convinced the wealthy citizens of the Dutch seaport of Hoorn (where the navigator was born) to invest in an expedition that would prove their theory correct. Isaac Le Maire's son, Jacob (1585–1616), would command the voyage. At the end of May in 1615, two ships set sail from the town: the *Eendracht* was captained by Willem Schouten, and the *Hoorn* was piloted by Jan Schouten (?–1616), Willem's brother.

Travelers lose ship

Before crossing the Atlantic, the ships stopped at Sierra Leone on the west coast of Africa. The travelers exchanged some of their trade goods for twenty-five thousand lemons, which would keep them—with their diet of dried meat and fish—from falling ill with scurvy. (All but three of the eighty-seven-man crew would survive the fifteen-month journey.)

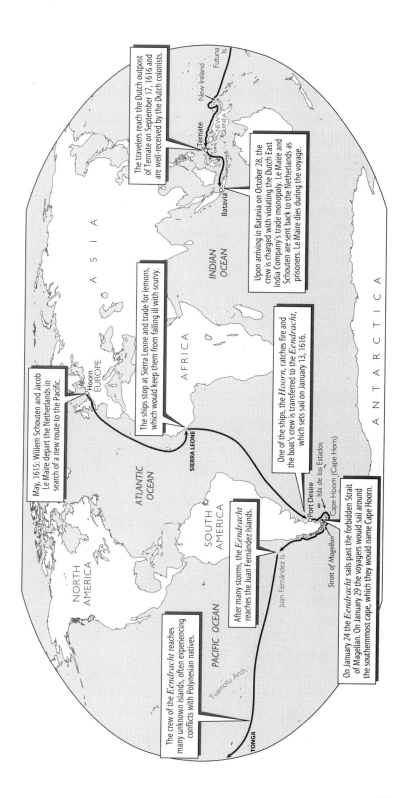

The travelers reach the Dutch outpost of Ternate on September 17, 1616 and are well-received by the Dutch colonists.

Upon arriving in Batavia on October 28, the crew is charged with violating the Dutch East India Company's trade monopoly. Le Maire and Schouten are sent back to the Netherlands as prisoners. Le Maire dies during the voyage.

May, 1615: Willem Schouten and Jacob Le Maire depart the Netherlands in search of a new route to the Pacific.

The ships stop at Sierra Leone and trade for lemons, which would keep them from falling ill with scurvy.

One of the ships, the *Hoorn*, catches fire and the boat's crew is transferred to the *Eendracht*, which sets sail on January 13, 1616.

After many storms, the *Eendracht* reaches the Juan Fernández Islands.

The crew of the *Eendracht* reaches many unknown islands, often experiencing conflicts with Polynesian natives.

On January 24 the *Eendracht* sails past the forbidden Strait of Magellan. On January 29 the voyagers would sail around the southernmost cape, which they would name Cape Hoorn.

Futuna Is.

New Ireland

Ternate

NEW GUINEA

Batavia

A S I A

EUROPE

Hoorn

AFRICA

INDIAN OCEAN

ATLANTIC OCEAN

SIERRA LEONE

NORTH AMERICA

SOUTH AMERICA

PACIFIC OCEAN

Juan Fernández Is.

Port Desire

Isla de los Estados

Cape Hoorn (Cape Horn)

Strait of Magellan

Tuamotu Arch.

TONGA

ANTARCTICA

On December 8 the ships anchored at Port Desire in Patagonia, in what is now southern Argentina. The men saw many curious sights there, like ostriches and llamas. But while in port the *Hoorn* caught fire and was burned beyond use. The boat's crew transferred to the *Eendracht,* which again set sail on January 13, 1616, heading south along the coast.

Eendracht passes through unknown strait into Pacific

On January 24 the *Eendracht* sailed past the forbidden Strait of Magellan. But not long after that the travelers came upon another passage to the west and were able to head toward the Pacific Ocean. Tierra del Fuego lay to their north and a small island (now called Isla de los Estados) lay to their south. They named the southernmost point of land they passed—on January 29—Cape Hoorn (Cape Horn) after the town that had sponsored their voyage.

The *Eendracht* followed a northerly course once it entered the Pacific. Its crew endured a month of storms before reaching the Juan Fernández Islands, located about four hundred miles off the coast of present-day Chile, in March. By then many of the men had become sick following their months of hard travel. Jan Schouten died on March 9.

Travelers discover numerous South Sea islands

The expedition sailed west, eventually coming upon the present-day island groups of the Tuamotu Archipelago and Tonga. The expedition members and the island natives often had difficulty understanding each other, which eventually led to conflicts and bloodshed. Many of the Polynesians fell victim to the superior weaponry of the Europeans.

In May the Dutchmen came upon more unknown islands. They named one group the Hoorns (later known as the Futuna Islands), again to honor their sponsors. There they enjoyed better relations with the natives, and were invited to participate in a feast held by a local king. The men so enjoyed themselves that they remained on the islands for more than two weeks—observing Polynesian culture—although they were still far from their destination.

At this point in the journey, Schouten and Le Maire argued about the best course to take next. Le Maire wanted to continue to discover and claim new trading lands not yet under the control of the Dutch East India Company, and perhaps even look for the legendary Solomon Islands or the great southern continent. Schouten, the practical navigator, did not want to sail into unknown waters. He wanted to head northwest toward the north coast of New Guinea, which was an established route that would lead to Batavia (now Jakarta), the capital of the Dutch East Indies, located on the island of Java. Schouten won the argument, and the expedition headed toward Dutch territories.

On the way, the expedition discovered more Pacific islands. The travelers sailed along the coast of what would later be known as New Ireland, sighted present-day New Hanover, and came upon several islands in the Admiralty group. During July and August they sailed along the northern coast of New Guinea, mapping it and stopping occasionally to get fresh water and food. (They named an island group off its northeast coast after Schouten.) The men reached the Dutch outpost of Ternate in the Moluccas (or Spice Islands) on September 17, 1616. There they were well-received by the Dutch colonists. But when the travelers landed in Batavia on October 28, their reception was anything but friendly.

Dutch authorities imprison *Eendracht* crew

In Batavia, the governor general of the Dutch East India Company refused to believe that Le Maire and Schouten had found a new passage into the Pacific. He charged them with violating the company's trade monopoly and seized the *Eendracht* and all its goods. Le Maire and Schouten and ten of their crew were sent back to the Netherlands as prisoners on a company ship. Le Maire, only thirty-one, died on the return trip. But Schouten lived to tell the story of their discoveries. His account of the expedition was published in Amsterdam in 1619. Le Maire's journal was published later that same year.

Trade monopoly broken

In the Netherlands, Jacob Le Maire's father Isaac sued the Dutch East India Company over the case. After two years of litigation, the Dutch courts accepted the claim that a passage existed south of the Strait of Magellan. The Dutch East India Company was forced to return the *Eendracht* and its cargo to the elder Le Maire, and to pay all related costs. What is more, the father made sure that the newly discovered waterway through which his son had passed into the Pacific was named Le Maire Strait in his honor.

Sources

Baker, Daniel B., ed. *Explorers and Discoverers of the World.* Detroit: Gale Research, 1993.

Bohlander, Richard E., ed. *World Explorers and Discoverers.* New York: Macmillan, 1992.

Marshall Cavendish Illustrated Encyclopedia of Discovery and Exploration, Volume 7: *Charting the Vast Pacific,* written by John Gilbert. Freeport, NY: Marshall Cavendish, 1990.

Freya Stark

Born January 31, 1893, Paris, France

Died May 9, 1993, Asolo, Italy

Born in Paris in 1893, Freya Stark seemed destined for a life of travel right from the start. Her parents were wealthy painters who moved freely about Europe, and some of Stark's earliest memories were of foreign landscapes rolling by her train window. Her father was English and her mother, who was of English and Italian heritage, had grown up in Italy. Stark's childhood was split between the English countryside and Italy's mountainous Piedmont region.

Stark's parents divorced when she was ten and her father eventually bought land in British Columbia, Canada, and settled there. He gave Freya and her younger sister a large sum of money before he left. In 1912 Stark used some of that money to study history at the University of London. It was the first formal schooling she had ever received. (Governesses had taught her as she had traveled from place to place.) Before she could earn her degree, though, World War I (1914–1918) broke out, and she returned to Italy, concerned for her mother's safety.

Englishwoman Freya Stark is well known for her decades of travel, especially to remote parts of Persia, Arabia, and Turkey. She also wrote numerous travel books about her experiences.

Stark served as a nurse in Italy during the war. At one point, she contracted typhoid and nearly died. Ever since childhood, her health had been very poor. (As a teenager, she had been terribly injured in an accident in a carpet factory when her long hair got caught in the machinery.)

Following the war, Stark was restless. She was eager to see more of the world but worried that her bad health and meager finances would keep her from traveling. Finally she decided that she would rather die than live like an invalid, and that the little money she had left from her father—while not enough for luxurious travel—would at least get her started. Particularly interested in seeing the countries of the Middle East, Stark began to study Arabic.

Begins life of travel

Ever since receiving a copy of the *Arabian Nights* for her ninth birthday, Stark had been captivated by that part of the world: its deserts, mountains, and ancient cities. In 1927 and 1928 she made her first visits to the Middle East, to Syria and Lebanon. She was not disappointed. In a letter to a friend Stark wrote: "I never imagined that my first sight of the desert would come as such a shock of beauty and enslave me right away."

In order to better study the history and culture of the area, Stark decided to move to Baghdad, the capital city of Iraq, in 1929. Too poor to live in the grand part of the city where foreign visitors stayed, she instead found lodgings with an Iraqi shoemaker and his family. While Baghdad's British residents were shocked by this unusual behavior, Stark was happy with the arrangement, speaking with her native hosts to perfect her language skills. Over the next few years, she explored parts of Iraq and its neighbor Persia (now Iran) while working for a newspaper in Baghdad.

Stark made one excursion to study the Lurs, a nomadic people who lived in Luristan, located in the Zagros Mountains of western Persia. The tribe was so untouched by civilization that they still dressed in clothing typically worn during medieval times. With a guide, and traveling on horseback, Stark

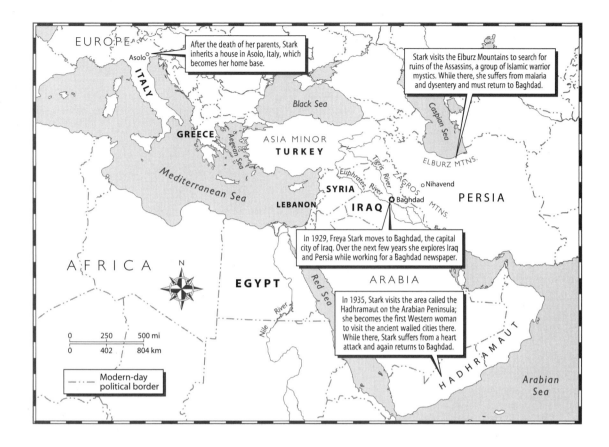

After the death of her parents, Stark inherits a house in Asolo, Italy, which becomes her home base.

Stark visits the Elburz Mountains to search for ruins of the Assassins, a group of Islamic warrior mystics. While there, she suffers from malaria and dysentery and must return to Baghdad.

In 1929, Freya Stark moves to Baghdad, the capital city of Iraq. Over the next few years she explores Iraq and Persia while working for a Baghdad newspaper.

In 1935, Stark visits the area called the Hadhramaut on the Arabian Peninsula; she becomes the first Western woman to visit the ancient walled cities there. While there, Stark suffers from a heart attack and again returns to Baghdad.

Modern-day political border

spent several weeks with the Lurs, talking to them and taking their photographs. She would be one of the last Westerners to see their primitive society before modern civilization changed it forever.

Hunts for buried treasure

Other excursions into Persia included a search for buried treasure. It was rumored that located in the hills near the city of Nihavend was a cave in which gold ornaments and coins, jewels, and other precious objects were buried. A young man from Luristan told Stark about the cave and gave her a map to follow, promising to meet her there. He needed the English-woman to smuggle the goods out of the country. With great effort Stark managed to make her way to the area in which the treasure was located. But the Persian police had also heard the rumors and watched her so closely that she could never get to the cave. Finally, she gave up the search.

Stark wrote a book about her life in Baghdad called *Baghdad Sketches,* published in 1933. In a second book, *The Valley of the Assassins,* she talked about her fascination with the Assassins, a notorious group of Islamic warrior mystics who—during medieval times—lived in a series of castles high in the peaks of the Elburz Mountains, located on the south shore of the Caspian Sea. Stark traveled to the rarely visited area, looking for ruins and other traces of the cult. She was especially interested in visiting the castle at Alamut, which had served as the Assassins' headquarters until their defeat by the Mongols in 1256. Over the course of several weeks, Stark managed to locate many mountaintop ruins, even discovering one that was unknown. She suffered from malaria and dysentery, though, which almost killed her. Thanks to the care provided by kind villagers, however, she was nursed back to health, and made her way back to Baghdad.

Receives awards for exploration efforts

The first Western woman to visit the "valley of the Assassins," Stark made maps of the area, noting her archaeological finds. (Existing maps had been inaccurate and incomplete.) Britain's Royal Geographical Society gave her an award for her work; in addition, she became the first woman to receive the honorary Burton Medal from the Royal Asiatic Society. After the publication of *The Valley of the Assassins* in 1934, Stark realized that she could earn a living as a travel writer. Thus began her lifelong pattern of making trips and then recounting her travels in essays and books.

Travels through Arabian Peninsula

In 1935 Stark decided to journey into the Arabian Peninsula. She was interested in visiting an area called the Hadramaut, which runs along the southern coast from the Red Sea to the Persian Gulf. The region—which had grown rich from the spice and incense trade—was infrequently visited by

Arabian Nights

Considered a classic of world literature, *Arabian Nights* (or *Thousand and One Nights*) is a collection of stories written long ago in Arabic. Their author or authors are unknown. There is a single plot device that runs throughout the tales of fantasy and adventure: they are told by a woman named Scheherezade, who for 1,001 nights tells a new story to her husband Schariar, the legendary king of Samarkand, to keep him entertained—otherwise he will kill her. The best known tales are those of Ali Baba and the forty thieves, Sinbad the sailor, and Aladdin and his magic lamp, which holds a genie that grants wishes. Over the centuries, *Arabian Nights* has been translated into many languages, including English.

Westerners because its inhabitants were devout Muslims who viewed strangers with suspicion. As an Englishwoman traveling alone there, Stark aroused great disapproval. Patient and respectful, she was eventually accepted, however, and was allowed to visit some of the Hadhramaut's ancient walled cities, the first Western woman to do so. Illness cut the trip short, though, when Stark suffered a heart attack and had to be returned to Baghdad by a Royal Air Force plane. Not long afterward she visited the area again, accompanying two female British scientists as they performed archaeological excavations. She wrote about her Arabian experiences in *The Southern Gates of Arabia,* published in 1936.

Aids British government

When World War II (1939–1945) broke out, Stark's knowledge about the Middle East and its peoples proved to be of great use to the British government. She worked for the British Ministry of Information in Arabia, Egypt, and Iraq, writing articles that tried to persuade those countries and their neighbors to join the side of Britain and its allies. At one point, she helped burn government records when the British embassy in Baghdad was overtaken by hostile Iraqi soldiers. (During that time she also met Stewart Perowne, a British co-worker whom she would marry in 1947, and divorce four years later.)

Following these war activities, Stark continued to aid the British government. In 1943 she visited the United States in an attempt to quiet negative feelings raised by Zionists—who wanted the establishment of a Jewish homeland in Palestine—about Britain's activities there. She also visited India as a good-will ambassador at a time when British rule there was nearing an end. In addition, she began work on her autobiography.

Other Middle East excursions

After the deaths of both her parents and the settling of their affairs (Stark inherited a house in Asolo, Italy, which be-came her home base), she took to traveling again. Over the next fourteen years, beginning in 1952, she would explore an area the ancient Greeks and Romans had called Asia Minor: Greece, Turkey, and Syria. She was especially interested in visiting the ancient sites connected with the life and travels of Alexander the Great (356–323 B.C.), the Macedonian king who had conquered much of Asia in the third century B.C. Stark followed the ancient ruler's route in Turkey, which resulted in a travel book titled *Alexander's Path*. Turkey was a favorite destination of Stark's, because it had been a cultural and religious center for so many peoples over the centuries: central Asians, Greeks, Romans, and Persians; Christians and Muslims alike. Among her other books was *Rome on the Euphrates*, a look at the Asian territories of ancient Rome.

Stark continued to travel until she was well into her seventies, including making her first visit to China. In 1969 she traveled to a remote part of Afghanistan so that she could see the Minaret of Djam—the tower of an ancient mosque (a Muslim place of worship), dating back before the thirteenth century. The site had just recently been discovered. The long journey over rocky terrain did little to ruin Stark's pleasure as the minaret came into view. Not long after, the dedicated traveler crossed Nepal's Himalaya Mountains by pony.

Internationally recognized as an explorer, historian, and exceptional travel writer, Stark was made a Dame of the British Empire—the female equivalent of a knight—in 1972.

Sources

Bohlander, Richard E., ed. *World Explorers and Discoverers*. New York: Macmillan, 1992.

Olendorf, Donna. *Contemporary Authors,* vol. 141. Detroit: Gale Research, 1994.

Stefoff, Rebecca. *Women of the World: Women Travelers and Explorers*. New York: Oxford University Press, 1992.

Tinling, Marion. *Women Into the Unknown: A Sourcebook on Women Explorers and Travelers*. Westport, CT: Greenwood Press, 1989.

Andrés de Urdaneta

Born c. 1508, Villafranca de Oria, Spain

Died June 3, 1568, Mexico City, New Spain (Mexico)

Andrés de Urdaneta was a Spanish navigator who took part in the second voyage around the world. Many years later he pioneered the first successful east-to-west sailing route across the Pacific Ocean.

In 1494 the Treaty of Tordesillas divided the non-Christian world between the two great maritime powers of Spain and Portugal to explore, convert, and colonize. The division essentially gave North and South America to Spain, and Africa, India, and the Orient to the Portuguese. Although the treaty allowed Portugal a trade monopoly with islands in the western Pacific, Spain still hoped to claim some of these countless islands as their own. Thus King Philip II (1527–1598) of Spain launched an expedition to the Philippines in 1564 to found a colony there and to convert the native population. Andrés de Urdaneta—one of the few survivors of a Spanish-led second voyage around the world begun in 1525—piloted the mission; on his return voyage he pioneered the first successful east-to-west sailing route across the Pacific Ocean to the colony of New Spain, now present-day Mexico. Known as Urdaneta's Passage, the route would change the nature of Pacific navigation, and give Spain a practical link to the Orient by way of Mexico.

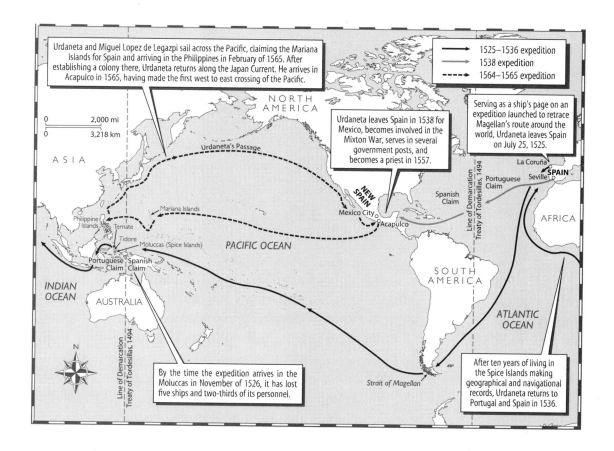

Urdaneta and Miguel Lopez de Legazpi sail across the Pacific, claiming the Mariana Islands for Spain and arriving in the Philippines in February of 1565. After establishing a colony there, Urdaneta returns along the Japan Current. He arrives in Acapulco in 1565, having made the first west to east crossing of the Pacific.

Urdaneta leaves Spain in 1538 for Mexico, becomes involved in the Míxton War, serves in several government posts, and becomes a priest in 1557.

Serving as a ship's page on an expedition launched to retrace Magellan's route around the world, Urdaneta leaves Spain on July 25, 1525.

	1525–1536 expedition
	1538 expedition
	1564–1565 expedition

By the time the expedition arrives in the Moluccas in November of 1526, it has lost five ships and two-thirds of its personnel.

After ten years of living in the Spice Islands making geographical and navigational records, Urdaneta returns to Portugal and Spain in 1536.

Joins round-the-world expedition

Urdaneta was born around 1508 in Villafranca de Oria, in the northern Spanish province of Guipœzcoa. In 1525, when Spanish king Charles I (1500–1558) launched an expedition to retrace the route of navigator Ferdinand Magellan (c. 1480–1521) around the world, the seventeen-year-old Urdaneta was on one of its seven ships, serving as a page to Juan Sebastián de Elcano (c. 1476–1526), the mission's pilot. The voyage was led by Francisco Garcia Jofre de Loaysa and its main purpose was to claim the Moluccas in eastern Indonesia (then known as the Spice Islands) for Spain. The expedition set sail from La Coruña, Spain, on July 25, 1525, traveled through the Strait of Magellan, and headed west across the Pacific. But disastrously, by the time it reached the islands in November 1526, it had lost five of its ships and two-thirds of its crew, including both leaders. The remaining Spanish sailors set up camp in Tidore, one of the Spice Islands, on January 1, 1527. Fighting began immediately with the Portuguese who occupied the neighboring island of Ternate. Finally, by the end of 1529, the men gave up their attempt to claim the islands for Spain; only seventeen Spaniards from the expedition crew remained. Urdaneta was among them.

Urdaneta stayed in Tidore under Portuguese rule, exploring the Spice Islands and making geographical and navigational records. In 1535, when word was received that Spain had sold its claims in the islands for 350,000 gold ducats, Urdaneta sailed back to Europe on a Portuguese ship. He traveled westward, by way of India and around Africa's Cape of Good Hope, arriving at Portugal's capital city of Lisbon in June 1536. He had just completed an around-the-world trip–begun more than ten years before.

Portuguese authorities kept Urdaneta in Lisbon for several months before allowing him to return to Spain. They took all his maps and expedition journals. But when the explorer finally reached the Spanish capital of Valladolid in February of 1537, he recreated his work from memory and presented it to Spain's Royal Council. King Charles gave Urdaneta a reward of money for his military and exploratory efforts on behalf of Spain.

Travels to Mexico

Because of his knowledge of the southwestern Pacific, Urdaneta was soon asked to join a voyage to the Spice Islands being planned by Pedro de Alvarado (c. 1485–1541), then governor of Spanish territories in Central America. Urdaneta left Seville, Spain, on October 16, 1538, to join him; but after arriving in Mexico, he became involved in an Indian uprising called the Míxton War. Alvarado, too, fought in the war, and was killed in 1541. All plans for the expedition were abandoned.

Urdaneta remained in Mexico, serving in various governments posts and continuing his geographical studies. In 1552, after a spiritual crisis, he joined the Order of Saint Augustine. Leading a secluded life in a monastery in Mexico City, he became a priest in 1557.

Leaves monastic life to pilot Pacific voyage

But in 1559, at the request of Spain's King Philip II, Urdaneta agreed to leave his quiet life and become chief pilot for an expedition to the western Pacific. Spain was still looking for a way to capture some of the spice trade, this time with a voyage departing from the west coast of Mexico. And because previous Spanish expeditions in the Pacific had been unable to find a west-to-east return route to the Americas (due to obstructing northeast trade winds), the king also wanted Urdaneta to use his considerable navigational skills to find such an ocean passage.

Because he was a priest, Urdaneta could not command the voyage. But he recommended that his friend Miguel Lopez de Legazpi (1510–1572), a former mayor of Mexico City who had also grown up in the Spanish province of Guipœzcoa, lead the expedition. Numerous delays stalled the voyage, which did not begin until November 21, 1564. Setting sail from the port of Acapulco on Mexico's Pacific coast, the fleet of five ships carried 150 sailors, 200 soldiers, and 5 Augustinian monks to help convert the native populations that the travelers would meet. The expedition was headed for the Philippines. Although—according to the Treaty of Tordesillas—the islands were in Portuguese territory, Spaniards had already made several landings there and Spain's King Philip was determined to claim them and establish a colony. Urdaneta and Legazpi guided their fleet west across the Pacific. On January 22 they came upon an island group later named the Marianas, and took possession of them for Spain.

Travelers claim Philippines for Spain

The fleet arrived in the Philippines on February 13, 1565. It traveled to the islands of Samar and Bohol, and finally to Cebu, where the ships anchored offshore on April 27. After bombarding the island with cannon fire, the Spaniards landed and claimed the territory for their king. They set up the first permanent Spanish settlement in the Philippines there, founding the city of San Miguel (now Cebu City). Legazpi and his forces remained on the islands, and the commander

The voyage of the *San Lucas*

While Urdaneta was recognized for making the first successful west-to-east passage across the Pacific, he was actually not the first Spanish sailor to do so. Shortly after Legazpi's fleet left Acapulco, the smallest ship—the *San Lucas* piloted by Alonso de Arellano—became separated from the other boats. According to Arellano's log book, his ship arrived in the Philippines some weeks before Legazpi and Urdaneta, and set sail on a return voyage to North America on April 22, 1565. Like the *San Pedro,* the *San Lucas* sailed at a higher latitude than usual and let the Japan Current and favorable winds carry it east across the Pacific. Arellano reached North America on July 17 and sailed down its coast to Acapulco, arriving there on August 8, about three months before Urdaneta. But because Arellano had made no records of his course—which would allow future navigators to travel it—he was not given credit for the passage. Arellano was viewed as merely lucky, while Urdaneta had developed a plan, followed it, and made detailed charts of the results. While at first receiving a hero's welcome when he arrived in port, Arellano would eventually be charged with disobedience and defection, authorities believing that he had left the fleet deliberately.

became their first governor. Urdaneta, with his royal instructions to find a return route to Mexico across the Pacific, prepared to leave at once.

Completes first west-to-east Pacific crossing

Urdaneta set sail on June 1, 1565, aboard the *San Pedro* (commanded by Legazpi's grandson Felipe de Salcado). In order to avoid adverse trade winds, he decided to follow a far more northerly course than those taken by previous navigators, sailing along the coast of Japan to latitude 42° N. There the winds blew mostly from the west, and–along with an eastern-flowing ocean current (later called the Japan Current)–he was able to easily cross the Pacific. He sighted the Channel Islands, located off the coast of present-day Santa Barbara, California, on September 18. He then sailed south to Acapulco, which he reached on October 8, 1565.

Although Urdaneta's course was twice as long as the western route across the Pacific (the wide arc he traveled covering more than eleven thousand miles), he had done what no Spanish navigator had done before: found a way to sail across the ocean from west to east. For the next 250 years Spanish traders would follow Urdaneta's Passage as they traveled regularly between western Mexico and the Philippines (after some protest, Portugal recognized Spain's claim to the islands). It would become the route of the famous "Manila Galleon," treasure-filled ships that made yearly runs between Manila—the Philippines's largest trade center—and Acapulco.

Shortly after Urdaneta's return to Mexico, his health began to deteriorate. He had hoped to return to the Philippines to do missionary work, but instead retired to his monastery. He died a few years later, on June 3, 1568.

Sources

Baker, Daniel B., ed. *Explorers and Discoverers of the World.* Detroit: Gale Research, 1993.

Bohlander, Richard E., ed. *World Explorers and Discoverers.* New York: Macmillan, 1992.

Delpar, Helen, ed. *The Discoverers: An Encyclopedia of Explorers and Exploration.* New York: McGraw-Hill, 1980.

Marshall Cavendish Illustrated Encyclopedia of Discovery and Exploration, Volume 7: *Charting the Vast Pacific,* written by John Gilbert. Freeport, NY: Marshall Cavendish, 1990.

Waldman, Carl and Alan Wexler. *Who Was Who in World Exploration.* New York: Facts on File, 1992.

Chronology of Exploration

As an aid to the reader who wishes to trace the history of exploration or the explorers active in a particular location, the major expeditions within a geographical area are listed below in chronological order.

*Explorers with entries in Explorers and Discoverers, Volume 6 are in **boldface** and have page numbers following their names; explorers whose names are not in boldface appear in Volumes 1–4 or Volume 5.*

Africa: central

1802–14	Pedro João Baptista and Amaro José
1854–56	David Livingstone
1858–64	David Livingstone
1872–73	David Livingstone
1873–77	Henry Morton Stanley
1877–80	Hermenegildo de Brito Capelo and Roberto Ivens
1884–85	Hermenegildo de Brito Capelo and Roberto Ivens
1888–90	Henry Morton Stanley
1896–98	Jean-Baptiste Marchand
1903	May French Sheldon
1924–25	Delia Akeley

Africa: coast

1416–60	Henry the Navigator
1487–88	Bartolomeu Dias
1765–68	**James Bruce 26**

Africa: east

c. 1493–92 B.C.	**Hatshepsut** (sponsored expedition) **90**
1490–1526	Pero da Covilhã
1768–73	**James Bruce 26**
1812–13	**Jean-Louis Burckhardt 35**
1814	Jean-Louis Burckhardt
1848	Johannes Rebmann
1848–49	Johann Ludwig Krapf
1848–49	Johannes Rebmann
1849	Johannes Rebmann

1851	Johann Ludwig Krapf
1855–57	Alexine Tinné
1857–59	Richard Burton and John Hanning Speke (with Sidi Mubarak Bombay)
1860–63	John Hanning Speke and James Augustus Grant (with Sidi Mubarak Bombay)
1862–63	Alexine Tinné
1862–64	Samuel White Baker and Florence Baker
1865–71	David Livingstone
1869	Alexine Tinné
1870–73	Samuel White Baker and Florence Baker
1871–73	Henry Morton Stanley (with Sidi Mubarak Bombay)
1883–84	Joseph Thomson
1891	May French Sheldon
1905–06	Delia Akeley
1909–11	Delia Akeley
1930s–1960s	Louis and Mary Leakey
1966–85	**Dian Fossey 57**
1968–	Richard Leakey

Africa: northwest

1763–65	**James Bruce 26**

Africa: south

1849	David Livingstone
1850	David Livingstone
1851–52	David Livingstone
1851–55	Ida Pfeiffer

Africa: west

1352–53	Abu Abdallah Ibn Battutah

1790–91	**Daniel Houghton 101**
1795–99	Mungo Park
1805	Mungo Park
1827–28	René Caillié
1850–55	Heinrich Barth
1856–60	Paul Du Chaillu
1861–76	Friedrich Gerhard Rohlfs
1863	Paul Du Chaillu
1867	Paul Du Chaillu
1875–78	Pierre Savorgnan de Brazza
1879	Henry Morton Stanley
1879–81	Pierre Savorgnan de Brazza
1883–85	Pierre Savorgnan de Brazza
1891–92	Pierre Savorgnan de Brazza
1893	Mary Kingsley
1894	Mary Kingsley
1903	May French Sheldon

Antarctica

1819–21	Fabian Gottlieb von Bellingshausen
1837–40	Jules-Sébastien-César Dumont d'Urville
1839–40	Charles Wilkes
1903–05	Jean-Baptiste Charcot
1907–09	Ernest Shackleton
1908–10	Jean-Baptiste Charcot
1910–12	Roald Amundsen
1914–16	Ernest Shackleton
1921–22	Ernest Shackleton
1928	Hubert Wilkins
1928–29	Richard Evelyn Byrd
1929	Hubert Wilkins
1933–34	Lincoln Ellsworth
1933–35	Richard Evelyn Byrd
1935–36	Lincoln Ellsworth

1937	Lincoln Ellsworth
1939–40	Richard Evelyn Byrd
1946–47	Richard Evelyn Byrd
1956	Richard Evelyn Byrd
1956–58	Vivian Fuchs
1989–90	Will Steger

Arabia

25 B.C.	Aelius Gallus
1812–13	Hester Stanhhope
1814–15	**Jean-Louis Burckhardt 35**
1854–55	Richard Burton
1877–78	Anne Blunt and Wilfrid Scawen Blunt
1879–80	Anne Blunt and Wilfrid Scawen Blunt
1913	Gertrude Bell
1935–36	**Freya Stark 181**
1990	Nicholas Clapp
1991–92	Nicholas Clapp

Arctic (see also Northwest Passage)

1827	Edward Parry
1858	Nils Adolf Erik Nordenskjöld
1860	Charles Francis Hall
1861	Nils Adolf Erik Nordenskjöld
1864	Nils Adolf Erik Nordenskjöld
1864–69	Charles Francis Hall
1868	Nils Adolf Erik Nordenskjöld
1871	Charles Francis Hall
1872	Nils Adolf Erik Nordenskjöld
1893–96	Fridtjof Nansen
1898–99	**Bob Bartlett** (with Robert Edwin Peary) **1**
1902	Jean-Baptiste Charcot

1902	Robert Edwin Peary
1905–06	Bob Bartlett (with Robert Edwin Peary)
1905–06	Robert Edwin Peary (with Matthew A. Henson)
1906–07	Vilhjalmur Stefansson
1908–09	Bob Bartlett (with Robert Edwin Peary)
1908–09	Robert Edwin Peary (with Matthew A. Henson)
1908–12	Vilhjalmur Stefansson
1913–14	Bob Bartlett (with Vilhjalmur Stefansson)
1913–18	Vilhjalmur Stefansson
1921–25	Vilhjalmur Stefansson
1925	Roald Amundsen
1925	Richard Evelyn Byrd
1926	Roald Amundsen and Umberto Nobile
1926	Louise Arner Boyd
1926	Richard Evelyn Byrd
1926–27	Hubert Wilkins
1928	Louise Arner Boyd
1928	Hubert Wilkins
1931	Hubert Wilkins
1940	Louise Arner Boyd
1955	Louise Arner Boyd
1958	U.S.S. *Nautilus*
1986	Will Steger

Asia: east

| Late 1960s | **Freya Stark 181** |

Asia: interior

| 1643–46 | Vasily Danilovich Poyarkov |
| 1649–50 | **Yerofey Pavlovich Khabarov 121** |

1650–54	Yerofey Pavlovich Khabarov
1866–68	Francis Garnier
1870–72	Nikolay Przhevalsky
1876	Nikolay Przhevalsky
1883–85	Nikolay Przhevalsky
1893–95	Sven Hedin
1895–97	Isabella Bird
1899	Fanny Bullock Workman
1899–1901	Sven Hedin
1900	Aurel Stein
1903–05	Sven Hedin
1906	Fanny Bullock Workman
1906–08	Aurel Stein
1913–15	Aurel Stein
1927–33	Sven Hedin
1932	Ella Maillart
1934	Ella Maillart
1934–36	Sven Hedin
1953	Edmund Hillary
1977	Edmund Hillary

Asia/Europe (see Eurasia)

Asia, south/China

629–45 B.C.	Hsüan-tsang
138–26 B.C.	Chang Ch'ien
399–414	Fa-Hsien
672–82	**I-Ching 106**
1321–30s or c. 1354	**Jordanus of Séverac 110**
1405–07	Cheng Ho
1407–09	Cheng Ho
1409–11	Cheng Ho
1413–15	Cheng Ho
1417–19	Cheng Ho
1421–22	Cheng Ho

1433–35	Cheng Ho
1847–48	Ida Pfeiffer
1851–55	Ida Pfeiffer
1857–64	**Robert Hermann Schomburgk 169**
1868	**Hari Ram 76**
1871–72	Hari Ram
1873	Hari Ram
1885	Hari Ram
1935	Ella Maillart
1939	Ella Maillart
1949	Ella Maillart
1994	Ella Maillart

Australia

1605–06	Willem Janszoon
1642	Abel Tasman
1644	Abel Tasman
1770	James Cook
1798–99	Matthew Flinders
1801–02	Matthew Flinders
1801–02	Joseph Banks
1802–03	Matthew Flinders
1813	Gregory Blaxland
1839	Edward John Eyre
1840–41	Edward John Eyre
1860–61	Robert O'Hara Burke and William John Wills
1869–70	John Forrest
1874	John Forrest
1876	John Forrest
1880	John Forrest

Aviation

| 1927 | Charles Lindbergh |
| 1928 | Amelia Earhart |

1930	Beryl Markham
1930	Amy Johnson
1931	Amy Johnson
1931	Wiley Post
1932	Amelia Earhart
1932	Amy Johnson
1933	Wiley Post
1935	Amelia Earhart
1936	Amelia Earhart
1936	Beryl Markham
1947	Chuck Yeager
1986	Dick Rutan and Jeana Yeager
1995	Steve Fossett
1996	Steve Fossett
1997	Steve Fossett

Central America
| 1523–26 | Pedro de Alvarado |

Circumnavigation
| 1525–36 | **Andrés de Urdaneta 188** |
| 1889–90 | **Nellie Bly 18** |

Eurasia *(see also* Tibet)
1454–43 B.C.	Herodotus
401–399 B.C.	Xenophon
334–23 B.C.	Alexander the Great
310–06 B.C.	Pytheas
921–22	Ahmad Ibn Fadlan
1159–73	Benjamin of Tudela
1245–47	Giovanni da Pian del Carpini
1271–95	Marco Polo
1280–90	Rabban Bar Sauma
1487–90	Pero da Covilhã
1492–93	Christopher Columbus
1497–99	Vasco da Gama

1502–03	Vasco da Gama
1537–58	Fernã o Mendes Pinto
1549–51	Saint Francis Xavier
1595–97	Cornelis de Houtman
1598–99	Cornelis de Houtman
1656–58	**Johann Grüber 70**
1661–64	Johann Grüber
1697–99	Vladimir Atlasov
1725–30	Vitus Bering
1733–41	Vitus Bering
1787	Jean François de Galaup, Comte de La Pérouse
1879–80	Nils Adolf Erik Nordenskjöld
1922–23	**Marguerite Baker Harrison 81**
1930s	Ella Maillart
1952–66	**Freya Stark 181**

Europe
1845	Ida Pfeiffer
1848	Ida Pfeiffer
1851	Ida Pfeiffer
1855	Alexine Tinné
1857	Alexine Tinné
1873	Heinrich Schliemann
1876–78	Heinrich Schliemann
1884–85	Heinrich Schliemann
1920	**Marguerite Baker Harrison 81**
1993	Barry Clifford

Greenland
982	Erik the Red
1870	Nils Adolf Erik Nordenskjöld
1871	Charles Francis Hall
1883	Nils Adolf Erik Nordenskjöld

1886	Robert Edwin Peary
1888	Fridtjof Nansen
1891–92	Robert Edwin Peary (with Matthew A. Henson)
1893–95	Robert Edwin Peary (with Matthew A. Henson)
1926–36	Jean-Baptiste Charcot
1931	Louise Arner Boyd
1933	Louise Arner Boyd
1937	Louise Arner Boyd
1938	Louise Arner Boyd

Middle East

1765–68	**James Bruce 26**
1809–12	**Jean-Louis Burckhardt 35**
1815	Jean-Louis Burckhardt
1842–43	Ida Pfeiffer
1847–48	Ida Pfeiffer
1856	Alexine Tinné
1857	Alexine Tinné
1924	**Marguerite Baker Harrison 81**
1927	**Freya Stark 181**
1928	Freya Stark
1929–33	Freya Stark
1952–57	**Kathleen M. Kenyon 114**

Muslim World

915–17	Abu al-Hasan 'Ali al-Mas'udi
918–28	Abu al-Hasan 'Ali al-Mas'udi
921–22	Ahmad Ibn Fadlan
943–73	Abu al-Kasim Ibn Ali al-Nasibi Ibn Hawkal
966–87	**Muhammed ibn-Ahmad al-Muqaddasi 138**

| 1325–49 | Abu Abdallah Ibn Battutah |

North America: coast

1001–02	Leif Eriksson
1493–96	Christopher Columbus
1497	John Cabot
1498	John Cabot
1500	**Gaspar Corte-Real 42**
1501	Gaspar Corte-Real
1502	**Miguel Corte-Real 42**
1502–04	Christopher Columbus
1508	Sebastian Cabot
1513	Juan Ponce de León
1513–14	Vasco Núñez de Balboa
1518–22	Hernán Cortés
1519–22	Pedro de Alvarado
1524	Giovanni da Verrazano
1534	Jacques Cartier
1534–36	Hernán Cortés
1535–36	Jacques Cartier
1539	Hernán Cortés
1540–41	Pedro de Alvarado
1541–42	Jacques Cartier
1542–43	João Rodrigues Cabrilho
1584	Walter Raleigh
1585–86	Walter Raleigh
1587–89	Walter Raleigh
1603	Samuel de Champlain
1604–07	Samuel de Champlain
1606–09	John Smith
1608–10	Samuel de Champlain
1609	Henry Hudson
1610	Samuel de Champlain
1614	John Smith
1792–94	George Vancouver

North America: interior

1618–20	**Jean Nicollet 147**
1620–29	Jean Nicollet
1634–35	Jean Nicollet
1666–71	Jacques Marquette
1673	Jacques Marquette
1674–75	Jacques Marquette
1678	**Louis Hennepin 95**
1679–80	Louis Hennepin (with René-Robert de La Salle)
1680–81	Louis Hennepin
1822	William Henry Ashley

North America: northwest

1805–06	**Simon Fraser 64**
1806–08	Simon Fraser

North America: southwest

1886	**Nellie Bly 18**
1987–	**Biosphere 2 9**

North America: sub-Arctic

1654–56	Médard Chouart des Groselliers
1668	Médard Chouart des Groselliers
1668	Pierre Esprit Radisson
1670	Pierre Esprit Radisson
1679	Louis Jolliet
1682–83	Médard Chouart des Groselliers
1684	Pierre Esprit Radisson
1685–87	Pierre Esprit Radisson
1689	Louis Jolliet
1694	Louis Jolliet

1725–30	Vitus Bering
1733–41	Vitus Bering
1789	Alexander Mackenzie
1795	Aleksandr Baranov
1799	Aleksandr Baranov
1819–22	John Franklin
1825–27	John Franklin

North America: west

1527–36	Álvar Núñez Cabeza de Vaca (with Estevanico)
1538–43	Hernando de Soto
1539	Estevanico
1540–42	Francisco Vásquez de Coronado
1611–12	Samuel de Champlain
1613–15	Samuel de Champlain
1615–16	Samuel de Champlain
1615–16	Ètienne Brulé
1621–23	Ètienne Brulé
1657	Pierre Esprit Radisson
1659–60	Médard Chouart des Groselliers
1659–60	Pierre Esprit Radisson
1669–70	René-Robert Cavelier de La Salle
1672–74	Louis Jolliet
1678–83	René-Robert Cavelier de La Salle
1684–87	René-Robert Cavelier de La Salle
1769–71	Daniel Boone
1775	Daniel Boone
1792–94	Alexander Mackenzie
1792–97	David Thompson
1797–99	David Thompson
1800–02	David Thompson

1804–06	Meriwether Lewis and William Clark
1805–06	**Sacagawea** (with Meriwether Lewis and William Clark) **161**
1805–06	Zebulon Pike
1806–07	Zebulon Pike
1807–11	David Thompson
1811–13	Wilson Price Hunt and Robert Stuart
1823	William Henry Ashley (with Jedediah Smith)
1823–25	Jedediah Smith
1824–25	William Henry Ashley
1824–25	Peter Skene Ogden
1825–26	Peter Skene Ogden
1826	William Henry Ashley
1826–27	Peter Skene Ogden
1826–28	Jedediah Smith
1828–29	Peter Skene Ogden
1829–30	Peter Skene Ogden
1842	John Charles Frémont
1843–44	John Charles Frémont
1845–48	John Charles Frémont
1848–49	John Charles Frémont
1850–51	Jim Beckwourth
1851–55	Ida Pfeiffer
1853–55	John Charles Frémont

North Pole *(see* Arctic)

Northeast Passage

1607	Henry Hudson
1878–79	Nils A. E. Nordenskjöld
1918–20	Roald Amundsen
1931	Lincoln Ellsworth

Northwest Passage

1610–13	Henry Hudson
1776–79	James Cook
1819–20	Edward Parry
1821–23	Edward Parry
1824–25	Edward Parry
1845–47	John Franklin
1850–54	Robert McClure
1903–06	Roald Amundsen

Oceans

1872–76	H.M.S. *Challenger*
1901	Jean-Baptiste Charcot
1912	R.M.S *Titanic*
1921	Jean-Baptiste Charcot
1925–27	**S.S. *Meteor* 134**
1942–42	Jacques Cousteau
1948	August Piccard
1954	August Piccard
1960s–	**Sylvia Earle 48**
1960	Jacques Piccard
1968–80	*Glomar Challenger*
1969	Jacques Piccard
1984	Barry Clifford
1985	R.M.S. *Titanic*

South America: coast

1498–1500	Christopher Columbus
1499–1500	Alonso de Ojeda
1499–1500	Amerigo Vespucci
1501–1502	Amerigo Vespucci
1502	Alonso de Ojeda
1505	Alonso de Ojeda
1509–10	Alonso de Ojeda
1519–20	Ferdinand Magellan

1526–30	Sebastian Cabot
1527	Giovanni da Verrazano
1528	Giovanni da Verrazano
1534	Pedro de Alvarado
1594	Walter Raleigh
1595	Walter Raleigh
1615	**Willem Corneliszoon Schouten 175**
1615	Pedro de Teixeira
1617–18	Walter Raleigh
1735–43	Charles-Marie de La Condomine
1743–44	Charles-Marie de La Condomine
1831–34	Charles Darwin
1847–48	Ida Pfeiffer
1851–55	Ida Pfeiffer

South America: interior

1524–25	Francisco Pizarro
1526–27	Francisco Pizarro
1531–41	Francisco Pizarro
1540–44	Álvar Núñez Cabeza de Vaca
1541–42	Francisco de Orellana
1620s	Pedro de Teixeira
1629	Pedro de Teixeira
1637–38	Pedro de Teixeira
1639	Pedro de Teixeira
1743	Charles-Marie de La Condomine
1760–62	**José Celestino Mutis 142**
1769–70	Isabel Godin des Odonais
1777–78	José Celestino Mutis
1782–92	José Celestino Mutis
1799–1803	Alexander von Humboldt

1835–36	**Robert Hermann Schomburgk 169**
1836–37	Robert Hermann Schomburgk
1838–40	Robert Hermann Schomburgk
1841–44	Robert Hermann Schomburgk
1900–06	**Cândido Rondón 153**
1903	Annie Smith Peck
1904	Annie Smith Peck
1906–09	Cândido Rondón
1908	Annie Smith Peck
1911	Hiram Bingham
1912	Hiram Bingham
1913–14	Cândido Rondón
1915	Hiram Bingham
1915–19	Cândido Rondón
1927–30	Cândido Rondón

South Pacific

671	**I-Ching 106**
682–95	I-Ching
1519–22	Ferdinand Magellan
1526–35	**Andrés de Urdaneta 188**
1564–65	Andrés de Urdaneta
1577–80	Francis Drake
1616	**Willem Corneliszoon Schouten 175**
1642–43	Abel Tasman
1721–22	Jacob Roggeveen
1766–68	Samuel Wallis
1766–69	Philip Carteret
1767–69	Louis-Antoine de Bougainville

1768–71	James Cook (with Joseph Banks)
1772–75	James Cook
1776–79	James Cook
1785–88	Jean François de Galaup, Comte de La Pérouse
1791	George Vancouver
1826–29	Jules-Sébastien-César Dumont d'Urville
1834–36	Charles Darwin
1838–39	Jules-Sébastien-César Dumont d'Urville
1838–42	Charles Wilkes
1847–48	Ida Pfeiffer
1851–55	Ida Pfeiffer
1923	Evelyn Cheesman
1928–30	Evelyn Cheesman
1930	Michael J. Leahy
1931	Michael J. Leahy
1932–33	Michael J. Leahy
1933–42	Evelyn Cheesman

Space

1957	*Sputnik*
1958–70	*Explorer 1*
1959–72	*Luna*
1961	Yury Gagarin
1962	John Glenn
1962–75	*Mariner*
1963	Valentina Tereshkova
1967–72	*Apollo*
1969	Neil Armstrong
1975–83	*Viking*
1977–90	*Voyager 1* and *2*
1983	Sally Ride
1986	**Christa McAuliffe 125**
1987	Mae Jemison
1990–	Hubble Space Telescope
1992	Mae Jemison
1986–	*Mir* space station

Tibet (*see also* Asia, south/China; Eurasia)

1624–30	Antonio de Andrade
1661	**Johann Grüber 70**
1811–12	Thomas Manning
1865–66	Nain Singh
1867–68	Nain Singh
1871	**Hari Ram 76**
1879–80	Nikolay Przhevalsky
1885	Hari Ram
1892–93	Annie Royle Taylor
1898	Susie Carson Rijnhart
1901	Sven Hedin
1915–16	Alexandra David-Neel
1923–24	Alexandra David-Neel

Explorers by Country of Birth

If an expedition were sponsored by a country other than the explorer's place of birth, the sponsoring country is listed in parentheses after the explorer's name.

Explorers with entries in Explorers and Discoverers, Volume 6 *are in **boldface** and have page numbers following their names; explorers whose names are not in boldface appear in Volumes 1–4 or Volume 5.*

Angola

Pedro João Baptista (Portugal)

Amaro José

Australia

John Forrest

Michael J. Leahy

Hubert Wilkins

William John Wills

Austria

Johann Grüber 70

Ida Pfeiffer

Belgium

Louis Hennepin (France) **95**

Brazil

Cândido Rondón 153

Canada

Bob Bartlett 1

Louis Jolliet

Peter Skene Ogden

Susie Carson Rijnhart

Vilhjalmur Stefansson

China

Rabban Bar Sauma

Chang Ch'ien
Cheng Ho
Fa-Hsien
Hsüan-Tsang
I-Ching 106

Denmark
Vitus Bering (Russia)

Ecuador
Isabel Godin des Odonais

Egypt
Hatshepsut 90

England
Samuel White Baker
Joseph Banks
Gertrude Bell
Isabella Bird
Gregory Blaxland
Anne Blunt
Wilfrid Scawen Blunt
Richard Burton
Philip Carteret
H.M.S. *Challenger*
Evelyn Cheesman
James Cook
Charles Darwin
Francis Drake
Edward John Eyre
Matthew Flinders
John Franklin
Vivian Fuchs
Henry Hudson (Netherlands)

Amy Johnson
Kathleen M. Kenyon 114
Mary Kingsley
Mary Leakey
Thomas Manning
Beryl Markham (Kenya)
Edward Parry
Walter Raleigh
John Smith
John Hanning Speke
Hester Stanhope
Freya Stark 181
Annie Royle Taylor
David Thompson
R.M.S. *Titanic* (built in Belfast, Ireland)
George Vancouver
Samuel Wallis

Estonia
Fabian Gottlieb von Bellingshausen (Russia)

Finland
Nils Adolf Erik Nordenskjöld (Sweden)

France
Louis-Antoine de Bougainville
Étienne Brulé
René Caillié
Jacques Cartier
Samuel de Champlain
Jean-Baptiste Charcot
Médard Chouart des Groselliers
Paul Du Chaillu (United States)
Jacques Cousteau
Alexandra David-Neel
Jules-Sébastien-César Dumont d'Urville

Francis Garnier
Jordanus of Séverac 110
Charles-Marie de La Condomine
Jean François de Galaup, Comte de La
    Pérouse
René-Robert Cavelier de La Salle
Jean-Baptiste Marchand
Jacques Marquette
Jean Nicollet 147
Pierre Esprit Radisson

Germany

Heinrich Barth (Great Britain)
Alexander von Humboldt
Johann Ludwig Krapf
Johannes Rebmann
Friedrich Gerhard Rohlfs
Heinrich Schliemann
Robert Hermann Schomburgk (Great
    Britain) **169**

Greece

Alexander the Great
Herodotus
Pytheas
Xenophon

Hungary

Aurel Stein (Great Britain)

Iceland

Leif Eriksson

India

Hari Ram (Great Britain) **76**
Nain Singh

Iraq

Abu al-Kasim Ibn Ali al-Nasibi Ibn Hawkal
Ahmad Ibn Fadlan
Abu al-Hasan 'Ali al-Mas'udi

Ireland

Daniel Houghton 101
Robert O'Hara Burke (Australia)
Robert McClure
Ernest Shackleton

Italy

Pierre Savorgnan de Brazza (France)
John Cabot (Great Britain)
Sebastian Cabot (England, Spain)
Giovanni da Pian del Carpini
Christopher Columbus (Spain)
Marco Polo
Giovanni da Verrazano (France)
Amerigo Vespucci (Spain, Portugal)

Kenya

Louis S. B. Leakey
Richard Leakey

Malawi

Sidi Mubarak Bombay (Great Britain)
James Chuma (Great Britain)

Morocco

Abu Abdallah Ibn Battutah
Estevanico

Netherlands

Willem Barents
Cornelis de Houtman
Willem Janszoon
Jacob Roggeveen
Willem Corneliszoon Schouten 175
Abel Tasman
Alexine Tinné

New Zealand

Edmund Hillary

Norway

Roald Amundsen
Erik the Red (Iceland)
Fridtjof Nansen

Palastine

**Muhammed ibn-Ahmad al-Muqaddasi
138**

Portugal

Antonio de Andrade
Hermenegildo de Brito Capelo
João Rodrigues Cabrilho (Spain)
Gaspar Corte-Real 42
Miguel Corte-Real 42
Pedro da Covilhã
Bartolomeu Dias
Vasco da Gama
Henry the Navigator
Roberto Ivens
Ferdinand Magellan (Spain)
Fernão Mendes Pinto
Pedro de Teixeira

Romania

Florence Baker

Rome

Aelius Gallus

Russia [see also Union of Soviet Socialist Republics

Vladimir Atlasov
Aleksandr Baranov
Yerofey Pavlovich Khabarov 121
Vasily Danilovich Poyarkov
Nikolay Przhevalsky

Scotland

James Bruce 26
David Livingstone
Alexander Mackenzie
Mungo Park
Robert Stuart (United States)
Joseph Thomson

Spain

Pedro de Alvarado
Benjamin of Tudela
Álvar Núñez Cabeza de Vaca
Francisco Vásquez de Coronado
Hernán Cortés
José Celestino Mutis 142
Vasco Núñez de Balboa
Alonso de Ojeda
Francisco de Orellana
Francisco Pizarro
Juan Ponce de León
Hernando de Soto

Andrés de Urdaneta 188
Saint Francis Xavier

Sweden
Sven Hedin

Switzerland
Jean-Louis Burckhardt (Great Britain) **35**
Ella Maillairt
Auguste Piccard
Jacques Piccard

Union of Soviet Socialist Republics
Yury Gagarin
Luna
Mir space station
Sputnik
Valentina Tereshkova

United States of America
Delia Akeley
Apollo
Neil Armstrong
William Henry Ashley
Jim Beckwourth
Hiram Bingham
Nellie Bly 18
Daniel Boone
Louise Arner Boyd
Richard Evelyn Byrd
Nicholas Clapp
William Clark
Barry Clifford
Sylvia Earle 48

Amelia Earhart
Lincoln Ellsworth
Explorer 1
Steve Fossett
Dian Fossey 57
Simon Fraser (Canada) **64**
John Charles Frémont
John Glenn
Glomar Challenger
Charles Francis Hall
Marguerite Baker Harrison 81
Matthew A. Henson
Hubble Space Telescope
Wilson Price Hunt
Mae Jemison
Meriwether Lewis
Charles Lindbergh
Mariner
Christa McAuliffe 125
National Geographic Society
U.S.S. *Nautilus*
Robert Edwin Peary
Annie Smith Peck
Zebulon Pike
Wiley Post
Sally Ride
Dick Rutan
Sacagawea 161
May French Sheldon
Jedediah Smith
Will Steger
Viking
Voyager 1 and *2*
Charles Wilkes
Fanny Bullock Workman
Chuck Yeager

Jeana Yeager

Wales
Henry Morton Stanley (United States)

Cumulative Index to Volumes 1-6

Boldface indicates main entries in Volume 6 and their page numbers; *1–4:* refers to entries in the four-volume base set; *5:* refers to entries in Volume 5; *6:* refers to entries in Volume 6; (ill.) following a page number refers to photos, drawings, and maps.

American Relief Administration *6:* 84, 86

American Revolution *1–4:* 120, 127, 192, 508, 529

American River *1–4:* 760

American Samoa *1–4:* 510

American West *6:* 168

Amiens, France *6:* 23

Amirante Islands *1–4:* 392

Amon-Ra *1–4:* 7; *6:* 91

Amritsar, India *1–4:* 105

Amsterdam, the Netherlands *1–4:* 455, 458, 486; *5:* 14, 16, 135; *6:* 176, 179

Amu Darya River *1–4:* 8, 808; *5:* 101

Amundsen, Roald *1–4:* 14–22, 56, 130, 158, 160, 337, 429, 641, 747, 859

Amundsen Gulf *1–4:* 17

Amundsen-Scott Base *1–4:* 377, 804

Amur *1–4:* 705

Amur River *5:* 22, 131–133; *6:* 121–124

"Amy, Wonderful Amy" *1–4:* 492

Anabasis 1–4: 868, 870

Anadyr River *1–4:* 41

Ancient Greeks *5:* 135

Andalusia, Spain *1–4:* 287

Andaman Islands *1–4:* 693

Anders, William *1–4:* 28

Anderson, Rudolph M. *5:* 147

Anderson, William R. *1–4:* 611, 613

Andes Mountains *1–4:* 99, 101, 157, 174, 299–301, 409, 479, 654, 768; *5:* 4, 88, 152; *6:* 143

Andrade, Antonio de *1–4:* 23–25

Andronicus II *1–4:* 67

Andronicus III *1–4:* 77

Andros Island *1–4:* 697

Anegada *6:* 170

Angareb River *1–4:* 45

Angediva Island *1–4:* 390

Angkor, Cambodia *1–4:* 395

Angmagssalik, Greenland *1–4:* 342

Angostura *1–4:* 479

Aneityum *5:* 37, 38

Annam, Vietnam *1–4:* 394

Annapolis Royal, Nova Scotia *1–4:* 214

Antanarivo, Madagascar *5:* 130

Antarctic Circle *1–4:* 91, 262; *5:* 32

Antarctic Peninsula *1–4:* 92–93, 803, 853

Antarctic Treaty *1–4:* 340

Anticosti Island *1–4:* 194–195, 498

Antioch, Syria *1–4:* 97, 220, 598

Antivari, Yugoslavia *1–4:* 186

Añasco Bay *1–4:* 248

Apalachen *1–4:* 769

Aparia *1–4:* 629, 630

Apollo 1–4: 26–33, 37, 402, 558

Appalachian Mountains *1–4:* 118, 529, 770

Appenine Mountains *1–4:* 31

Apuré River *1–4:* 478

Aqualung *1–4:* 282–284

Arab Bureauscuba *1–4:* 89

Arabian Desert *5:* 127; *6:* 140

Arabian Nights 6: 182, 185

Arabian Peninsula *1–4:* 108, 223, 772; *5:* 40, 42; *6:* 39, 139, 184

Arabian Sea *1–4:* 435; *6:* 75

Aral Sea *1–4:* 78, 597

Arawak (tribe) *1–4:* 248–249

Archimedes Crater *1–4:* 556

Arctic Circle *1–4:* 328, 612, 640; *6:* 44

Arctic Ocean *1–4:* 14, 21, 469, 509, 801, 821, 857; *5:* 13, 120, 123, 131, 147

Arctic Researches and Life Among the Esquimaux 5: 71

Arellano, Alonso de *6:* 192

Arequipa, Peru *1–4:* 99

Areta (tribe) *1–4:* 384

Arghūn *1–4:* 67

Argo 5: 166

Arguin Island *1–4:* 426

Arias, Pedro *1–4:* 767

Arikara (tribe) *1–4:* 483, 532

Aristotle *1–4:* 5, 9; *6:* 52

B

Bird Woman's River *6:* 165

Birú *1–4:* 670

Biscoe, John *1–4:* 853

Bishop, John *1–4:* 105

Bisland, Elizabeth *6:* 23, 24

Bismarck, North Dakota *1–4:* 532

Bitter Root River *1–4:* 535

Bitterroot Range *1–4:* 534

Bjaaland, Olav *1–4:* 19

Black, Campbell *1–4:* 593

Black, Tom Campbell *1–4:* 591

Black Death *1–4:* 80

Black Flags *1–4:* 398

Black Sea *1–4:* 44–45, 67, 91, 597, 694, 763, 869; *5:* 99

Blackbeard *5:* 50, 52

Blackfoot (tribe) *1–4:* 82, 483, 535

Blackwell's Island *6:* 21, 22

Blaha, John *5:* 111, 114

Blaxland, Gregory *1–4:* 55; *5:* 24–27, 24 (ill.), 25 (ill.)

The Blessing of Burntisland 5: 52

Bligh, William *1–4:* 54, 189, 264, 359

Blom, Kristin *5:* 44

Blom, Ron *5:* 42–44

Blue Mountains *1–4:* 484; *5:* 24–27

Blue Nile River *1–4:* 54; *5:* 158; *6:* 26

Blunt, Anne *1–4:* 107–111

Blunt, Wilfrid Scawen *1–4:* 107–111

Bly, Nellie *6:* **18–25,** 18 (ill.), 22 (ill.)

Bobadilla, Francisco de *1–4:* 251

Bobonaza River *1–4:* 411, 412

Boca del Sierpe *1–4:* 251

Bodega y Quadra, Francisco de la *1–4:* 833

Bodleian Library *6:* 31, 32, 32 (ill.)

Bogotá, Colombia *1–4:* 99, 479; *6:* 143–146

Bohol *6:* 191

Bolivar, Simon *1–4:* 99

Bolling Advanced Weather Station *1–4:* 161

Boma, Zaire *1–4:* 4, 795

Bombay, India *1–4:* 112

Bombay, Sidi Mubarak *1–4:* 112–116, 153–155, 231, 233, 773, 790

Bomokandi River *1–4:* 4

Bonner, T. D. *1–4:* 84

Bonpland, Aimé *1–4:* 474, 476–480, 482; *6:* 146

Book of Joshua *6:* 114

Book of Ser Marco Polo 1–4: 687, 694

Boone, Daniel *1–4:* 117–121, 531

Boone, Daniel Morgan *1–4:* 121

Boone, Rebecca Bryan *1–4:* 117

Boonesboro, Kentucky *1–4:* 119–120

Boothia Peninsula *1–4:* 368

Bora Bora *5:* 36

Bora Island *1–4:* 733

Bordeaux, France *1–4:* 68

Borman, Frank *1–4:* 28

Bornu, Nigeria *1–4:* 71

Bororo (tribe) *6:* 154

Boston, Massachusetts *1–4:* 227

Botany Bay *1–4:* 260, 360, 510–511

Botletle *1–4:* 546

Bou-Am *1–4:* 736

Boudeuse 1–4: 123, 127, 190

Bougainville, Louis-Antoine de *1–4:* 122–128, 190, 510

Bougainville Island *1–4:* 126

Bougainvillea 1–4: 122

Boulogne, France *1–4:* 151

Bounty 1–4: 54, 188

Boxer Rebellion *1–4:* 584

Boyarsky, Victor *1–4:* 803

Boyd, Louise Arner *1–4:* 129–132

Bozeman Pass *1–4:* 536

Braddock, Edward *1–4:* 117

Brahe, William *1–4:* 145–148

Brahmaputra River *1–4:* 421, 752

Bransfield, Edward *1–4:* 91

C

Cabeza de Vaca, Alvar Núñez *1–4:* 164–168, 270, 346, 348

Cabo da Roca, Portugal *1–4:* 247

Cabot, John *1–4:* 169–171, 172; *6:* 44

Cabot, Sebastian *1–4:* 170, 172–175

Cabot Strait *1–4:* 194

Cabral, Pedro Alvares *1–4:* 313, 391, 840

Cabrilho, Joao Rodrigues *1–4:* 176–178

Cache Valley *1–4:* 759

Cadamosto, Alvise da *1–4:* 426

Cádiz, Spain *1–4:* 248, 250, 252, 320, 710, 716; *6:* 143

Caillié, René *1–4:* 73, 179–182, 736

Caillié Travels through Central Africa to Timbuktoo 1–4: 182

Caingangue (tribe) *6:* 155

Cairo, Egypt *1–4:* 45, 49, 51, 55, 76, 89, 111, 114, 152, 289, 416, 506, 578, 583, 591, 721, 786; *5:* 127, 156, 157, 159; *6:* 28, 31, 33, 35, 37, 40, 102

Cajamarca, Inca empire *1–4:* 481, 672, 768

Cajon Pass *1–4:* 621

Calais, France *1–4:* 320

Calcutta, India *1–4:* 421, 491, 575, 577, 755, 807

Calicut, India *1–4:* 78, 222–223, 289, 389–392

California Gold Rush *1–4:* 81, 83; *5:* 136

Caliph al-Muktadir, Abbasid *5:* 75

Callisthenes *1–4:* 9

Callisto *1–4:* 848

Caloris 588

Calypso 1–4: 285

Cambridge, England *1–4:* 499

Cambridge Bay *1–4:* 17

Cambridge University *5:* 92; *6:* 36, 61

Camden, Arkansas *1–4:* 770

Cameahwait *6:* 165

Camelford, Baron *1–4:* 835

Cameron, Verney Lovett *1–4:* 116, 234

Camp VIII *1–4:* 451

Canaan *6:* 114

Canadian Arctic Expedition *1–4:* 856; *5:* 147; *6:* 1, 5

Canadian Rockies *1–4:* 701

Canary Islands *1–4:* 174, 244, 248, 288, 426, 455, 500, 568, 631; *6:* 143

Cannanore, India *1–4:* 289

Canton, China *1–4:* 79, 105, 577, 667, 866; *5:* 57, 128; *6:* 107, 109

Cañar *1–4:* 481

Cao, Diogo *1–4:* 311

Cap Haitien, Haiti *1–4:* 246

Capara *1–4:* 696

Cape Blanco *1–4:* 426

Cape Bojador *1–4:* 425

Cape Breton Island *1–4:* 170; *6:* 2

Cape Canaveral, Florida *1–4:* 26, 28–29, 37, 353, 725; *5:* 82

Cape Chelyuskin *5:* 124

Cape Cod, Massachusetts *1–4:* 213–215; *5:* 47

Cape Columbia *1–4:* 430, 431, 650, 652; *6:* 3

Cape Cross *1–4:* 311

Cape Dan *1–4:* 605

Cape Delgado *1–4:* 505

Cape Disappointment *1–4:* 832

Cape Fear, North Carolina *1–4:* 837–838

Cape Hatteras *1–4:* 837

Cape Hecla *1–4:* 648, 650

Cape Hood *1–4:* 832

Cape Horn *1–4:* 258, 297, 510, 732, 834, 853; *5:* 128; *6:* 178

Cape Leeuwin *1–4:* 361

Cape Maria van Diemen *1–4:* 811

Cape Mendocino *1–4:* 178

Cape of Good Hope *1–4:* 116, 127, 190, 192, 241, 258, 260–262, 265, 288, 311,

Boldface indicates main entries in Volume 6 and their page numbers; *1–4:* refers to entries in the four-volume base set; *5:* refers to entries in Volume 5; *6:* refers to entries in Volume 6; (ill.) following a page number refers to photos, drawings, and maps.

219 | Index

Challenger (space shuttle) *1–4:*
39, 467, 725–726; *5:* 42; *6:*
125, 129–132, 132 (ill.)
H.M.S. *Challenger 1–4:*
209–211, 406
Challenger Flight 51-L *6:* 129
Chalybes *1–4:* 868
Champlain, Samuel de *1–4:*
141–143, 212–217; *6:*
147–149, 148 (ill.)
Ch'ang-an *1–4:* 460–461
Chang Ch'ien *1–4:* 218–220
Channel Islands *1–4:* 178; *6:*
193
Charbonneau, Pomp *1–4:* 532,
534, 536; *6:* 163, 167, 168
Charbonneau, Toussaint *1–4:*
532; *6:* 162, 163, 165–167
Charcot, Jean-Baptiste *5:* 28–34,
28 (ill.), 29 (ill.)
Charcot Land *5:* 33
Charles I (of England) *5:* 51
Charles I (of Spain) *1–4:* 168,
175, 629–630, 768; *6:* 189
Charles II (of England) *1–4:* 227
Charles III (of Spain) *1–4:* 123;
6: 142
Charles V (of Spain) *1–4:* 277,
280–281, 567, 570, 573, 671
Charles X (of France) *1–4:* 326
Charlesbourg, Quebec *1–4:* 196
Charlotte Harbor *1–4:* 697
Charlottesville, Virginia *1–4:*
120, 528
Charlton Island *1–4:* 472
Chasseloup-Laubat, Marquis de
1–4: 395
Chatham 1–4: 832
Chatham Island *1–4:* 301
Cheesman, Evelyn *5:* 35–38, 35
(ill.), 37 (ill.)
Cheirosophus *1–4:* 868–869
Chen Tsu-i *1–4:* 222
Cheng Ho *1–4:* 221–224
Ch'eng-tu *1–4:* 460
Cherokee *1–4:* 118, 119
Chesapeake Bay *1–4:* 142, 470,
764–765
Cheyenne *1–4:* 85
Cheyenne Peak *1–4:* 663

Chiaha *1–4:* 770
Chibcha *1–4:* 479
Chicago River *5:* 107
Chickahominy River *1–4:* 764
Chickasaw (tribe) *1–4:* 770
Chiengmai, Thailand *6:* 174
Chihuahua, Mexico *1–4:* 348,
663
Childersburg, Alabama *1–4:* 770
Children's Crusade *1–4:* 96
Chillicothe, Ohio *1–4:* 120
Chiloe Island *1–4:* 300
Chimbu Valley *1–4:* 521
Chin-liu, China *1–4:* 460
China Illustrata 6: 75
China Inland Mission *1–4:* 814
China Sea *6:* 149, 150, 152
Chinese Nationalists *5:* 98
Chira River *1–4:* 672
Chirikov, Alexei Ilyich *5:* 22, 23
Chitambo *1–4:* 554
Cho Oyu *1–4:* 450
Chobe River *1–4:* 547–548
Choctaw Bluff, Alabama *1–4:*
770
Cholon (Saigon, Vietnam) *1–4:*
394
Cholula, Mexico *1–4:* 278
Choqquequirau, Peru *1–4:* 99
Chouart des Groseilliers, Médard
1–4: 225–230
Christa McAuliffe Fellowship *6:*
133
Christian, Fletcher *1–4:* 189
Christmas Island *1–4:* 265
Chryse Planitia *1–4:* 845
Chu Chan-chi *1–4:* 223
Chu Ti *1–4:* 222
Ch'üan-chou, China *1–4:* 79
Chukchi (tribe) *6:* 6
Chukchi Peninsula *1–4:* 62
Chukchi Sea *1–4:* 611
Chuma, James *1–4:* 116,
231–237, 552, 554, 826
Church Missionary Society *1–4:*
503, 505
Church of England *1–4:* 316
Church of Vidigueira *1–4:* 392
Churchill, Winston *1–4:* 748
Churchill River *1–4:* 561

Cooper's Creek *1–4:* 145–147

Coos Bay *1–4:* 318

Coosa River *1–4:* 770

Copiapó, Peru *1–4:* 301

Coppermine River *1–4:* 366–367, 641

Coptic Christians *1–4:* 598

Coptos, Egypt *6:* 92

Coquivacoa *1–4:* 624

Coqville 1–4: 326

Cordillera Mountains *1–4:* 299

Cordoba, Francisco Hernandez de *1–4:* 275, 767

Córdoba, Spain *1–4:* 241, 415

Corinthian War *1–4:* 870

Cornwallis Island *1–4:* 368

Coronado, Francisco Vásquez de *1–4:* 164, 167, 176, 268–273, 281, 345, 349; *5:* 5

Coronation Gulf *5:* 147

Corps of Discovery *6:* 161, 163–165, 168

Corrective Optics Space Telescope Axial Replacement (COSTAR) *1–4:* 468

Corrigan, Sharon Christa. *See* McAuliffe, Christa

Corte-Real, Gaspar *1–4:* 171; ***6: 42–47,*** 43 (ill.)

Corte-Real, Joäo Vaz *6:* 42

Corte-Real, Miguel *6: 42–47,* 43 (ill.)

Cortés, Hernán *1–4:* 176–177, 274–281, 669, 672; *5:* 1, 2

Coryndon Memorial Museum *5:* 92

Cosa, Juan de la *1–4:* 623

Cosa *1–4:* 770

Cosmonauts *5:* 109, 113

Cosmopolitan 1–4: 332; *6:* 85

Cossacks *1–4:* 40–42, 421; *5:* 19, 128, 131, 133

Council of Clermont (1095) *1–4:* 96

Courantyne River *6:* 174

Coureur de bois (forest runner) *6:* 147, 149

Cousteau, Jacques *1–4:* 282–286; *5:* 116; *6:* 53

The Cousteau Almanac of the Environment 1–4: 285

Covilha, Pero da *1–4:* 287–291

Cozumel, Cuba *1–4:* 275–276

Craterus *1–4:* 11, 12

Cree (tribe) *1–4:* 227

Crèvecoeur *1–4:* 514

Crichton, Michael *5:* 76, 79

Crimea, Ukraine *1–4:* 77, 433, 773

Crimean War *1–4:* 153, 773; *5:* 136

Crippen, Robert *1–4:* 725

Crocker, George *1–4:* 649

Crocker Land *1–4:* 649

Crooked Island, Bahama Islands *1–4:* 245

The Crossing of Antarctica 1–4: 377

Crow *1–4:* 81–82, 85

Crown Point, New York *1–4:* 215

Croydon Airfield *1–4:* 490

Crusades *1–4:* 96–97, 186, 424

Cuauhtémoc *1–4:* 279

Cuba *1–4:* 165, 249, 481, 625, 696–698, 768–769

Cubagua Island *1–4:* 630–631

Cueva, Beatriz de la *5:* 5

Cuiabá, Argentina *6:* 154

Culiacán, Mexico *1–4:* 167, 270

Cumaná *1–4:* 476

Cumberland 1–4: 363

Cumberland Gap *1–4:* 118, 119

Cumberland Peninsula *1–4:* 525

Cumberland valley *1–4:* 119

Cunene River *1–4:* 139

Cunningham, Walter *1–4:* 28

Curaçao Island *1–4:* 624; *6:* 143

Curtiss Field *1–4:* 539

Custer, George Armstrong *1–4:* 789

Cutler, W. E. *5:* 92

Cuzco, Peru *1–4:* 99, 627, 672, 768

Cyrene, Libya *1–4:* 434

Cyrus *1–4:* 867–868

Boldface indicates main entries in Volume 6 and their page numbers; *1–4:* refers to entries in the four-volume base set; *5:* refers to entries in Volume 5; *6:* refers to entries in Volume 6; (ill.) following a page number refers to photos, drawings, and maps.

223 | Index

D

d'Orville, Albert *6:* 70, 71, 73, 74

Dahar-June *1–4:* 787

Dahe, Qin *1–4:* 803

Daily Mail 1–4: 492

Dakar, Senegal *1–4:* 426

Dalai Lama *1–4:* 307–309, 575–577, 753

The Dalles, Oregon *1–4:* 621

Damascus, Syria *1–4:* 76, 88, 97, 109, 157, 597

Damietta, Egypt *1–4:* 97

Danube River *1–4:* 44

Dardanelles *1–4:* 6

Darién *1–4:* 616

Darien Peninsula *1–4:* 625, 670

Darius I (of Persia) *1–4:* 434

Darius II (of Persia) *1–4:* 867

Darius III (of Persia) *1–4:* 7, 8

Darling, William *1–4:* 357

Darling River *1–4:* 145, 147

Dartmouth, England *1–4:* 472

Dartmouth College *5:* 148

Darwin, Charles *1–4:* 292–305, 474

Darwin, Erasmus *1–4:* 292

Darwin, Australia *1–4:* 491–492

Daurians *5:* 133; *6:* 122

David, Edgeworth *1–4:* 747

David-Neel, Alexandra *1–4:* 306–310

Davis, John *1–4:* 458

Davis Strait *1–4:* 472, 525; *6:* 44

De Long, George Washington *1–4:* 606; *6:* 5

De Pere, Wisconsin *5:* 107

De Soto, Hernando. *See* Soto, Hernando de

Dead Sea *1–4:* 597; *6:* 114

Dean Channel *1–4:* 564

Deccan, India *1–4:* 596

Deena *1–4:* 633

Deep Flight 6: 55, 56

Deep Ocean Engineering *6:* 54

Deep Rover 6: 54, 54 (ill.), 55

Deep Sea Drilling Project *1–4:* 406

Deganawidah *1–4:* 215

Deimos *1–4:* 587

Delabarre, Edmund B. *6:* 45, 47

Delaware Bay *1–4:* 470

Delaware River *1–4:* 470

Delft 1–4: 487

Delhi, India *1–4:* 23; *6:* 75

Demerara, Guyana *6:* 169

Denbei *1–4:* 42

Denmark Strait *6:* 44

Denver, Colorado *1–4:* 84

Derb-el-Haj *1–4:* 76

Derendingen *1–4:* 502

Descartes Mountains *1–4:* 32

Déscription de la Louisiane 6: 99

A Description of New England 1–4: 765

Desideri, Ippolito *1–4:* 576

Detroit, Michigan *1–4:* 120, 485, 538

Detroit Arctic Expedition *1–4:* 857

Devil's Ballroom *1–4:* 20

Devon Island *1–4:* 16

Dhofar Mountains *5:* 42

Dias, Bartolomeu *1–4:* 241, 288, 311–314, 386, 388, 426

Dias, Dinis *1–4:* 426

Días, Melchor *1–4:* 270, 271

Dickson, James *1–4:* 633, 635

Diderot, Denis *1–4:* 127

Diebetsch, Josephine *1–4:* 645

Diemen, Anthony van *1–4:* 810

Dieppe, France *1–4:* 837

Diestel, Bernard *6:* 70

Dietrich, Rosine *1–4:* 504

Digges Island *1–4:* 473

Digging Up Jericho 6: 119

Dighton, Massachusetts *6:* 45

Dighton Rock *6:* 45–47, 46 (ill.)

Dingri, Tibet *6:* 78, 79

Diomede Islands *5:* 20

Dione, moon *1–4:* 849

Discoverie of Guiana 1–4: 715

Discovery 1–4: 264–266, 464, 472–473, 830–833

Discovery: The Autobiography of Vilhjalmur Stefansson 5: 149

Disko Bay *5:* 125

Dispatch 6: 19–21

District of Orleans *1–4:* 536

Diyarbakir *1–4:* 77

Djakarta, Indonesia *1–4:* 127, 190

Djenné, Mali *1–4:* 180, 579

Dnieper River *1–4:* 41

Dolak Island *1–4:* 487

Dolphin 1–4: 188, 190, 191, 257

Donn River *1–4:* 41

Donnacona *1–4:* 194, 195

Dorantes, Andres *1–4:* 165–166, 347–348

Doudart de Lagrée, Ernest *1–4:* 396

Drake, Francis *1–4:* 315–320

Druid 1–4: 296

Druses *1–4:* 786–787

Druze *1–4:* 87

Dry Tortugas *1–4:* 697

Du Chaillu, Paul *1–4:* 321–324

Du Pont, François Gravé *1–4:* 213

Dubois River *1–4:* 530

Dudh Kosi River *1–4:* 752; *6:* 79

Duifken 1–4: 486–487

Duke, Charles *1–4:* 32

Dulhut, Daniel Greysolon *6:* 98

Duluth, Minnesota *1–4:* 142, 823

Dumont d'Urville, Jules-Sébastien-César *1–4:* 325–329, 511, 853

Dundee Island *1–4:* 339

Dunhuang, China *5:* 55

Dupuis, Jean *1–4:* 396–398

Dusky Sound *1–4:* 263

Dutch East India Company *1–4:* 454–455, 469, 486, 732, 809–810; *6:* 175, 176, 179, 180

Dutch East Indies (Indonesia) *1–4:* 328; *5:* 19, 129, 130

Dwyer, Michael *1–4:* 520

Dyak (tribe) *5:* 129

Dza-chu River *1–4:* 706

Dzungaria *1–4:* 707

E

Eagle 1–4: 37–38

Eagle, Alaska *1–4:* 18

Eaglet 1–4: 227

Eannes, Gil *1–4:* 426

Earhart, Amelia *1–4:* 330–335, 493

Earle, Sylvia *6:* **45–56,** 48 (ill.), 50 (ill.), 55 (ill.)

Earp, Wyatt *1–4:* 337

East Africa *1–4:* 502–505, 507; *5:* 91–93, 95, 140

East India Company *1–4:* 151, 564, 575, 811, 733

Easter Island *1–4:* 263, 732

Eastman, Charles *6:* 166

Eaters of the Dead 5: 76

Ebierbing *5:* 70, 71, 73

Ebro River *1–4:* 94

Ecbatana (Hamadan, Iran) *1–4:* 220

Edmonton, Alberta *1–4:* 701, 703

Edward I (of England) *1–4:* 68

Edward VI (of England) *1–4:* 175

Edwards Air Force Base *1–4:* 726, 742, 872, 874

Edy, Montana *1–4:* 759

Eendracht 6: 176, 178–180

Effie M. Morrissey 7, 8

Eielson, Carl *1–4:* 858

Eight Years' Wanderings in Ceylon 1–4: 44

Einstein Cross *1–4:* 467

Eisele, Don *1–4:* 28

Eisenhower, Dwight D. *1–4:* 428, 542

El Carmen, Patagonia *1–4:* 298

El Haura, Arabia *1–4:* 384

El-Mahdi *1–4:* 580, 582, 583

El Misti *1–4:* 654

Elburz Mountains *6:* 184

Elcano, Juan Sebastián de *1–4:* 571–573; *6:* 189

Elephant Island *1–4:* 748–749

Eletrophorus electricus 1–4: 477

Elgon, Mount *1–4:* 828

Boldface indicates main entries in Volume 6 and their page numbers; *1–4:* refers to entries in the four-volume base set; *5:* refers to entries in Volume 5; *6:* refers to entries in Volume 6; (ill.) following a page number refers to photos, drawings, and maps.

225 | Index

Boldface indicates main entries in Volume 6 and their page numbers; *1–4:* refers to entries in the four-volume base set; *5:* refers to entries in Volume 5; *6:* refers to entries in Volume 6; (ill.) following a page number refers to photos, drawings, and maps.

227 | Index

Gama, Paolo da *1–4:* 387

Gama, Vasco da *1–4:* 224, 288, 313, 386–392

Gambia River *1–4:* 426, 633; *6:* 103

Gandak River *6:* 78

Ganges River *1–4:* 24, 453, 462–463, 598; *5:* 56; *6:* 107, 108

Ganymede *1–4:* 848

Garhwal, India *1–4:* 24

Garnier, Francis *1–4:* 393–399

Garstang, John *6:* 115

Gaspé Bay *1–4:* 194

Gaspé Peninsula *1–4:* 194–195, 214

Gatty, Harold *1–4:* 700–702

Gaugamela, Assyria *1–4:* 8

Gauhati *1–4:* 463

Gautama, Siddhartha. *See* Siddhartha Gautama

Gaza *1–4:* 7

Gedrosia *1–4:* 12

Gemini 6 1–4: 28

Gemini 8 1–4: 36, 37

Genesee River *1–4:* 142

Genesis Rock *1–4:* 32

Geneva, Switzerland *5:* 98, 99

Genghis Khan *1–4:* 66, 67, 184

Genoa, Italy *1–4:* 95, 694

Geodesy *5:* 86

Geographical Magazine 1–4: 755

George III (of England) *1–4:* 53; *6:* 33

Georges River *1–4:* 360

Georgetown, British Guiana *6:* 170, 173

Georgian Bay *1–4:* 142; *6:* 148, 151

Geraldton, Australia *5:* 60

Gerlache, Adrien de *1–4:* 15

German Atlantic Expedition *6:* 134, 136

Ghat, Libya *1–4:* 71

Gibson Desert *5:* 60

Gila River *1–4:* 271

Gilbert, Humphrey *1–4:* 712

Gilbert Island *1–4:* 326

Gilgit *5:* 56

Gilgit range *1–4:* 807

Ginuha Genoa, Italy *1–4:* 67

Gjöa 1–4: 16–18

Gjöa Haven *1–4:* 16–17

Gladstone, William *1–4:* 105

Glenn, John *1–4:* 31, 400–405; *6:* 126

Glomar Challenger 1–4: 406–408

Gloster Meteor 1–4: 872

Goa, India *1–4:* 25, 289, 636, 666, 667–668, 865–866

Gobi Desert *1–4:* 308, 420, 461, 691, 705, 707; *6:* 86

Godin des Odonais, Isabel *1–4:* 409–414

Godin des Odonais, Jean *1–4:* 409–411, 413–414

Godthaab, Greenland *1–4:* 606; *5:* 122

Goering, Hermann *1–4:* 703

Goethe, Johann Wolfgang von *1–4:* 475

Golden Hind 1–4: 318, 319

Gombe National Park *5:* 117; *6:* 58

Gomes, Diogo *1–4:* 427

Gomez, Fernao *1–4:* 291

Gonçalves, Antao *1–4:* 426

Gonam River *5:* 132, 133

Gondar, Ethiopia *6:* 29–31

Gondokoro, Sudan *1–4:* 45, 48–51, 114, 156, 776–777; *5:* 158

Góngora, Antonio Caballero y *6:* 145

Goodall, Jane *5:* 117; *6:* 58–60

Gordon, Charles "Chinese" *1–4:* 51, 580, 796

Gordon, George *1–4:* 358

Gordon, Richard *1–4:* 30

Goree Island *1–4:* 636; *6:* 102

Gorgan, Iran *1–4:* 416

Gorges, Ferdinando *1–4:* 765

Gorillas in the Mist 6: 61

Goroka Valley *1–4:* 521

Gouda *1–4:* 454

Graf Zeppelin 1–4: 338

Graham Land *1–4:* 15; *5:* 31

Boldface indicates main entries in Volume 6 and their page numbers; *1–4:* refers to entries in the four-volume base set; *5:* refers to entries in Volume 5; *6:* refers to entries in Volume 6; (ill.) following a page number refers to photos, drawings, and maps.

229 | Index

Gulf of Suez *1–4:* 384
Gulf of Taranto *1–4:* 434
Gulf of Tonkin *1–4:* 396
Gulf of Urabá *1–4:* 615, 625, 670
Gulf St. Vincent *1–4:* 362
Gunnbjörn's Skerries *1–4:* 342
Gurgan, Persia *6:* 139
Gustav V (of Sweden) *1–4:* 422
Güyük *1–4:* 185, 186
Gwadar, Pakistan *1–4:* 10
Gymnias *1–4:* 868

H

Haakon VII (of Norway) *1–4:* 19, 130
Hab River *1–4:* 10
Hadhramaut, Yemen *1–4:* 384; *6:* 184, 185
Hadjui *1–4:* 736
Hagia Sophia *1–4:* 67, 96
The Hague, the Netherlands *5:* 18, 155
Hail, Saudi Arabia *1–4:* 88
Haiphong, Vietnam *1–4:* 398
Haise, Fred *1–4:* 30
Half Moon 1–4: 469–470
Halicarnassus *1–4:* 6
Hall, Charles Francis *5:* 68–74, 69 (ill.)
Hall, F. C. *1–4:* 700
Hall Land *5:* 72
Hallett, Goody *5:* 47
Hamadan, Iran *1–4:* 8
Hamburg, Germany *1–4:* 16; *6:* 134
Ha-mi *1–4:* 461
Hamid, Abdul *1–4:* 751
Hankow, China *1–4:* 396, 397
Hanoi, Vietnam *1–4:* 393, 398–399
Hanssen, Helmer *1–4:* 19
Harana, Diego de *1–4:* 246
Harar, Ethiopia *1–4:* 153
Harbor Grace, Newfoundland *1–4:* 333

Hari Ram *1–4:* 752; *6: 76–79,* 77 (ill.)
Harrison, Marguerite Baker *6: 81–89,* 81 (ill.), 85 (ill.), 87 (ill.)
Harrison, Thomas Bullitt *6:* 82
Harrison, William Henry *1–4:* 82
Hartog, Dirk *1–4:* 488
Hassel, Sverre *1–4:* 19
Hatshepsut *6: 90–94,* 90 (ill.), 93 (ill.)
Hatton, Denys Finch *1–4:* 590
Hauptmann, Bruno *1–4:* 541
Hawaiian Islands *1–4:* 104, 255, 265, 408, 484, 510, 542, 832, 834, 854
Hawikuh, New Mexico *1–4:* 270, 349
Hawkes, Graham *6:* 53–55
Hearne, Samuel *1–4:* 509, 821
The Heart of the Antarctic 1–4: 747
Hebard, Grace *6:* 166
Hebron, Jordan *1–4:* 97
Hecla 1–4: 639–642
Hecla Bay *1–4:* 640
Hecla Strait *1–4:* 641
Hedges, George *5:* 43, 45
Hedin, Sven *1–4:* 418–423, 728, 807
Heemskerk, Jacob van *5:* 16, 17
Heemskerk 1–4: 810
Hejaz, Saudi Arabia *6:* 39
Heligoland Island *1–4:* 711
Hellenism *1–4:* 5, 12
Henderson, Richard *1–4:* 118–119
Hendrik, Hans *5:* 73
Hennepin, Louis *1–4:* 513–514; *6: 95–100,* 95 (ill.), 97 (ill.), 99 (ill.)
Henrietta Bird Hospital *1–4:* 105
Henry, Andrew *5:* 6
Henry IV (of France) *1–4:* 213, 215
Henry VII (of Norway) *1–4:* 170
Henry VIII (of England) *1–4:* 316

Hudson River *1–4:* 470; *6:* 149
Hudson Strait *1–4:* 472
Hudson's Bay Company *1–4:* 225, 227, 230, 366, 564, 618–619, 622, 759, 761, 821–823
Hulagu Khan *1–4:* 688
Humber River *1–4:* 142
Humboldt, Alexander von *1–4:* 293, 474–482, 505; *6:* 145, 145 (ill.), 146, 173
Humboldt, Alexander von (son) *1–4:* 474
Humboldt, Wilhelm von *1–4:* 474–475
Humboldt Current *1–4:* 481
Humboldt River *1–4:* 620
Humboldt Sink *1–4:* 620–621
Humphreys, Jack *1–4:* 492
Hunt, John *1–4:* 451
Hunt, Wilson Price *1–4:* 483–485
Hupei *5:* 54, 57
Huron (tribe) *1–4:* 141–143, 215–217, 226; *6:* 151
Hwang Ho River *1–4:* 707
Hyksos people *6:* 91

I

I-Ching *6:* **106–109,** 108 (ill.)
Iberian Peninsula *1–4:* 95; *6:* 138
Ibn Abdullah, Ibrahim *6:* 36
Ibn Battutah, Abu Abdallah 75–80, 181
Ibn Fadlan, Ahmad *5:* 75–79, 77 (ill.), 78 (ill.)
Ibn Hawkal, Abu al-Kasim Ibn Ali al-Nasibi *1–4:* 415–417
Ice Fjord *1–4:* 131
Ice Haven *5:* 17, 18
Ictis Island, St. Michael's Mount, Cornwall *1–4:* 710
Id-al-Khabir *1–4:* 152
Iditarod *5:* 62
Igloolik Island *1–4:* 641
Iguaçu Falls *1–4:* 168

Il-Khan Abaga *1–4:* 67–68, 693
Ile-a-la-Crosse *1–4:* 561, 619
Ili River *1–4:* 219
Iliad 5: 135, 137, 138
Illinois (tribe) *5:* 104, 107
Illinois River *1–4:* 497, 516; *5:* 107; *6:* 96, 98, 152
Illyria *1–4:* 6
Imperial Herbarium *5:* 159
In Darkest Africa 1–4: 799
Inca Empire *1–4:* 98–102, 174, 627, 669, 671, 768; *5:* 5
Independence Bay *1–4:* 429, 647
Indian Ocean *1–4:* 10, 11, 456, 488, 504, 598; *6:* 49
Indus River *1–4:* 5, 9, 11, 78, 421, 434–435, 463, 598, 754–755, 808; *5:* 56; *6:* 75
Indus Valley *1–4:* 9, 596
Innocent IV *1–4:* 183
Inquisition *1–4:* 95
Inside Passage, Alaska *1–4:* 834
International Date Line *1–4:* 573
International Geophysical Year *1–4:* 93, 340, 351, 376, 801; *6:* 136
International Memorial *5:* 168
International Space Station (ISS) *5:* 109, 110, 114
International Trans-Antarctica Expedition *1–4:* 803
International Women's Peace Congress *1–4:* 820
Inuit (tribe) *1–4:* 344, 368, 428–432, 473, 498, 641, 645, 647–648, 650; *5:* 68, 70, 71, 73, 74, 122, 145–147; *6:* 1–3, 6
Investigator 1–4: 361–364, 600–603
Investigator Strait *1–4:* 362
Iraq Museum *1–4:* 89
Irish Sea *1–4:* 711
Irkutsk *1–4:* 701, 703
Iron Gates *1–4:* 461
Iroquois (tribe) *1–4:* 142, 194–196, 215, 217, 225–227, 513, 765; *6:* 148, 152

John F. Kennedy Space Center *1–4:* 402, 587

John I (of Portugal) *1–4:* 240, 247, 288, 424, 425

John II (of Portugal) *1–4:* 288, 290, 291, 311, 313, 386

John III (of Portugal) *1–4:* 864

John XXII (Pope) *6:* 111

John of Monte Corvino *1–4:* 68; *6:* 110

Johns Hopkins University *1–4:* 337

Johnson, Amy *1–4:* 333, 489–493

Johnson, Lyndon B. *1–4:* 404

Johnson, Samuel *6:* 33

Johnson Space Center *5:* 114; *6:* 128, 132

Johnston, Keith *1–4:* 235, 236, 826

Johore *1–4:* 458

Joinville Land *1–4:* 328

Joliba *1–4:* 636, 637

Jolliet, Louis *1–4:* 494–498, 513, 516; *5:* 104, 106–108

Jordan River *6:* 37, 114

Jordan Valley *1–4:* 597

Jordanus of Séverac *6:* **110–112,** 112 (ill.)

José, Amaro *1–4:* 57–60 139

Josephine Ford *1–4:* 160

Joshua era *6:* 115, 116

A Journey in Ashango Land *1–4:* 324

Journal of a Voyage by Order of the King to the Equator *5:* 89

Journal of the Royal Geographical Society *6:* 170

"J.T." : The Biography of an African Monkey *1–4:* 2

Juan Fernández Islands *1–4:* 124, 188, 569, 732; Juan Fernández Islands *6:* 49, 178

Juba, Somalia *1–4:* 223

Juba, Sudan *1–4:* 591; *5:* 160

Jumano (tribe) *1–4:* 347

Jumla, Nepal *6:* 78

Jungle Portraits *1–4:* 4

Junkers, Hugo *1–4:* 422

Jupiter *1–4:* 464, 468, 847–850

Jupiter Inlet *1–4:* 697

Jur River *1–4:* 582

K

Ka'abah *1–4:* 152

Kabalega Falls *1–4:* 43

Kabara *1–4:* 636; *6:* 59

Kabul, Afghanistan *1–4:* 8, 434, 808

Kabul River *1–4:* 434, 462; *5:* 56

Kabylia campaigns *1–4:* 736

Kadiköy *1–4:* 869

Ka-erh *1–4:* 754–755

Kafu River *1–4:* 47

Kagoshima *1–4:* 667

Kai Island *1–4:* 487

K'ai-feng *1–4:* 687

Kailas Mountains *1–4:* 421

Kalahari Desert *1–4:* 544, 546

Kalami River *1–4:* 10

Kalgan, China *1–4:* 705

Kalomo River *1–4:* 549

Kalongosi River *1–4:* 553

Kamalia *1–4:* 634

Kamchadals *1–4:* 42

Kamchatka *1–4:* 511

Kamchatka Mountains *1–4:* 41

Kamchatka Peninsula *1–4:* 40–42, 267, 510; *5:* 20

Kamchatka River *1–4:* 41, 42

Kamehameha (of Hawaii) *1–4:* 64, 832, 834

Kanawha valley *1–4:* 121

Kanbaya, port *1–4:* 596

Kan-chou River *1–4:* 808

Kane, Elisha Kent *1–4:* 644; *5:* 71, 72

Kangaroo Island *1–4:* 362

Kannauj *1–4:* 462

Kano, Nigeria *1–4:* 71

Kanpur *1–4:* 462

Kansas (tribe) *1–4:* 662

Kansu *5:* 102

Kapuas River *5:* 129

Kara Sea *5:* 16

Boldface indicates main entries in Volume 6 and their page numbers; *1–4:* refers to entries in the four-volume base set; *5:* refers to entries in Volume 5; *6:* refers to entries in Volume 6; (ill.) following a page number refers to photos, drawings, and maps.

235 | Index

Kircher, Athanasius *6:* 75

Kirghiz (Kazakh) *5:* 100

Kiribati Islands *1–4:* 733

Kisangani, Zaire *1–4:* 4, 795

Kisulidini *1–4:* 721, 722

Kisumu *1–4:* 3

Kitchener, Horatio Herbert *1–4:* 583

Kitty Hawk, North Carolina *1–4:* 837

Kitui *1–4:* 505

Kivoi, King *1–4:* 506

Klamath Lake *1–4:* 621

Klamath River *1–4:* 620

Kmeri (of Usambara) *1–4:* 504

Knife River *6:* 162

Knorr 5: 165

Knox Coast *1–4:* 853

Kodiak Island, Alaska *1–4:* 62–63

Koko Nor *1–4:* 705, 707, 728, 752

Kolobeng *1–4:* 544, 548

Kootenay (tribe) *1–4:* 824

The Koran *6:* 36, 138

Korean War *1–4:* 35, 401

Korntal *1–4:* 506, 507

Korolov, Sergei *1–4:* 380, 778–779

Korosko *5:* 158

Kosmos 1–4: 482

Koundian *1–4:* 579

Kouroussa, Guinea *1–4:* 180

Krapf, Johann Ludwig *1–4:* 152, 502–507, 718, 721–722, 827

Krestovka River *1–4:* 41

Kronshlot, Russia *1–4:* 91, 93

Kublai Khan *1–4:* 65–66, 687–689, 691–693

Kucha *1–4:* 461

Kukawa, Nigeria *1–4:* 72–74, 737

Kukukuku (tribe) *1–4:* 521

Kuldja *1–4:* 706

Kumara River *6:* 124

Kumbum *1–4:* 728

Kun Lun Shan mountains *1–4:* 219, 707, 807

K'un-ming, China *1–4:* 221, 396, 692

Kurdistan, Turkey *5:* 128

Kurdistan Mountains *1–4:* 868

Kuril Islands *1–4:* 40; *5:* 22

Kuruman *1–4:* 544

Kuskov, I. A. *1–4:* 64

Kuti Pass *6:* 78

Kwango River *1–4:* 138, 549

Kyakhta, Russia *1–4:* 420, 705

Kyasha *1–4:* 667

Kyi-Chu River *1–4:* 753

Kyirong *1–4:* 753

Kyoto, Japan *1–4:* 865

Kyrgyzstan *1–4:* 461

Kyushu *1–4:* 667, 865–866

Kyzyl Kum Desert *5:* 101

L

La Boussole 1–4: 509, 511

La Concepción de Urbana *1–4:* 478

La Condamine, Charles-Marie de *1–4:* 409–410, 476–477, 481; *6:* 144

La Coruña, Spain *6:* 189

La Dauphine 1–4: 837–838

La Guajira *1–4:* 624–625

La Hogue 1–4: 638

La Motte, Dominique *1–4:* 513

La Navidad (Limonade-Bord-de-Mer, Haiti) *1–4:* 246, 248

La Paz, Bolivia *1–4:* 654

La Paz Bay *1–4:* 280–281

La Pérouse, Jean-François de Galaup, comte de *1–4:* 326, 508–511

La Pérouse Strait *1–4:* 510

La Relación y Comentarios 1–4: 168

La Rochelle, France *1–4:* 766; *5:* 87

La Salle, René-Robert Cavelier de *1–4:* 512–518; *6:* 95, 100

La Salle, Illinois *1–4:* 516

Lacerda, Francisco José de *1–4:* 57–58

Boldface indicates main entries in Volume 6 and their page numbers; *1–4:* refers to entries in the four-volume base set; *5:* refers to entries in Volume 5; *6:* refers to entries in Volume 6; (ill.) following a page number refers to photos, drawings, and maps.

237 | Index

Lassen Volcanic National Park *1–4:* 83

L'Astrolabe 1–4: 509–511

Latakia, Syria *1–4:* 787

Lavaca River *1–4:* 518

Lawrence, T. E. *1–4:* 87, 89; *5:* 41

Lawrence, Wendy *5:* 114

Lawrence of Arabia. *See* Lawrence, T. E.

Lazarev, Mikhail *1–4:* 91

Le Bourget Field *1–4:* 540

Le Havre, France *5:* 30, 32

Le Jeune, Paul *6:* 149

Le Maire, Isaac *6:* 176, 181

Le Maire, Jacob *6:* 179–181

Le Maire Strait *6:* 180

League of Nations *1–4:* 522

Leahy, Dan *1–4:* 521–523

Leahy, Michael J. *1–4:* 519–523

Leahy, Patrick "Paddy" *1–4:* 521

Leakey, Louis S. B. *5:* 91–97, 91 (ill.), 94 (ill.); *6:* 58, 58 (ill.), 59

Leakey, Mary *5:* 91–97, 92 (ill.), 94 (ill.), 117; *6:* 58

Leakey, Richard *5:* 91–97, 93 (ill.), 94 (ill.)

Ledyard, John *1–4:* 55, 632; *6:* 101

Leech Lake *1–4:* 662

Leeward Islands *1–4:* 357

Legazpi, Miguel Lopez de *6:* 191, 192

Legion of Honor *1–4:* 128, 579

Leh, India *1–4:* 421, 755

Leicester, England *6:* 115

Leichhardt, Friedrich Wilhelm Ludwig *5:* 58

Leif Eriksson *1–4:* 251, 343, 524–527

Leifrsbudir *1–4:* 526–527

Leif's Booths *1–4:* 526

Leigh, Linda *6:* 15

Leith (Edinburgh, Scotland) *5:* 51

Lemhi River *1–4:* 533–534

Lena River *5:* 124, 131, 134

Lennon, Patrick *1–4:* 296

Leopold II (of Belguim) *1–4:* 134–136, 738, 796–797, 799

Lesseps, Jean de *1–4:* 510

Leticia, Colombia *6:* 158

Lett River *5:* 26

Levant *1–4:* 787

Lewis, Meriwether *1–4:* 458, 528–537; *5:* 6; *6:* 64, 65, 161–163, 162 (ill.), 165–168

Lhasa, Tibet *1–4:* 24, 306, 308–309, 421, 574–577, 707, 727–729, 753, 813–815; *6:* 71–73, 72 (ill.)

Liang-chou *1–4:* 461

Liber Tatarorum 1–4: 186

Libreville, Gabon *1–4:* 135–136

Liegnitz, Poland *1–4:* 184

The Life and Adventures of James P. Beckwourth, Mountaineer, Scout, Pioneer, and Chief of the Crow Nation 1–4: 84

Lillooet, British Columbia *6:* 66

Lima, Rodrigo da *1–4:* 291

Lima, Peru *1–4:* 99, 157, 481, 627, 673; *5:* 88

Lincoln, Abraham *1–4:* 374

Lincoln, Nebraska *1–4:* 538

Lindbergh, Ann Morrow *1–4:* 542

Lindbergh, Charles *1–4:* 160, 492, 538–542, 592, 743

Linenger, Jerry *5:* 114

Linnaean Society *1–4:* 304

Linnaeus, Carolus *1–4:* 53; *6:* 144, 145

Linschoten, Jan Huyghen van *1–4:* 455; *5:* 14–17

Linyanti *1–4:* 549

Lippershey, Hans *1–4:* 464

Lisa, Manuel *1–4:* 483

Lisbon, Portugal *1–4:* 239, 241, 312–313, 387, 390, 454–455, 666, 668; *6:* 43–45, 190

Lisiansky, Yuri *1–4:* 63

Little Abbai River *6:* 30

Little America 1–4: 160–161

Little America II 1–4: 338–339

Little Falls, Minnesota *1–4:* 538

Livingstone, David *1–4:* 60, 74, 115–116, 134, 231–236, 397,

Machiparo *1–4:* 630
Machu Picchu *1–4:* 98, 100, 102
Mackenzie, Alexander *1–4:* 367,
    560–565, 834; *6:* 65, 66
Mackenzie, Charles Frederick
    1–4: 231
Mackenzie Bay *5:* 146
Mackenzie Delta *1–4:* 601
Mackenzie Pass *1–4:* 563
Mackenzie River *1–4:* 18, 367,
    560, 562, 601, 801; *5:* 146
Mackinac *1–4:* 496, 514
Macquarie Island *1–4:* 92
Mactan Island *1–4:* 570
Madeira Islands *1–4:* 19, 239,
    425
Madeira River *1–4:* 630
Madison, James *1–4:* 533
Madison River *1–4:* 533
Madras, India *6:* 110
Madrid, Spain *6:* 142, 146
Madura *1–4:* 457
Magadha, India *1–4:* 462; *5:*
    56; *6:* 108
Magdalen Islands *1–4:* 194
Magdalena River *1–4:* 479, 615;
    6: 143, 145, 146
Magellan, Ferdinand *1–4:* 174,
    566–573; *6:* 189
Magomero, Africa *1–4:* 231
Maharashtra *1–4:* 463
Mahdia, Tunisia *1–4:* 415
Maigaard, Christian *1–4:* 645
Maillart, Ella *5:* 98–103, 98
    (ill.), 100 (ill.)
Makatéa Island *1–4:* 733
Makololo *1–4:* 546–550
Makran Coast, Pakistan *1–4:*
    10–11
Malabar Coast *6:* 111
Malacca, Malaya *1–4:* 223, 667,
    865
Malaga, Spain *1–4:* 79
Malagarasi River *1–4:* 790
Malakal *1–4:* 591
Malange, Angola *1–4:* 138
Malay Archipelago *1–4:* 327,
    459, 666, 742, 865
Malay Peninsula *1–4:* 105, 666,
    692; *6:* 109, 174

Maldive Islands *1–4:* 78, 223
Maldonado, Pedro Vicente *5:*
    87, 88
Malheur River *1–4:* 620
Malindi, Kenya *1–4:* 223, 290,
    389–390
Malta Island *1–4:* 785
Malthus, Thomas
Mambirima Falls *1–4:* 140
Mana, India *1–4:* 24
Mana Pass *1–4:* 24, 754
Manacupuru *5:* 152
Manaus, Brazil *6:* 155
Manco *1–4:* 672
Manco II *1–4:* 99
Mandan (tribe) *1–4:* 532, 823; *6:*
    162, 167
Mandarin *1–4:* 460
Mandingo language *6:* 102, 103
Manhattan *1–4:* 470
S.S. *Manhattan* *1–4:* 17
Manila, Philippines *6:* 193
Manila Galleon *6:* 193
Mankinga (of the Chagga)
    719–721
Manning, Thomas *1–4:* 574–577
Manta *5:* 87
Manoa, South America *1–4:* 715
Manuel Comnenus *1–4:* 95, 96
Manuel I (of Portugal) *1–4:* 313,
    386, 390–391; *6:* 42
Manuel II *1–4:* 566
Maori (tribe) *1–4:* 259, 260,
    302, 810
A Map of Virginia, 1–4: 764
Maragheh, Azerbaijan *1–4:* 66
Marañón River *1–4:* 411, 413;
    5: 88, 89
Marchand, Jean Baptiste *1–4:*
    136, 578–584
Marcos, Fray *1–4:* 176
Mare Crisium *1–4:* 559
Mare Imbrium *1–4:* 556
Margarita Island *1–4:* 251, 624
Margarita, Venezuela *1–4:* 630
Mariame (tribe) *1–4:* 347
Mariana Islands *1–4:* 569, 573;
    6: 191
Mariana Trench *1–4:* 211, 659
Marias River *1–4:* 533

Boldface indicates main entries in Volume 6 and their page numbers; *1–4:* refers to entries in the four-volume base set; *5:* refers to entries in Volume 5; *6:* refers to entries in Volume 6; (ill.) following a page number refers to photos, drawings, and maps.

245 | Index

Boldface indicates main entries in Volume 6 and their page numbers; *1–4:* refers to entries in the four-volume base set; *5:* refers to entries in Volume 5; *6:* refers to entries in Volume 6; (ill.) following a page number refers to photos, drawings, and maps.

247 | Index

Olaf I (Norway) *1–4:* 524
Old Jericho *6:* 115, 118
Old Testament *6:* 37, 114
Olduvai Gorge, Tanzania *5:* 93,
    95, 117; *6:* 58
Ollantaitambo, Peru *1–4:* 99
Olympias *1–4:* 5–6
Olympic Games (1924) *5:* 99
Olympic Games (1936) *1–4:*
    423
Omagua Indians *5:* 89, 153
Omaha (tribe) *1–4:* 531
Omanum Emporium *5:* 42, 43
On the Ocean 1–4: 709
On the Shape of the World 1–4:
    415
Oneida (tribe) *1–4:* 215
Onizuka, Ellison S. *6:* 129
Onondaga (tribe) *1–4:* 215
Onondaga, New York *1–4:* 226
Operation Highjump *1–4:* 163
Opium War *1–4:* 544
Oracle, Arizona *6:* 9
Oran *1–4:* 737
Orchomenus, Greece *5:* 138
Order of Christ *1–4:* 425
Ordos Desert *1–4:* 705; *6:* 71
Oregon River *1–4:* 530
Oregon Trail *1–4:* 372, 484, 485
Orellana, Francisco de *1–4:*
    627–631; *5:* 152
Organization of African Unity *5:*
    83
The Orient *6:* 44, 151, 175, 188
The Origin of Species 1–4:
    304–305
Orinoco River *1–4:* 251,
    476–479, 715–717; *6:* 173
Orkney Islands *1–4:* 711
Ormuz, Persia *6:* 70, 75, 111
Oromo *1–4:* 503
Orteig Prize *1–4:* 539
Ortiz, Juan *1–4:* 770
Osage (tribe) *1–4:* 662
Oscar (of Sweden and Norway)
    1–4: 608
Oscar II (of Sweden) *1–4:* 419;
    5: 123
Oslo, Norway *1–4:* 16, 19

Oswell, William Colton *1–4:*
    546–548
Oto (tribe) *1–4:* 531
Ottawa (tribe) *1–4:* 226–227
Ottawa River *1–4:* 142, 195,
    216; *6:* 148
Ottoman Empire *1–4:* 44, 49; *6:*
    70
Otumba *1–4:* 279
Ouango *1–4:* 581
Ouessant Island *1–4:* 710
Ouezzane *1–4:* 736
Ovando, Nicolás de *1–4:*
    252–254
Overweg, Adolf *1–4:* 70, 72
Ovimbundu *1–4:* 58
Oxford University *6:* 31, 32, 47,
    89, 115, 187
Oxus River *1–4:* 416
Oyster Bay, New York *6:* 3
Ozark Mountains *1–4:* 770

P

Pacific Ocean *1–4:* 28, 39, 210,
    408, 472, 511, 529–530, 535;
    5: 4, 13, 19–21, 62–64, 104,
    124, 131–133; *6:* 51, 64–67,
    84, 121, 161, 165, 167, 178,
    188
Padilla, Juan de *1–4:* 271
Paez, Pedro *6:* 30
Pai River *1–4:* 394
Paiva, Afonso de *1–4:* 288, 290
Palembang, Sumatra *6:* 107, 109
Palermo, Sicily *1–4:* 417
Palmer, Nathaniel *1–4:* 91–92
Palmer Archipelago *5:* 31, 32
Palmer Peninsula *1–4:* 93, 748
Palmyra, Syria *1–4:* 87, 109,
    385, 597, 786; *6:* 37
Palo de vaca 1–4: 477
Palos de la Frontera, Spain *1–4:*
    240, 243
Pamir Mountains *1–4:* 419, 420,
    807–808; *5:* 56
Pamir Plateau *1–4:* 690
Pamlico Sound *1–4:* 837

Boldface indicates main entries in Volume 6 and their page numbers; *1–4:* refers to entries in the four-volume base set; *5:* refers to entries in Volume 5; *6:* refers to entries in Volume 6; (ill.) following a page number refers to photos, drawings, and maps.

249 | Index

Project Vanguard *1–4:* 352, 353
Prussian Geographical Society
 1–4: 74
Przewalski's horse *1–4:* 707
Przhevalsky, Nikolay *1–4:*
 418–419, 704–708
Ptolemy *1–4:* 798; *5:* 42, 43
Pueblo (tribe) *1–4:* 347
Pueblo, Colorado *1–4:* 83, 663
Puerto de los Reyes, Paraguay
 1–4: 168
Puget, Peter *1–4:* 835
Puget Sound *1–4:* 832
Pulitzer, Joseph *6:* 21, 22
"Pundit-explorer" *6:* 76
Pundits *1–4:* 751–753
Punjab, India *1–4:* 462, 754
Punjab Plains *5:* 56
Punta Alta, Argentina *1–4:* 297
Puquiura, Peru *1–4:* 100
Purari River *1–4:* 520
Pushkin Museum *5:* 139
Putnam, George Palmer *1–4:* 332
Pygmies *1–4:* 1, 4, 321, 324, 797
Pyrenees Mountains *1–4:* 872
Pytheas *1–4:* 709–711

Q

Qagssiarssuk, Greenland *1–4:*
 343
Quapaw *1–4:* 497
Quebec City, Quebec *1–4:* 195,
 215, 494
Quebrabasa Falls *1–4:* 549
Quebrabasa Rapids *1–4:* 550
Queen Charlotte Islands *1–4:*
 834
Queen Charlotte Sound *1–4:*
 259, 263–264, 833
Queen Maud Gulf *1–4:* 17
"Queen of the Air," *1–4:* 492
Queensland, Australia *1–4:* 360,
 520, 523
Quelimane, Mozambique *1–4:*
 140, 232, 550
Quesada, Gonzalo Jimenez de
 1–4: 479

Quetzalcoatl *1–4:* 276, 278
Qui Nhon, Vietnam *1–4:* 222
Quindio Pass *1–4:* 480
Quiros, Pedro Fernandez de *1–4:*
 125
Quito, Ecuador *1–4:* 410,
 479–480, 628; *5:* 4, 5, 85,
 87–89, 152, 153
Qumis *1–4:* 596

R

Rabai *1–4:* 721, 828
Rabbai Mpia *1–4:* 504–506
Radisson, Pierre Esprit *1–4:*
 225–230
Rae, John *1–4:* 368
Raleigh, Walter *1–4:* 712–717
Ram, Hari. *See* Hari Ram
Ramotobi *1–4:* 546
Ramsay, William *1–4:* 88
Ramses II *5:* 157; *6:* 37, 38
Ramu *1–4:* 520
Ranavola *5:* 130
Rangpur, Bangladesh *1–4:* 575
Rappahannock River *1–4:* 764,
 765
Ras Michael of Tigre *6:* 29, 30
Reagan, Ronald *6:* 125, 127, 132
Rebmann, Johannes *1–4:* 113,
 504–505, 718–722
Recife, Brazil *1–4:* 174
Red River *1–4:* 396, 398,
 662–663; *6:* 67
Red Sea *1–4:* 4, 13, 76, 285,
 290, 384, 503, 580, 583, 584,
 666, 773; *5:* 86, 156; *6:* 23,
 29, 39, 40, 92, 139, 184
Rejaf, Sudan *5:* 158
Reliance 1–4: 360
Repulse Bay *1–4:* 640
Research Institute for the Explo-
 ration of the Sea (IFREMER)
 5: 165, 168
Resolution 1–4: 261–264, 266,
 830
Resolution Island *1–4:* 472
Restello, Portugal *1–4:* 392

Boldface indicates main entries in Volume 6 and their page numbers; *1–4:* refers to entries in the four-
volume base set; *5:* refers to entries in Volume 5; *6:* refers to entries in Volume 6; (ill.) following a page
number refers to photos, drawings, and maps.

251 | Index

Scoresby, William *1–4:* 56

Scoresby Sound *5:* 33

Scott, David *1–4:* 29, 31, 36

Scott, Robert Falcon *1–4:* 19, 21, 453, 744

Scott, Walter *1–4:* 635

Scott Base *1–4:* 452, 453

Scottish Geographical Society *1–4:* 745

SCUBA *6:* 49, 53

Scurvy *5:* 22, 23

Scylax of Caryanda *1–4:* 434–435

Sea of Crises *1–4:* 557

Sea of Galilee *6:* 114

Sea of Japan *1–4:* 510

Sea of Marmara *1–4:* 6

Sea of Okhotsk *1–4:* 510, 701; *5:* 20, 131, 133

Sea of Plenty *1–4:* 558

Sea of Tranquility *1–4:* 37

Sealab *1–4:* 286

Seal Nunataks *1–4:* 803

Seaman, Robert L. *6:* 24

Seattle, Washington *1–4:* 18, 857

Sebituane *1–4:* 547

Second Kamchatka Expedition *5:* 21

Sedgwick, Adam *1–4:* 293

Ségou *1–4:* 579, 634

Seine River *1–4:* 540

Seistan *1–4:* 596

Sekelutu *1–4:* 548–550

Seleucia-Ctesiphon, Iraq *1–4:* 220

Seminole *1–4:* 83

Seneca (tribe) *1–4:* 142, 215, 513

Senegal River *1–4:* 426

Sennar, Sudan *6:* 31

Seoul, Korea *5:* 62

Serengeti Plain *5:* 95

Serpa Pinto, Alexandre Alberto da Rocha de *1–4:* 138

Sesheke *1–4:* 547

Sesostris II *6:* 92

Setúbal *1–4:* 666

Seuthe *1–4:* 870

Seven Cities of Cíbola *1–4:* 164, 167, 270, 281, 345, 348, 349, 768; *5:* 5

Seven Pillars of Wisdom 1–4: 87

Seven Years' War *1–4:* 187, 255, 410, 508

Seville, Spain *1–4:* 254; *6:* 190

Shackleton, Ernest *1–4:* 20, 375, 744–749, 857

Shackleton Base *1–4:* 376, 452

Shackleton Ice Shelf *1–4:* 854

Shanapur, India *1–4:* 231

Shang-ch'uan Island *1–4:* 866

Shanghai, China *1–4:* 397, 399, 692, 728; *6:* 23

Shang-tu *1–4:* 691

Shantung Peninsula *5:* 57

Shaw, T. E. *1–4:* 87

Shawnee (tribe) *1–4:* 118, 120

Sheffield University *1–4:* 489

Sheldon, May French *5:* 140–144, 140 (ill.), 141 (ill.)

Shelekhov, Gregory *1–4:* 62

Shendi, Sudan *6:* 38, 39

Shensi *1–4:* 692

Shepard, Alan *1–4:* 31, 402; *6:* 126

Shepard, Sam *1–4:* 874

Sherpa *1–4:* 451, 453

Shewa, Ethiopia *1–4:* 290, 503

Shi'ite Muslims *1–4:* 77, 88

Shigatse, Tibet *1–4:* 421; *6:* 78

Shipton, Eric *1–4:* 450

Shiraz, Iran *1–4:* 77; *6:* 139

Shire River *1–4:* 550

Shoemaker-Levy 9 *1–4:* 468

Shoshone (tribe) *1–4:* 532–534; *6:* 162, 165, 166

Shuga Mountains *6:* 71

Shuttle Imaging Radar (SIR) *5:* 25, 42, 68–70, 74, 85

Sian *1–4:* 461, 463, 692

Sicily, Italy *1–4:* 67, 95, 434, 710

Sidayu *1–4:* 457

Siddhartha Gautama *1–4:* 307; *5:* 56

Siebe, Augustus *6:* 52

Sierra de Quareca *1–4:* 616

Boldface indicates main entries in Volume 6 and their page numbers; *1–4:* refers to entries in the four-volume base set; *5:* refers to entries in Volume 5; *6:* refers to entries in Volume 6; (ill.) following a page number refers to photos, drawings, and maps.

255 | Index

Boldface indicates main entries in Volume 6 and their page numbers; *1–4:* refers to entries in the four-volume base set; *5:* refers to entries in Volume 5; *6:* refers to entries in Volume 6; (ill.) following a page number refers to photos, drawings, and maps.

Takla Makan *1–4:* 420, 690, 706, 708, 807–808; *5:* 55

Talavera Commission *1–4:* 241

Tallahassee, Florida *1–4:* 165

Taloi Mountains *1–4:* 11

Talon, Jean *1–4:* 496

Tampa Bay, Florida *1–4:* 165, 769

Tamralipti *1–4:* 463; *5:* 56; *6:* 107, 108

Tana River *1–4:* 3, 506

Tangier, Morocco *1–4:* 79, 426, 736

Tankar, China *1–4:* 420

Tao-chou *1–4:* 814

Taos, New Mexico *1–4:* 83

Tapirapuã, Brazil *6:* 155, 156

Tarim Basin *1–4:* 420–421, 706

Tashkent, Uzbekistan *1–4:* 419, 461; *5:* 101

Tasman, Abel *1–4:* 258–259, 809–812

Tassili-n-Ajjer Plateau *1–4:* 71

Ta-T'ang Si-Yu-Ki *1–4:* 463

Tatar Straits *1–4:* 510

Tatars *1–4:* 41, 666

Taunton River *6:* 45, 47

Taveta *5:* 142

Tawang *1–4:* 755

Taxila, Pakistan *1–4:* 9, 462

Taylor, Annie Royle *1–4:* 813–816

Taylor, Jim *1–4:* 521–523

Tecla Haimanot *6:* 29

Tegulet, Ethiopia *1–4:* 290

Tehachapi Mountains *1–4:* 760

Tehran, Iran *1–4:* 87, 105, 419

Teixeira, Pedro de *5:* 150–154, 151 (ill.)

Tekeze River *1–4:* 45

Tektite II *6:* 49

Telefomin *1–4:* 522

Tenerife Island *1–4:* 568

Tengri Nor Lake *1–4:* 755

Tennessee River *1–4:* 770

Tennyson, Alfred *1–4:* 358

Tenochtitlán (Mexico City, Mexico) *1–4:* 276–279; *5:* 1, 2

Tensas (tribe) *1–4:* 516

Tereshkova, Valentina *1–4:* 723, 817–820

Terhazza, Mali *1–4:* 80

Ternate, Indonesia *1–4:* 304; *6:* 179, 190

Terra Australis *1–4:* 188, 256–257, 487, 731, 810

Terra Verde (Newfoundland) *6:* 44, 45

Terror *1–4:* 368

Tete, Africa *1–4:* 58–59, 550

Teton Sioux (tribe) *1–4:* 532

Thagard, Norman *5:* 114

Thames River *1–4:* 493, 835

Thana, Salsette Island *6:* 111

Thank God Harbor *5:* 72

Thar Desert *1–4:* 463

Thebes, Egypt *1–4:* 6, 95; *5:* 138; *6:* 91

Theodore Roosevelt *1–4:* 648–649, 652; *6:* 2–4, 2 (ill.)

There's Always Tomorrow *6:* 89

Thessaly *1–4:* 6

Thok Jalung, Tibet *1–4:* 754

Thomas, Bertram *5:* 42

Thompson, David *1–4:* 821–824

Thomson, Charles Wyville *1–4:* 209–210

Thomson, Joseph *1–4:* 231, 235–236, 825–829

Thousand and One Nights *6:* 185

Thrace *1–4:* 6, 433, 870

Through the Dark Continent *1–4:* 798

Thucydides, Historian *1–4:* 870

Thurii, Greece *1–4:* 434

Thutmose I *6:* 91

Thutmose II *6:* 91

Thutmose III *6:* 94

Thuzkan, Tuscany, Italy *1–4:* 67

Tib, Tippu *1–4:* 794–795, 797

Tibetan Buddhism *1–4:* 307, 576, 689

Tibetan Pioneer Mission *1–4:* 816

Tibetan Plateau *6:* 71

Tider, Morocco *1–4:* 426

Tidore Island *1–4:* 571, 573; *6:* 190

Boldface indicates main entries in Volume 6 and their page numbers; *1–4:* refers to entries in the four-volume base set; *5:* refers to entries in Volume 5; *6:* refers to entries in Volume 6; (ill.) following a page number refers to photos, drawings, and maps.

259 | Index

Tuat, Algeria *1–4:* 737
Tübingen *1–4:* 502
Tucker, HL *1–4:* 101
Tudela, Spain *1–4:* 94, 97
Tukulors *1–4:* 579
Tulloch, George *5:* 168
Tumba Lake *1–4:* 796
Tumbes *1–4:* 671, 672
Tun-huang *1–4:* 691, 807
Tunis, Africa *1–4:* 307; *6:* 27
Touré, Samory *1–4:* 579
Turkestan Solo 5: 101
Turks *6:* 29
Turktol *5:* 101
Turtle Lake *1–4:* 823
Tuscaloosa, Chief *1–4:* 770
Tutuila *1–4:* 510
Tutankhamen *6:* 119
Tuvalu Islands *1–4:* 733
Twenty Thousand Leagues under the Sea 1–4: 610
Tyre, Lebanon *1–4:* 7, 433
Tyson, George *5:* 72–74

U

Ubangi River *1–4:* 581
Ubar *5:* 40–46
Ugogo *1–4:* 774
Ujiji, Tanzania *1–4:* 115–116, 233, 552–553, 774, 790
Ukambani *1–4:* 505–506
Ulan Bator *1–4:* 705
Ulfsson, Gunnbjörn *1–4:* 342
Ulloa, Francisco de *1–4:* 281
Ulya River *5:* 133
Umbriel *1–4:* 850
Umivik Fjord *1–4:* 605
Umpqua (tribe) *1–4:* 761
Umpqua River *1–4:* 761
Unalaska, Aleutian Islands *1–4:* 62
Unbeaten Tracks in Japan 1–4: 105
The Undersea Odyssey of the "Calypso" 1–4: 286
United States Biological Survey *1–4:* 337

University of Heidelberg *6:* 134
Unyanyembe *1–4:* 773
Ural Mountains *5:* 121
Uranus *1–4:* 847, 849, 850
Urban II *1–4:* 96
Urdaneta, Andrés de *6:* 188–193, 189 (ill.)
Urdaneta's Passage *6:* 188, 193
Urga *1–4:* 705
Urubamba River *1–4:* 99, 100
Uruguay River *1–4:* 174
U.S. Bureau of Indian Affairs *6:* 166
U.S. Congress *5:* 167
U.S. Navy *6:* 6, 8
U.S. Virgin Islands *6:* 49
Usambara *1–4:* 504, 506
Ussuri River *1–4:* 705

V

Vaca, Alvar Núñez Cabeza de. *See* Cabeza de Vaca, Alvar Núñez
Valenzuela, Eloy *6:* 145
Valladolid, Spain *1–4:* 254; *6:* 190
Valles Marineris *1–4:* 587
Valley of Añaquito *1–4:* 480
Valley of Mexico *1–4:* 278, 279
Valley of Taurus-Littrow *1–4:* 32
The Valley of the Assassins 6: 184
Valparaíso, Chile *1–4:* 300, 301, 328
Valparaíso, Spain *1–4:* 318
Van Allen radiation belts *1–4:* 352, 376
Van Diemen's Land *1–4:* 810
Van Thillo, Mark *6:* 15
Vancouver, George *1–4:* 62, 263–264, 361, 564, 830–835
Vancouver, British Columbia *6:* 66
Vancouver Island *1–4:* 833
Vanguard 1 1–4: 351, 353, 354
Vanikoro Island *1–4:* 511

Boldface indicates main entries in Volume 6 and their page numbers; *1–4:* refers to entries in the four-volume base set; *5:* refers to entries in Volume 5; *6:* refers to entries in Volume 6; (ill.) following a page number refers to photos, drawings, and maps.

261 | Index

Boldface indicates main entries in Volume 6 and their page numbers; *1–4:* refers to entries in the four-volume base set; *5:* refers to entries in Volume 5; *6:* refers to entries in Volume 6; (ill.) following a page number refers to photos, drawings, and maps.

X

X-1 *1–4:* 872, 873
X-1A *1–4:* 874
Xanadu *1–4:* 691
Xavier, Saint Francis *1–4:* 497, 667–668, 864–866
Xenophon *1–4:* 867–870
Xingu River *5:* 151; *6:* 159
Xining, China *5:* 55
Xocotla, Mexico *1–4:* 277
XS-1 project *1–4:* 872

Y

Yadkin valley *1–4:* 118–119
Yakutat Bay *1–4:* 63, 510
Yakutsk, Russia *5:* 131, 134; *6:* 121, 122
Yang-chou *1–4:* 692
Yangtze River *1–4:* 106, 222, 396, 692, 728
The Yangtze River and Beyond *1–4:* 106
Yao (tribe) *1–4:* 112, 231
Yaqui *1–4:* 167
Yaqui River *1–4:* 270
Yarkand, China *1–4:* 421, 690, 755
Yarmuk *6:* 118
Yarqui plains *5:* 88
Yatung, Sikkim *1–4:* 816
Yauri, Hausa 636–637
Yeager, Chuck *1–4:* 871–874
Yeager, Jeana *1–4:* 739–743
Yeager *1–4:* 874
Yelcho *1–4:* 749
Yellow River *1–4:* 460, 691; *6:* 71
Yellowstone River *1–4:* 533, 536; *6:* 167
Yenba, Saudi Arabia *1–4:* 152; *6:* 40
Yenisei River *1–4:* 482; *5:* 123; *6:* 121
Yeti *1–4:* 453

Yokohama, Japan *1–4:* 106; *5:* 63, 124; *6:* 23
Yongden *1–4:* 308–310
York *1–4:* 530, 534, 664
York Factory, Canada *1–4:* 366
Young, Brigham *1–4:* 372
Young, John *1–4:* 29, 32
Younghusband, Francis *1–4:* 577
Yucatán Peninsula *1–4:* 275
Yucay, Peru *1–4:* 99
Yüeh-chih *1–4:* 218
Yukagirs *1–4:* 41
Yukon Arctic coast *5:* 147
Yukon River *1–4:* 18, 801
Yule, Henry *1–4:* 750
Yuma, Arizona *1–4:* 271
Yungay *1–4:* 654
Yung-lo *1–4:* 222–223
Yunnan, China *1–4:* 396, 692

Z

Zagros Mountains *6:* 182
Zambezi *1–4:* 547, 549–550
Zambezi River *1–4:* 58, 139–140, 232
Zanzibar, Tanzania *1–4:* 112–116, 153–154, 156, 223, 234–236, 504, 552, 776, 789, 792, 795–796, 798, 826–827; *5:* 141
Zanzibar Island *1–4:* 721
Zardeh Kuh mountain *6:* 87
Zarins, Juris *5:* 43
Zaysan *1–4:* 707
Zeehaen *1–4:* 810
Zeeland *1–4:* 458
Zeila, Somalia *1–4:* 77, 290
Zelée *1–4:* 327, 328
Zen Buddhism *1–4:* 307
Zenag *1–4:* 523
Zenobia *1–4:* 786
Zeya River *5:* 132; *6:* 124
Zinga *1–4:* 581
Zinjanthropus *5:* 95
Zionists *6:* 186
Zoar *1–4:* 498

Greenland

Baffin Bay

Beaufort Sea

Bering Sea

NORTH PACIFIC OCEAN

Hudson Bay

Labrador Sea

NORTH ATLANTIC OCEAN

NORTH

Vancouver
Seattle
Calgary
Minneapolis
Ottawa Montréal
Toronto Boston
Chicago New York
Washington, DC

AMERICA

San Francisco
Atlanta

Los Angeles
Dallas
Houston
Miami

Monterrey
Gulf of Mexico
Havana
Port-au-Prince
Santo Domingo

Guadalajara

México

ATLANTIC OCEAN

Guatemala
San Salvador

Caribbean Sea

PACIFIC   OCEAN

Caracas

Medellín
Cali Bogotá
Quito
Guayaquil
Belém
Manaus

SOUTH

Recife

Lima
Salvador

La Paz
Brasília

AMERICA

Rio de Janeiro
Asunción
São Paulo
Curitiba

Córdoba
Pôrto Alegre

SOUTH PACIFIC OCEAN

Santiago
Rosario
Buenos
Aires Montevideo

New
Zealand

SOUTH ATLANTIC OCEAN